ROCK ROCK ROCK ROCK RO

CK ROCK ROCK ROCK R

K ROCK ROCK ROCK RO

ROCK ROCK ROCK

THE ROCK

ROCK ROCK ROCK ROC
K ROCK ROCK ROCK R
ROCK ROCK ROCK RO
ROCK ROCK ROCK

ARNOLD SHAW

REVOLUTION

CROWELL-COLLIER PRESS
Collier-Macmillan Limited, London

ROCK ROCK ROCK ROCK ROCK ROCK ROCK ROCK ROCK ROCK ROCK ROCK ROCK ROCK ROCK ROCK ROCK ROCK ROCK

To
Mindy Sura, Ruth Ellen, Elizabeth Hilda
and the future of the rock generation

CONTENTS

PRELUDE

The phrase Rock Revolution may sound like a metaphor or hyperbole. It is neither a figure of speech nor a rhetorical exaggeration. It quite literally characterizes what has happened to American music in the 1960s—a complete upending of the pop music scene.

When it first manifested itself in the mid-50s, rock was dismissed as an aberration and an abomination. At one end of the spectrum, Pablo Casals termed it "poison put to sound" while, at the other, Frank Sinatra damned it as "a rancid-smelling aphrodisiac." Repeated prophecies of its early demise, however, proved futile cries of frustration, as a St. Louis radio station demonstrated when it smashed stacks of rock 'n' roll disks over the air. Before the Presley rockabilly movement subsided, there was a rising tide of Negro rhythm-and-blues. Then came Bob Dylan and folk rock. Beatlemania took England and Europe by storm and proceeded to inundate American teenagers. Today, we have soul, raga rock, psychedelic rock and an influx of exotic instruments, electronic sounds and magnetic-tape music that is rattling the rafters of the entire music world, art as well as pop.

1

The year of Dylan's embrace of the electric guitar and the Big Beat, 1965, was the year in which the teenage rebellion matured into full-scale musical revolution. By then it was clear that the old days of so-called good music were not coming back. The era of the Big Bands, the Big Ballads and the Big Baritones was gone, along with crewcuts. Rock was not just a passing fad, but the sonic expression of the Now, the Turned-On, the Hair Generation. Literature had the antinovel and antihero. The stage had its Theater of the Absurd. In painting, there were mixed media, op, pop and ob art. And in pop, it was rock.

The main features of the overthrow of the older generation's popular music culture may be listed as follows:

1. The guitar and other plucked, picked and strummed string instruments have superseded bowed instruments (violin), blown instruments (reeds and brass) and the piano as vocal accompaniment.

2. Control of pop has been taken out of the hands of major record companies, staff Artist and Repertoire (A & R) executives and Broadway-Hollywood publishing companies. The choice and character of material are now dictated by under-thirty artist-writers and independent record producers, and no major record company is today without a "house hippie," a hirsute A & R man in search of rock artists.

3. Established song forms, like the 32-bar chorus-cum-bridge, have given way to new forms characterized by odd-numbered formations, shifting meters, radical stanza patterns and changing time signatures.

4. The traditional division of labor among performer, writer and record producer has broken down. Instrumentalists sing and singers play instruments. Originators of material tend to account for the total product. "The medium is the message," and the record *is* the song.

5. Just as blues singers treated their voices as musical instruments, and balladeers of the 1940s handled the microphone as if it were an instrument, rock artists have made the recording studio their instrument and the amplifier their tool.

6. We are in the midst of an electrical explosion of sound. Magnetic tape and electronics have made the 1960s an era of echo chambers, variable speeds, and aleatory (chance) and programmed (computer) composition. New procedures include manipulation of texture as a developmental technique, "wall-of-sound" density and total enveloping sound. Philosophical as well as esthetic concepts underlie these developments: a concern with sensory overload as a means of liberating the self, expanding consciousness and rediscovering the world.

7. New subject matter includes an exploration of the cosmos of strange experiences, from the psychedelic expansion of the mind back into the world of medievalism and beyond time into transcendental meditation. We are in an era of meaningful lyrics, protesting, probing and poetic.

8. But we are also in a period when sound itself, as in jazz but in a more complex way, frequently is theme and content. If the folk orientation of rock emphasizes *meaning*, the psychedelic stresses tone color, texture, density and volume.

9. The record is being transformed into a miniature theater of playlets with music. The integrated suite, the extended pop song and unstructured music are becoming commonplace. *Continuity* becomes a compelling concern as more and more rock albums are for listening, not dancing.

10. Superalbums represent a new driving force, with outrageous sums of money being lavished not only on recording but on packaging.

11. Rock groups are concerned not merely with uniqueness of sound, long a requirement of singing and instrumental suc-

and appearance

cess, but with total image. Hair styles, wardrobe, LP covers and liners, and even the styling of promotion matter are no longer left to professionals but are the subject of personal and group expression.

12. The era of the raucous disk jockey is in a transitional stage. FM and progressive radio stations are receptive to recordings that by-pass traditional restrictions on time, treatment, outlook and even language.

13. The discotheque, a melange of vibrating colors, blinding images and deafening sound, has superseded the night club, cocktail lounge and jazz club as after-hour pads for teenagers.

14. For the first time in the history of popular music, we are developing canons of criticism. Just as there has long been a phalanx of concert and jazz critics, we now have an under-thirty group of reviewers whose work appears regularly in rock publications like *Crawdaddy, Rolling Stone, Cheetah* and *Eye* and is beginning to find space in *The New Yorker, Esquire, Life, Vogue* and other over-thirty periodicals.

15. Rock has brought a renascence of the bardic tradition. Like the medieval troubadours, Celtic bards and epic Homers, Leonard Cohen, Bob Dylan, Paul Simon and John Lennon are poets, singing rather than reciting or just printing their verses.

16. Rock is a collage, capable of absorbing the most diverse styles and influences: folk, blues, bluegrass, jazz, soul, country-and-western (c&w), rhythm-and-blues (r&b), motion picture themes, Broadway show tunes, Indian ragas, baroque, tape, computer and chance music. There is an increasing crossover between popular songwriting and serious composition.

17. In the outlook of the under-thirty generation, as reflected in rock, romanticism is dead. Realism, naturalism, mysticism and activism are the new acceptable and conflicting ideologies. Young people appear restless, tough, alienated, hostile, defiant,

4

aggressive, frustrated—looking to the East rather than the West, more concerned with black than white, and vacillating between the put-down and the put-on, the hippie withdrawal from society and the yippie assault on it.

18. Rock is reaching an audience once impervious to and snobbish about pop music and rock 'n' roll. Whereas the college crowd once went for jazz, folk and symphony, it is now buying rock records and supporting rock groups.

19. The traditional tension between generations has grown to a point where the gap is almost like that between classes in a revolutionary era. The teeny-boppers, flower children, hippies and yippies all represent something more than mere rebellion against over-thirty values. Condemning the supermaterialism, duplicity and hypocrisy of the older generation, they are raising the banners of a new ideology embodying communal sharing, nonviolence, plain talk and equality. This is the first song culture, not only *for* under-thirty but *of* and *by* under-thirty.

How all this happened and *why* are among the questions I propose to answer. We also want to learn *who* made the revolution, details of their contribution, the varied manifestations of change, and the present direction and possible future of the insurrection. In short, I am concerned with the sociology and psychology as well as esthetics of what *Life* has called "the most popular music of all time."

In *Billboard*'s year-end survey published early in 1968, the Artist of the Year was a forty-seven-year-old sitar player whose records never made pop bestseller charts. The curious choice of Ravi Shankar was sound recognition of his tremendous impact on teenage musicians and listeners. It was also an index to the vast expansion of outlook and content that pop and rock have undergone. In the classical field, traditionally separated from popular music by a deep moat of snobbery, record companies have also begun breaking out of their cramped confines. Suddenly, their new releases include large samples of modern European and American music, with increasing stress on electronic and avant-garde composers. "Without The Beatles," one company executive conceded, "we would have had no success with *Silver Apples,* an electronic work." And another stated, "There is no longer a fixed division between pop and classical." In other words, something of a revolution is beginning to develop in the classical field. Is it too much to suggest that the open-minded attitude of rock musicians and listeners is beginning to carry over into so-called serious music?

Having been patronized and reviled during much of its frenetic existence, American popular music is today being accorded the status and recognition of an art form. This, too, is a major, if not revolutionary, change that rock has effected.

ARNOLD SHAW

Labor Day, 1968

1 WHERE IT'S AT : *The Recording Studio Is the Instrument*

In 1967, a twenty-three-year-old girl from Chickasaw County, Mississippi, went into a Hollywood recording studio and cut "demos" of two of her songs. After the demonstration cuts were transferred from magnetic tape to disk, she took the "dub" to Capitol Records. Although she had been singing and dancing in Los Angeles and Las Vegas clubs, Bobbie Lee Gentry was trying to sell her songs, not her singing. Capitol executives were so impressed by both, not to mention her good looks, that they signed her and released her "Ode to Billie Joe" backed with "Mississippi Delta" as her first disk. Within weeks, the tragic-blues tale of "Billie Joe" had outdistanced competitive records by The Monkees, The Supremes and others to become # 1 on the record charts of all music tradepapers—*Billboard, Cash Box* and *Record World*. Overnight, Miss Gentry became a new singing sensation whose voice was heard all over the radio dial, whose face was seen on major TV shows, and whose swift rise was celebrated in newspaper and magazine accounts.

A similar experience was enjoyed by Rudy Martinez, a twenty-two-year-old Mexican musician living near Saginaw, Michigan.

Since recording studios are now almost as omnipresent as pizza parlors—the average charge seems to run about twenty dollars an hour for monaural taping—Martinez took his small combo into a local studio and cut several sides. These were released by Pa-Go-Go Records, a local label owned by a motel operator and food executive, who puts out disks as a sideline. As soon as the disk made an appearance on local record charts, sales executives of several New York record companies phoned Pa-Go-Go. One executive, from Cameo-Parkway in Philadelphia, even flew to Texas where the owner of the Michigan label was transacting some business. Before the executive was on his way back to Philadelphia, the Pa-Go-Go owner had a check for $2,500, an advance against royalties to be paid on the sale of each disk pressed from the master tape. By the end of the year, "Ninety-Six Tears" had sold over a million disks and Rudy Martinez, who had cut the master, became widely known as the leader of ? and the Mysterians, as the group called itself.

Today, the recording studio is not merely an instrumentality. It is *the* instrument that established artists play with a dedication and high seriousness characteristic of classical masters of the piano or violin. In 1966 The Beach Boys spent ninety hours in a studio to produce a single 45 r.p.m. disk. The Beatles' *Sgt. Pepper's Lonely Hearts Club Band* was four months in the making and cost over $56,000. Songs are no longer written and then recorded. They are most frequently conceived in the recording studio, with the process of recording entering actively into the shape and form and sound that the song ultimately takes.

But even after the time-consuming process of recording or creating has been completed, the disk is not yet ready for duplication. It now has to be edited or "mixed." This procedure frequently takes longer than the original step, for each instrument and each voice may be cut on a separate track. Major studios are now equipped to cut as many as twenty-four separate tracks at a time. These have to be combined or "mixed" to produce the single groove that activates a needle. In the editing process, each track can be electronically altered as to dynamics (soft or loud), frequencies (high or low), texture (smooth or rough), echo (much or little, fuzz, feedback or tape reverb), and so forth. Today's rock and pop scene is a reverberating cosmos of microphones, amplifiers and magnetic tape recorders.

James Michener, author of *Tales of the South Pacific* and other bestsellers, once served as a judge in a competition of forty-three amateur rock bands. The event took place at the Music Circus, a theater in a tent at Lambertville, New Jersey. Michener was present when the more than two hundred young musicians tuned up their instruments, loosened up their fingers through practice runs and warmed up their amplifiers. "It was noise," he later wrote, "such as the world has rarely heard—absolute cacophony, metallic, brash, the sound of our age. . . . It hurtled at me from all sides, from some four hundred amplifiers and was as near total noise as anything I have so far experienced." Michener found that five amplifiers and four microphones were "about the least a self-respecting band could get away with," and it seemed to him that the musical instrument in itself was less important "than the electronic system that reproduces it and throws it full volume at the listener."

Clearly, this is a strange world by comparison either with what the popular music scene once was or is even today in non-rock areas. When Jack Jones or Johnny Mathis enters a recording studio, he has learned the songs he is about to cut and has gone over them with an arranger, who prepared the scores for the orchestra. Union regulations permit the recording of a maximum of four songs in three hours, after which musicians are paid overtime at increased rates. The average Sinatra or Como or Streisand LP is cut in about ten hours. The editing or mixing may take as long on rock records. But the recording studio in this case is not an instrument. It is a medium, a means to an end, not a form of expression.

Before 1950, in the period of the Big Bands, the Big Balladeers (Crosby, Sinatra, Como) and the Big Belters (Fisher, Laine, Ray), the key to success was a network radio program, *Your Hit Parade.* Each Saturday night, from April 20, 1935, until June 7, 1958, after the advent of rock 'n' roll, the *Hit Parade* presented the Top Ten songs of the week. To the Now generation, it will doubtless come as a surprise that what counted most in making a hit were not record sales or disk jockey plays, but *live* performances on the radio. These were tabulated numerically by services that monitored the four major networks in New York, Chicago and Los Angeles. To secure such performances, publishers employed song-pluggers or contact men who solicited, cajoled and pressured "plugs" from those who sang or played on the radio. (Contact men are still part of the music scene today, but their present function revolves entirely around records: getting songs recorded and getting the records played by disk jockeys.)

Before a publisher knew whether he had a *Hit Parade* song or a "dog," weeks of concentrated work were required, as was an investment of between $10,000 and $25,000 per song. The *Hit Parade* period is known in music business history as the Era of the # 1 Plug, because each publisher concentrated for a given period on the exploitation of one tune. To assist his plugging staff, a publisher printed "pros" (professional copies) and "stocks" (orchestrations), which were given away free to performers. Staff pianists and arrangers taught new songs to singers and re-arranged them in keys suitable for their vocal range. After a time, a "drive" was set up, a week in which plugs were bunched on the air. It generally took several drives to discover whether a song would make it. A strong ballad might remain on the *Hit Parade*, climbing up and sliding down, for twelve weeks, giving a hit song a life span of about six months. (Curiously, the longest-lived song on the *Hit Parade* was "Too Young," a ballad with a teenage slant. It started on the *Parade* on May 19, 1951, and remained in the Top Ten for twenty-two weeks. It was the only song in the *Parade's* twenty-three-year history to maintain the # 1 spot for twelve weeks.)

The dictators of the business were a small group of powerful publishers then affiliated with the American Society of Composers, Authors and Publishers (ASCAP). These publishers could not tell the public what to buy, but they could determine what was exposed for the public's aural consideration. Equally potent in the shaping of public taste were the big name bandleaders like Glenn Miller, Tommy Dorsey, Benny Goodman, Sammy Kaye, Guy Lombardo and star vocalists like Bing Crosby, Kate Smith, and Frank Sinatra. Even though there were "rocking chair hits"—songs that were runaway smashes and that made it possible for a publisher and his staff to sit back in their chairs and rock—it was not easy for a new writer to break into the business or even to get into ASCAP. There were also severe restrictions on the form, subject matter, vocabulary and emotions of songs, and, though taboos were sometimes successfully broken, popular songwriting tended to be communication on a low musical and verbal level.

A number of developments changed this situation. These included the growth of television, which led to the demise of costly network radio shows and the rise of the Knights of the Turntable, the disk jockeys; the introduction of magnetic tape and tape recording, which brought the making of masters within the reach of small capital and broadened the base of the recording industry; the formation and growth of Broadcast Music, Inc. (BMI) as a competitive performing rights society to ASCAP, a development which broadened the base of the publishing industry and opened the doors of professional songwriting to new writers around the country, especially those in the rhythm-and-blues (r&b) and country-and-western (c&w) areas; and finally, the sharp change of taste that accompanied the entry of a new generation into the record and song market. The new buyers, more affluent and more articulate than previous generations, were the offspring of World War II parents. They were the first generation that grew up in a world of television, electronics, jets and the atom bomb—a world of heightened communication, accelerated speeds and unanticipated potential destructiveness.

In the latter days of the *Hit Parade* era, the *live* performance began to give way to the *recorded* performance as a hit-making medium. This situation developed apace as the emergence of TV drew major advertising revenue away from network radio and led to the less costly use of spot plugs and jingles, sandwiched between the inexpensive playing of records on local radio stations. Although the *Make Believe Ballroom* of WNEW in New York, regarded as the pioneer program of this type, was launched in 1935, the record did not become King until the early 1950s. Its new potency derived from the emergence of a group of personality platter-spinners—Bill Randle at WERE, Cleveland; Bob Clayton at WHDH, Boston; Ed McKenzie at WJBK, Detroit; and many others. Their power to make hits grew by leaps and bounds as the radio audience expanded tremendously with the vast increase in car radios and portable transistor sets.

In this period, the power of old-line music publishers began to decline and passed into the hands of those who decided what was to be recorded: namely, Artist and Repertoire executives (A & R men) at the major record companies. Their reign was largely terminated with the rise of rock, when young producers, functioning independently, began coming up with the record hits. Today, there is a new group of music "millionaires," mostly men under thirty who not only produce records, but generally manage the groups they produce and publish their songs. A number of them have launched their own record labels. Among the more successful of these independent producers are Phil Spector, who is responsible for the Righteous Brothers and who owns Philles Records; Bob Crewe, who produces The Four Seasons, Frankie Valli, and Mitch Ryder and The Detroit Wheels;

Koppelman and Rubin, who struck oil with The Lovin' Spoonful; Lou Adler, whose productions include The Mamas and The Papas; and Burt Bacharach and Hal David, who write and produce Dionne Warwick's record hits. Quite a number of rock artists and groups also function as their own producers. Among these are The Young Rascals, The Tokens, Dave Clark and James Brown. Because so few top singles are produced by A & R men at the major record companies, tradepapers now give the names of producers along with other label information.

The word "payola," which came into national prominence in 1959, harks back to the Era of the # 1 Plug. In the 1930s, there was, in fact, a payola scandal inside the music business: it involved publishers and live performers. When the Congressional investigation of payola hit the headlines in 1959, record distributors were paying disk jockeys for plugs. One of the casualties of the probe was a disk jockey at WINS in New York named Alan Freed, who pioneered the raucous, rapid-fire style of announcing that still tends to be characteristic of rock programming. To add drive and excitement to the records he played, Freed frequently accompanied them by slamming a phone book hard on the afterbeat. Freed came to New York by way of Cleveland, where he worked mainly with r&b disks; that is, disks aimed primarily at the segregated Negro market. As we shall see, rock 'n' roll was, in its beginnings, a merger of two basic but regional, or ghetto, streams of music: the hillbilly songs of white rural folk of the Southeastern mountain regions with the r&b songs of urban Negro communities. It was Alan Freed who named the new type of music that germinated in the mid-50s, rock 'n' roll, appropriating the phrase from an old blues: "My baby rocks me with a steady roll."

2 WHEN IT STARTED : *Rockabilly,*

Haley and Presley

During the summer of 1955, as General Professional Manager of Edward B. Marks Music Corporation, I paid one of my periodic visits to Nashville, then known as the home of the Grand Ole Opry and now known as Music City. At the home of Colonel Tom Parker, who had managed Eddy Arnold from his beginnings as the Tennessee Plowboy, I heard recordings issued by a Memphis label, Sun Records. I was not familiar with the artist, who sounded like a Negro blues-shouter, but who also sang with a nasal quality characteristic of hillbilly white. It was a curious mixture, but it had drive and a sensuality that interested rather than impressed me. To be candid, I could not make out most of the lyrics. The Colonel, a canny promoter, informed me that the singer was "sending" deep-South females the way Sinatra had once stirred the bobby soxers. He wondered how Elvis Presley—that was the singer's name—would do north of the Mason-Dixon line where he had not then been heard at all.

On my return to New York, I brought Presley's disks to the attention of Bill Randle, a midwest disk jockey who did a Saturday show over WCBS in New York. Uneasy about programming Presley in the big city, Randle agreed to try the disks over his daily shows on WERE in Cleveland. Within days, an excited Randle was on the long-distance phone, exclaiming that he had never had such fantastic responses to any disks he had ever programmed.

That was late August, 1955. It was the beginning of rockabilly, a style cultivated by Presley and pioneered by the owner of Sun Records, Sam Phillips. Responsible for launching the careers of Johnny Cash, Carl Perkins, Jerry Lee Lewis and Roy Orbison, Phillips encouraged all his hillbilly singers to study bluesmen like Muddy Waters, B. B. King, Roscoe Gordon and Howlin' Wolf, all of whom he had recorded in his early years. Within days of Randle's tremulous phone call to me, record companies from coast to coast were trying to buy out Phillips' contract with Presley. The spirited bidding rose until finally RCA Victor and a New York publisher, Hill & Range, effected the shift by jointly paying Phillips the sum of $40,000.

The nationwide frenzy was yet to come. The Pelvis, as he came to be called because of his knocking knees and swivelling hips, made his first appearance on TV in the fall of 1955. His debut was, surprisingly, on the *Tommy Dorsey Show*. Adult viewers were so outraged by his highly suggestive body movements and dissolute appearance—the hair in the face, the glazed eyes, the long sideburns and the frenzied voice—that there was talk of cancelling his second and third appearances. It was only talk. Soon, the very proper *Ed Sullivan Show* booked him. Sullivan tried to mollify his viewers by keeping the camera focussed entirely on Presley's face. The compromise did not include the fee, which until then was the highest ever paid a guest performer.

Beginning with "Heartbreak Hotel," Presley's first Gold Record—it sold enough to earn two—the pace and quantity of his record sales shook up the entire industry. In 1956 the *Hit Parade* was still on radio and by then also on TV. After "Hotel," which went to the top, "Love Me Tender" made # 1 while "Don't Be Cruel" and "Blue Suede Shoes" each went to # 2. The latter, written by a Sun Record colleague, Carl Lee Perkins, and originally cut by him, was typical of early rock songs in which teenagers were finding an identity through the offbeat clothes they wore.

Presley's impact was troubling to adults because his influence seemed more nonmusical than musical. It was both. Musically speaking, his disks were danceable. In a period when jazz had gone bop and was turning cool—with jazzmen playing for listeners, not dancers—and when pop balladry was ear-catching but not foot-tempting, danceability was an important factor. However, the intensity of teenage reaction suggested that youngsters were responding to him for deeper psychological, emotional and social reasons. To them, he was in fact the first rock symbol of teenage rebellion—made so in part by adults because they did not like him, were outraged by him, and condemned him as depraved. Anti-Negro prejudice doubtless figured in adult antagonism. Regardless of whether parents were aware of the Negro-sexual origins of the phrase "rock 'n' roll," Presley impressed them as the visual and aural embodiment of sex. Curiously, to female adolescents, he seemed to have a slightly different meaning: "He had the lustre," a writer observed, "of being secretly 'bad,' but with no apparent evidence to support this mysterious quality." Youngsters could thus vicariously enjoy the forbidden without facing the responsibility, or suffering the cost. This toying with sex through song was linked with the James Dean syndrome: frustration in the face of authority, originating in suppressed hostility.

Within a two-year period, Presley's disks aggregated the staggering sale of over 28 million records. On its release in 1957, "Jailhouse Rock" skyrocketed to second place in tradepaper charts in just two weeks. Although RCA Victor stated that it had by then shipped 2 million disks, a Boston disk jockey announced: "Rock 'n' roll has had it." The basis of his prediction:

the revival of an old ballad, "Love Letters in the Sand." Marty Faye, a Chicago disk jockey, disagreed: "The kids have accepted this twanging guitar," he said, "this nasal, unintelligible sound, this irritating sameness of lyrics, this lamentable croak. They've picked a sound of their own, apart from anything adults like. Rock 'n' roll is as strong as ever, and we'll have to live with it." To the attendant controversy, the producer of *Bandstand*, one of the last live-music shows on network radio, contributed a cogent thought: "It is becoming apparent that the interpretation of a song or the 'sound' of a record is the selling factor. This makes it almost impossible to use the best-selling record charts as a guide for programming a live show, since we must pick numbers in which an artist . . . doesn't suffer by comparison with a tricked-up echo chamber." (Here is the explanation for the "lip-synchronization" technique that most teenage TV shows soon adopted: the singer does not sing but merely synchronizes the movements of his lips with his phrasing on the record being played.)

Despite the dire predictions—a reflection of the futile hopes of older artists, writers and publishers—there was no slump in Presley's popularity even when a two-year stint in the Army took him away from his fans. "Stuck Up," the initial release after his discharge from the Army, became a Gold Record overnight. A "Welcome Elvis" appearance on TV with Frank Sinatra—an electric confrontation of the idols of two generations— brought him $125,000, a fee which no TV show had been willing to pay before his Army stint. Since then, Presley has sold so many disks that he reportedly has fifty Gold Records hanging in Graceland, his Memphis, Tennessee, home. As for his films: "Presley pictures don't need titles," an MGM executive has said. "They could be numbered and they would still sell." The numbers would now pass the thirty mark. Although he has received fees of over a million dollars for many of them, on movie sets, Presley still addresses even movie directors he knows well as "Sir."

In the spring of 1968, shortly after he received a Grammy for "How Great Thou Art" as the Best Sacred Recording of the Year, Presley was awarded his forty-second Gold Disk for the album of the same name. At the time, the claim was made that Elvis was "still the indisputable all-time Gold Disk champ, far outranking the runner-up Beatles." Statistics revealed that The Pelvis had received thirty-two Disks for singles and ten for albums while The Beatles had captured only twenty-six. Of course, Elvis' career was then almost thirteen years old while The Beatles' popularity spanned only a four-year period.

Before Elvis Aaron Presley's explosion on the teenage music scene, at least one other artist foreshadowed the rise of rockabilly. Like Presley, Bill Haley of Highland Park, Michigan, grew up in the hillbilly tradition. The instrumentation of his band was typically c&w, consisting of accordion, steel guitar or dobro, acoustic guitar (Haley's own instrument) and bass. For the "Rock Around the Clock" recording, which brought him international recognition, he added drums, tenor sax and Spanish electric guitar—instruments more characteristic of r&b. Haley and his Comets also sang the song behind the credits of *The Blackboard Jungle,* the interracial film that served to introduce Sidney Poitier on the screen. The success of the film set off a nuclear reaction that sent the record soaring to the top. It was on the *Hit Parade* in July, 1955, before Presley had been heard north of the Mason-Dixon line. As the film travelled around the world, teenagers in other countries began discovering rockabilly. Soon, the teenage world was expectantly waiting for the god of rock to appear—and Presley did. His prophet was featured in a 1956 film titled *Rock Around the Clock,* which also yielded a hit for Haley in "See You Later, Alligator." But prophet Haley lacked the charisma of his god, and faded from the limelight in which Presley still remains. (As this volume is being completed, word comes of the re-release in England of the Haley disk of "Rock Around the Clock," together with a new version he has just cut, and of the impending re-release of such r 'n' r originals of the 1950s as Buddy Holly's "Peggy Sue," Gene Vincent's "Be-Bop-A-Lula" and Carl Perkins' "Blue Suede Shoes." Whether this revival will also become an American phenomenon should be clear by the time this book is in print. Incidentally, shortly after The Beatles emerged in 1964, Haley's disk was re-released in Australia, where it climbed bestseller charts; personal appearances he made in Germany and on the continent were huge sellouts.)

Historically, the immediate origin of rock antedates even Bill Haley and his Comets. In the spring of 1954, an unknown group of young Negroes cut some sides for Atlantic Records. One was called "Sh-Boom." It was credited to the five singers who made up The Chords. All five received credit because the song was written, as many rock songs have since been written, in the studio. Writing, singing and recording were a single act. Or, as a memorable catch phrase of Marshall McLuhan puts it, "the medium is the message." That is, the recording *is* the song. Atlantic executives were so uncertain about "Sh-Boom"—"It had something," they said, "but what?"—that they decided not to release it on their own label. Instead, they created a new label, Cat, which, despite its historic contribution, died with "Sh-Boom." What happened to "Sh-Boom" startled not only Atlantic but most other music business pros, including the writer of this book.

I was then Vice-President and General Professional Manager of Hill & Range Songs. One morning in the late spring of 1954, I discovered quite by accident that at the Music City Record Shop in Los Angeles—I was in New York at the time—a song I had never heard of, by an unknown group, on an unknown label, was outselling all the top artists in the business. By the middle of the following week, I had purchased for the firm I managed a half interest in the unknown song—it was "Sh-Boom" —for $6,000. It was a gamble but the surprising sales of the disk in Los Angeles, which motivated me to act, also soon stirred Mercury Records to make a competitive copy, or cover, with a white group. "Sh-Boom" not only launched The Crew Cuts, then an unknown, teenage group from Canada, but it remained on the *Hit Parade* through the summer of 1954, causing music business pros to sit up and wonder whether a new sound was on the way in.

"Sh-Boom" was a signpost to the future in several respects. In addition to the method of composition and the big Negro beat it represented, it touched a theme that became central in teenage songs: dissatisfaction with the world as it is and the yearning for a better world: "Life can be a dream, sh-boom, sh-boom." It was also a harbinger of a development that prevailed in the record field through 1955: the more flexible and cannier white artists came up with hits by copying records made by Negroes for the segregated Negro market. Early in the year, the Top Ten included "Ko Ko Mo (I Love You So)." The r&b ballad was a hit for Perry Como on RCA Victor, which cut a polished version of an r&b disk by Combo No. 64, Gene and Eunice. Toward the end of the year, The Fontane Sisters had a # 1 hit in "Seventeen," a song recorded originally by writer Boyd Bennett and his Rockets on King, a Cincinnati-based record company. The McGuire Sisters scored with "Sincerely," an r&b ballad co-authored by deejay Alan Freed and cut originally by The Moonglows, a Negro group on Chess, a Chicago label. Perhaps the most successful of the imitators was Georgia Gibbs, who racked up a two-million-copy seller in "Tweedle Dee," patterned after a LaVern Baker disk, and "Dance With Me Henry," originally cut by Etta James on Modern, a modest west coast label. The point of this recital is that Negro artists were then unable to penetrate the national record market. It required a white artist to make more than a regional seller of a song. This recital also underlines the areas in which the rock impulse originated.

Although the white takeover of Negro material continued intermittently—in 1958 "Lollipop" was a smash for The Chordettes, who became interested in the song as the result of a disk I made with a mixed couple, Ronald and Ruby—the demand for the Negro original grew as teenage buyers began to dominate the singles record market. Teresa Brewer, who once outdistanced Ivory Joe Hunter on "A Tear Fell," later ran a weak second to Sam Cooke on "You Send Me." Georgia Gibbs failed to top Jerry Lee Lewis's r&b treatment of "Great Balls of Fire." Sometime in 1956, r&b came roaring out of the Negro ghettoes, began placing black artists on national bestseller charts, and led to the rise of new publishing companies, new writers, new record companies, and new sounds like the Detroit and the Memphis Sound. It also brought prosperity to a group of regional labels that had for years sold only the limited quantities bought in Negro ghettoes. One such label was Atlantic Records, a New York company purchased in 1967 by Warner Brothers–Seven Arts for 17 million dollars.

3 WHERE IT STARTED : *Blues, Race*

and Rhythm-and-Blues

"We sing more colored than the Africans," said John Lennon, boastfully acknowledging the debt of The Beatles to Negro music. But two young Americans who derive their name from the gospel expression "That's righteous, brother!" really have a blacker sound than the Liverpool lads. So does the British group that took its name from the title of a Muddy Waters' blues, "Rollin' Stone." The debt of rock to the Negro was quite apparent even in Elvis Presley, who freely admitted the influence of Arthur "Big Boy" Crudup, a deep-South singer remembered for the popular blues "Mean Old Frisco."

No understanding of the Rock Revolution, of its esthetics, psychology or sociology, is really possible without some background in Afro-American music. For, as anthropologist Charles Keil has noted: "The rhythmic complexity and subtlety, the emphasis on percussive sound qualities, the call-and-response pattern, the characteristic vocal elements (shout, growl, falsetto and so on), blues chromaticism, blues and gospel chord progressions, Negro vocabularly, Afro-American dance steps—all have become increasingly prominent in American music." Chronologically, the development was from country and folk blues to classic blues to race records to rhythm-and-blues and finally to soul, today a basic phase of the Rock Revolution.

THE BLUES

Although the first blues did not appear in print until 1912, the form and style was a post-Civil War development—an expression of the Negro made mobile, rather than free, by the Emancipation Proclamation. The blues is a migratory music of men in search of work, food, money, sex, love and self-respect. A music of nasal moans, spoken delivery and on-the-beat phrasing, it originated in the Delta region of Mississippi. "We sang the blues," said bluesman Big Bill Broonzy, who was born in Mississippi. "In New Orleans, they played jazz."

As a form, the blues is the simplest of three that have dominated pop music since the turn of the century. Tin Pan Alley has traditionally worked with a 32-bar form, structured into four 8-bar segments with an A-A-B-A arrangement. Since "the bridge," "channel," or "release," as the B section is variously called, involves a change of key and rhythm from the A sections, the Tin Pan Alley song consist of two melodic strains. Although the patterns of show tunes vary greatly, they also frequently follow a 32-bar form, but one divided into two 16-bar units. Not only is the melodic line longer, but the chord sequences and rhythmic patterns are generally more complex. Contrasting with these two forms, the blues is traditionally a 12-bar sequence, employing only three chords—those on the first, fourth and fifth notes of the scale. Like Gregorian chant and c&w music, early rock 'n' roll also used little more than these three basic chords, key changes being effected through direct, chromatic leaps rather than slow modulation. The twelve bars divide into three groups (A-A-B), with each set of four bars embodying a call-and-response, statement-and-comment pattern.

23

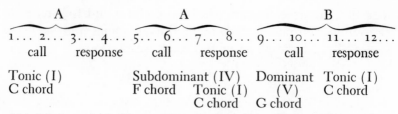

```
            A                    A                    B
    ┌─────────────┐    ┌─────────────┐    ┌─────────────┐
  1... 2... 3... 4... 5... 6... 7... 8... 9... 10... 11... 12...
    call     response    call     response    call     response
```

Tonic (I)   Subdominant (IV)   Dominant   Tonic (I)
C chord   F chord   Tonic (I)   (V)   C chord
                                   C chord   G chord

(A) My home's in Texas, what am I doin' up here? (Bars 1 and 2)
(A) My home's in Texas, what am I doin' up here? (Bars 5 and 6)
(B) Yes, my good corn whiskey, baby, and women brought me here.
    (Bars 9 and 10)

Into this simple form, the Negro poured the woes of human beings trying to effect the transition from chattel slavery to individual independence. Under slavery, all he could hope for was a heaven after death: his spirituals employed idealized imagery, swathing a coarse reality in the soft cotton of an imagined paradise. As a free man, albeit segregated and discriminated against, he could hope for a heaven on earth: the language of the blues was vivid and tough, recording the raw emotions of a people dispossessed, ostracized but undefeated.

"The most astonishing aspect of the Blues," novelist Richard Wright has written, "is that though replete with a sense of defeat and down-heartedness, they are not intrinsically pessimistic; their burden of woe and melancholy is dialectically redeemed through sheer force of sensuality into an exultant affirmation of life, of love, of movement, of hope."

This duality of blues feeling found perfect tonal expression in the shifting major-minor sound of the music—the melodies minor, abounding in "blue" notes (flatted thirds, fifths and later sevenths and ninths) but sounding against major chords. And not only blue notes, but notes that are slurred, quartered, sharped, moaned and growled, adding tension and intensity.

The earliest exponents of country or folk blues were men like Blind Lemon Jefferson and three bluesmen, all of whom served as his lead-boys and learned their art from this poor Texan who sang, as one perceptive admirer noted, "in a high crying voice with the biting tone of the guitar whining behind him." Huddy Ledbetter, one of the lead-boys who became known as Leadbelly, sang his way out of a penitentiary where he was serving a sentence for murder and went on to write the tender love ballad "Goodnight Irene." Lightnin' Hopkins, another lead-boy, became an exponent of the crying vocal style associated with the poor farm country of central Texas. The third, Aaron "T-Bone" Walker, eventually was able to swim successfully into the urban tributary of the blues that became known as rhythm-and-blues.

Of this early group, the bluesman whose influence carried to The Beatles and other British groups, was McKinley Morganfield, known as Muddy Waters. It was not alone through his Chess recordings of the 1940s that Waters was known abroad. In 1958 he made a sensational tour of England that gave a growing generation of rockers personal contact with him. He was still the tough cotton picker from Rolling Fork, Mississippi, and he still delivered in his old primitive "down-home" shout style—save that the din of amplified instruments drove an English critic to a remote men's room where he listened to the concert. Despite the ear-splitting decibels, he was so stirred by Waters earthiness and animal vitality that he could not leave. Muddy was no longer using the neck of a bottle as a guitar fret—indigent guitarists would actually break off the neck of a soda bottle and convert it into a fret by inserting their little finger into the opening. But he was still crying "I Be's Troubled" and "I Can't Be Satisfied," a screamer that became a hit for The Rolling Stones.

The latter song sums up a significant trend in blues literature— the boastfulness of the male filled with vanity over his virility, a concept given more polite expression by Brook Benton and less restrained utterances by Britain's Stones. In *Poetry of the Blues*, Samuel Charters notes that the blues are blunt about the pleasure of sexual love and adds: "It is often in the colorful and elaborate sexual imagery that the blues is most vividly poetic."

25

Today, Waters, who has been a Chicago dweller since he began recording for Chess in the 1940s, is part of the burgeoning Chicago Sound, a revival of the cobblestone school of r&b exemplified by raw shouters like B.B. King, Bo Diddley, Smokey Hogg, Howlin' Wolf and Big Mama Thornton. Willie Mae Thornton, incidentally, made the original recording of "Hound Dog," an r&b hit three years before it became a pop smash for Presley.

Currently, all of these early proponents of urban blues are enjoying a revival, not only in personal appearances that bring them into contact with white audiences, but through the re-issue of their vintage recordings. Just as their imitators, the white blues bands, have been growing by binary fission, so the black blues bands are now producing offspring. After twelve-and-a-half years, James Cotton, who was Paul Butterfield's teacher for a time, surfaced from the Muddy Waters Blues Band. His superlative mouth-organ playing, ranked with that of Rice Miller (Sonny Boy Williamson) from whom he learned the instrument, may be heard on *Pure Cotton*. More recently, pianist Otis Spann, who worked with Cotton in the Waters combo, also stepped out on his own. And most recently, guitarist Buddy Guy, whose flamboyant style has been likened to Jimi Hendrix's histrionics, split from the Junior Wells band. His debut album *A Man and His Blues* has been greeted with superlatives, including its characterization as "one of the great blues recordings of all time" by *Rolling Stone*. Of Guy, who imitates bassist Slam Stewart's bit of humming unison with his instrument, pioneer bluesman B. B. King has said, "When I'm through, Buddy Guy is the only one who can take my place."

CLASSIC BLUES

Although Bessie Smith became known as Empress of the Blues, it was Mamie Smith (no relation) who launched the era of classic blues and race records in 1920. The unanticipated sales of Mamie's Okeh disk of "Crazy Blues" set record companies to recording other blues singers. Unlike folk and country blues, classic blues were sung by professional rather than amateur performers, and mostly by women rather than men. Many of them were composed and published rather than improvised and circulated by word of mouth. As public entertainment rather than personal plaints, they reached larger audiences through the media of records and vaudeville. Theatre Owners Booking Agency gave employment to Negro performers, who claimed that the initials T.O.B.A. stood for Tough on Black Artists. Classic blues singers were accompanied, not by harmonica and/or guitar, but by ragtime or "stride" pianists and frequently by instrumental combos.

Among the many females who recorded for the race labels of the day were Alberta Hunter, writer of "Down Hearted Blues," Bertha "Chippie" Hill, and a number of Smiths (Clara, Laura, Trixie) who were not related to each other. The most important of the Smiths was, of course, Bessie, who learned her art as a member of Gertrude "Ma" Rainey's touring troupe of Rabbit Foot Minstrels. Ma Rainey is credited with the authorship of "See See Rider," a classic blues revived by The Animals and other British rock groups. Bessie recorded one hundred and sixty blues in a voice that many feel could have done well in opera. "She could make entire audiences weep," says John Hammond, Talent Coordinator of Columbia Records.

The classic blues era came to an end long before Bessie's inhuman death in a 1937 automobile accident—an incident memorialized in Edward Albee's play *The Death of Bessie Smith.* It went down the flue of time, along with other cultural and social institutions, and businesses (including the record business), when the Great Depression struck in 1929. But it was in the period of classic blues that the public became acquainted with the pioneer country blues singers (Blind Lemon Jefferson *et al.*), who were put on wax for the first time.

RHYTHM-AND-BLUES

Although the era of the Big Bands (1935–46) took its impetus, sound and even its arrangements from the Negro bands of Fletcher Henderson, Jimmie Lunceford, Count Basie and others, swing was white man's music. But just as the white name bands nurtured the vocalists who became star singers after World War II, so Negro bands in the Southwest, in Kansas City, Oklahoma City, St. Louis and elsewhere, served as the training ground for a new generation of urban blues singers. With the big baritones (white) accounting for huge sales at the major labels, it fell to small, independent recording companies to showcase Negro artists and bands. When record executives and trade-paper editors, in a spirit of postwar liberalism, found the terms "race records" and "sepia blues" objectionable, the music of this new generation became known as rhythm-and-blues.

In Cincinnati, in the early 1940s, Syd Nathan, a successful record retailer, moved into a deserted icehouse and began recording Negro singers who drifted in from towns to the south. Bullmoose Jackson, discovered by r&b bandleader Lucky Millinder, was one of King Record's earliest artists. Then, there was Ivory Joe Hunter of New Orleans, a more sophisticated singer-writer whose ballad "I Almost Lost My Mind" was a hit later for teen-singer Pat Boone. From The Dominoes, who sold 2.5 million records of the spicy *Sixty Minute Man*, came Clyde McPhatter and Jackie Wilson, who scored later as individual soul artists. Most impressive of the King groups was The Midnighters, led by songwriter Hank Ballard, who had a # 1 ballad in 1958 in "Teardrops on Your Letter." On the back of this record was a rocking tune nobody noticed until four years later, when it exploded as one of the biggest hits and biggest dance crazes since the Lindy Hop. It was "The Twist," which became a runaway hit for Chubby Checker, a former Philadelphia chicken-plucker. Unquestionably, the biggest instrumental in the r&b

field is "Honky Tonk," a number that is reputed to have sold 4 million disks for the Bill Doggett quartet in 1956–57. It was the King label that also started The Platters, Little Willie John, Joe Tex, Nina Simone and Otis Redding.

About the same time that Syd Nathan was getting started in Cincinnati, two immigrant brothers, Leonard and Phil Chess, began recording some of the talent that appeared in their South Side Chicago club, The Macomba. One of the first artists who dropped into their store-front office was McKinley Morganfield, whose first single was "I Can't Be Satisfied," followed in 1948 by "Rollin' Stone." The Chess label, which succeeded the rather unsuccessful Aristocrat venture—despite Muddy Waters' contribution—produced two artists who have exerted a strong influence on rock. One was Ellis McDaniel, better known as Bo Diddley, a raucous and sometimes ribald performer who originated the swivelling hip motion copied by Presley. "We all owe a debt to The Beatles," Bo has said. "They started playing r&b with c&w rhythm and changes. It had to come from over there first for American kids to listen."

The other was Chuck Berry who worked with a small combo in East St. Louis and was studying to be a professional hairdresser. One weekend in Chicago, at the suggestion of Muddy Waters, whom he heard in a blues club, Berry went to see the Chess brothers with "Ida Red," a country music takeoff. Acting as their own engineers, the brothers recorded the tune in their two-by-four studio, but they gave it an r&b instead of a c&w sound and feeling. "Mabelline," as it was renamed—Berry claims that the title had no relationship to his abortive career as a cosmetician—became one of the first Triple Crowns on *Billboard*'s charts: # 1 r&b, # 1 c&w, and # 1 pop.

Another Chess artist whose impact continues to be felt, particularly among British rock singers, is Chester Burnett, known as Howlin' Wolf. Leonard Chess says he found him in West Memphis, Arkansas, on one of his periodic field trips, during which he would set up his tape recorder in a bean or cotton field and run a long extension cord to an electric outlet in a farmhouse. Chess recorded Arthur Crudup, who influenced Presley, in a cotton field in Forest, Mississippi. According to Burnett, he cut records for Sun in Memphis and for RPM in Los Angeles before he recorded for Chess. Born and raised on a plantation in West Point, Mississippi, he early idolized the Father of Country Music, Jimmie Rodgers. Finding that he could not "blue yodel" as his idol did, he took to growling. This form of expression became Howlin' when he adopted his nickname. The Wolf came from tales that his grandfather told him of pioneering days in Mississippi. He has written many successful songs, including "Killing Ground," recorded by The Electric Flag, and "Sittin' On Top of the World," recorded by The Grateful Dead, The Cream and other rock groups.

R&b labels did not spring up in the Midwest alone. More appeared on the west coast, to which Negro singers emigrated from Texas and the Southwest, bringing with them a tradition of unison, screaming saxes, loud, driving drumming, and "riffing" (the repetition of a phrase, over and over, sometimes with minor variations). Three of the more important coast labels were Specialty, responsible for Little Richard; Imperial, today a subsidiary of Liberty Records; and Modern, founded in the mid-40s and located today against a spur of railroad track on the "outskirts of town."

In the 1950s the diminutive was a favorite nickname of male Negro artists. Little Walter was on Checker. Little Willie John was on King. Little Jr. Parker was on Duke. (By contrast, female singers did not balk at being called Big: Maybelle, for one.) But none was more influential than Specialty Records' Little Richard, who amassed four # 1 disks in Presley's miraculous year, 1956. The titles are familiar since some of today's rock groups have revived them: "Long Tall Sally," "Ready Teddy," "Rip It Up" and "Slippin' and Slidin'." Singing in a strident, high-pitched voice that occasionally rose to an impassioned scream, Little Richard (Penniman) scored with five Top

Ten tunes the following year. At this time, he exhibited a fondness for women's names: "Jenny, Jenny," "Lucille" and "Miss Ann." But two of the songs were peremptory demands: "Keep A-Knockin' " and "Send Me Some Lovin'." In a recent essay, Albert Goldman contends that Little Richard's popularity with ghetto buyers was the result of his "erotic defiance." Little Richard was not really having a good time—he was vigorously asserting his right to have one. "Reckless and rebellious," Mr. Goldman writes, "he gave us the first taste of the voice that was later to holler 'Burn, baby, burn!' " But defiance was hardly a new note in Negro song, considering old blues like " 'Taint Nobody's Biz-ness If I Do" and "A Graveyard of My Own" or a then recent Top Ten swinger by Bo Diddley, "I'm a Man." In 1954 Muddy Waters had made hits of the boastfully erotic "I'm Ready" and "I'm Your Hootchie Kootchie Man." No, Little Richard's impact was based on the unbuttoned intensity of his style, the orgiastic frenzy that Jerry Lee Lewis tried to capture at the time in "Great Balls of Fire" and that Jackie Wilson and James Brown later imitated and elaborated. He was the first of the ecstasy singers.

B. B. King, the most influential of Modern's finds, was born in Mississippi, and came to the coast label in 1940 from a successful disk jockey career in Memphis. King was known there as the Beale Street Blues Boy. In *Urban Blues*, Charles Keil hails his style as "pure" and "authentic" blues singing. But a reviewer of a recent LP, *Blues Is King*, characterizes his style as "frenzy bordering on hysteria," and dismisses it as unconvincing, "strained . . . affectation." Keil praises King for not modulating his style to attract a white or teenage audience and for not attempting to enlarge his following by using gospel chord progressions or churchlike effects, as have Ray Charles and Bobby Bland. King's churchlike imitators include Lou Rawls, who also interpolates monologues in his songs.

In the year that B. B. left Memphis for California, Fats Domino hit paydirt for the Imperial label with a song appropriately called "Fat Man." Since then, Antoine Domino, who was born in Louisiana in 1928 and was performing in New Orleans honky tonks when he was just ten, has collected eighteen Gold Records. Written in collaboration with Dave Bartholomew, the New Orleans bandleader who brought him to Imperial's attention, his hits include "Ain't That a Shame," a bestseller also for young Pat Boone; "I'm Walkin'," a hit also for young Ricky Nelson; and "Boll Weevil," a hit also for Teresa Brewer. Although Domino's feeling for the blues is implicit in everything he sings, his is a "manicured" style that appeals to pop, white audiences. He was also able to take country hits, "Blueberry Hill," for example, and, like Ray Charles later, move them into the Top Ten on r&b charts. (The 1968 revival of r&b brought him back on the national record scene with a new album, *Fats Is Back*, on Reprise.)

The year 1949 saw another west coast independent open shop. Like the Chess Brothers in Chicago, Don Robey operated a club (The Bronze Peacock) in Houston. The delay of another r&b label, Aladdin, in releasing records of an artist playing his club, motivated Robey to record Gatemouth Brown himself and to start the successful Peacock label. Those were the days, Robey recalls, when "r&b music was felt to be degrading . . . low, and not to be heard by respectable people." This attitude was manifested not only by whites but by middle-class Negroes as well. Robey's great find was a young man from Memphis, Bobby Bland. As a result of listening to B. B. King during his Memphis sojourn and to gospel singer Ira Tucker of the Dixie Hummingbirds, Bland developed a style that is a cross between, but not a wedding of, gospel and blues.

The east coast had a score of independent r&b record companies, several of which contributed to the jazz discography— Savoy's catalogue includes early Charlie "Bird" Parker, while Prestige's includes early Miles Davis. Of labels like Apollo, National, Jubilee, Herald, Bethlehem, Savoy and Prestige, the strongest and most important is Atlantic. "What we managed

32

to achieve," Ahmet Ertegun, one of the founders, has said, "was something like the authentic blues, but cleaner, less rough and perforce more sophisticated. The first important vocalist whom we signed, Ruth Brown, was not a country blues singer, but a jazz and pop singer who had in her childhood been exposed to gospel, and to a lesser extent, to blues." When Ertegun asked Brown to sing some blues, she told him that she did not like blues. "As a result, the blues records we made with her came out like urbanized, watered-down versions of real blues. But we discovered white kids started buying these records because the real blues were too hard for them to swallow."

Ruth Brown cut "So Long" on her first date in 1949, became a star overnight, and made Atlantic a label to reckon with. The following year, when Ruth had "Teardrops from My Eyes," the label acquired The Clovers, for whom Ertegun, writing under the pen name of Nugetre (his name spelled backward), produced a # 1 song in "Don't You Know I Love You." Big Joe Turner was signed in 1951—his first disk, "Chains of Love," a Nugetre collaboration; Ray Charles in 1952; Clyde McPhatter and LaVern Baker in 1953. By then, the winds of r&b were developing hurricane force. As they swept over the music scene, setting up tides in pop and country, Atlantic's domination of the r&b scene took on major proportions. (Nor did its impact as a jazz label lessen.) Today, it maintains its potent position, not only because of such powerhouse soul artists as Wilson Pickett, Percy Sledge and Aretha Franklin, but because it is able to attract rock groups like The Young Rascals, The Bee Gees and The Cream.

R&b was an urbanized and less raucous form of blues than country or folk blues, but more vulgar and more exhibitionistic than classic blues. More so than the classic blues, its accompaniment consisted of small and large combos in which the tenor sax, honking style, was dominant. "The riff itself was the basis," LeRoi Jones observes in *Blues People*, "the saxophonist repeating it much past any useful context, continuing it until he and the crowd were thoroughly exhausted physically and emotionally. The point, it seemed, was to spend oneself with as much attention as possible, and also to make the instruments sound as unmusical, or as *non-Western*, as possible."

R&b flourished as a segregated music in the days when Negro jazzmen developed bop. If one accepts Jones' reasoned contention that Negro music is "the result of certain specific ways of thinking about the world (and only ultimately about the *ways* in which music can be made)," then it is clear that bop was an expression of frustration, hostility and alienation. The end of World War II did not bring an end to segregation, discrimination and deprivation. Although Negro musicians were now conservatory-trained, symphony orchestras, recording studios, radio house bands and motion picture studio orchestras were still off limits. Musically crude, r&b was an expression of similar urban emotions. In its heyday, saxophonists in blues bands would often engage in contests to see who could squeal, screech, or honk louder and longer. One well-known tenorman, Jay Mc-Neely, would throw himself on the floor and, lying on his back, kick his feet in the air as he kept honking one loud note repeatedly. Can anyone conceive a more graphic representation of frustration and anger, almost childlike in character?

In the r&b era, that is, before 1954, the walls of musical segregation were tall enough to keep Negro labels out of the white market, but low enough to give white disks access to Negro markets. In 1950, for example, Ivory Joe Hunter had three r&b bestsellers, but none of these made *Billboard*'s pop Honor Roll of Hits. Neither did Ruth Brown's tremulous "Teardrops from My Eyes" or her "Mama, He Treats Your Daughter Mean," recently a hit for Herman's Hermits. During this period, the bestsellers of Howlin' Wolf, Muddy Waters and B. B. King remained marooned on ghetto charts. But Johnnie Ray's "Cry" (1951) went to # 1 on r&b charts, as did Les Paul and Mary Ford's "How High the Moon."

By 1954, however, the flow of hits began to move in the opposite direction. And by October of 1955, *Billboard's* pop Honor Roll included Negro disks as well as white cover records in the Top Ten: "Seventeen's" success was based on the sales of Boyd Bennett's King disk as well as that of the Fontane Sisters, and "Ain't That a Shame" was a hit for Fats Domino as well as for Pat Boone. But there were also songs that owed their prosperity entirely to Negro artists. The Platters had "Only You" by themselves and Chuck Berry had "Mabelline" to himself. (In this period, Dot Records, originally a country label out of Gallatin, Tennessee, developed into a major company—bought not too long ago for several million by Paramount Pictures—by covering r&b hits with white artists.)

In studying bestsellers of the early 1950s, one can see, as from a plane flying over two converging sets of railroad tracks, the approaching entente of white and black music that came with rockabilly. For while r&b was then shut out of the white pop market, hillbilly was not. In 1950 "Slipping Around," a c&w hit by Floyd Tillman, was high on *Billboard's* pop Honor Roll, as a result of Tillman's recording. So was "Chattanooga Shoe Shine Boy" on Red Foley's cloth-snapping platter. In the next few years, pop artists began covering country hits like "Tennessee Waltz" and the many fine songs by the Hillbilly Shakespeare, Hank Williams. In short, by the mid-1950s when r&b began infiltrating pop, it met hillbilly in a head-on collision, as it were. The contact resulted in a merger—a mixed marriage that produced the sound heard round the world.

4 TEENAGE ROCK : *Buckskins,*
Triplets and Falsettos

Early rock 'n' roll was white, monotonous, juvenile and in search of identity. Like most young generations, the children of World War II felt themselves an alien group in an unfriendly, adult world. But unlike many generations, and particularly the depression generation of its parents, this one had buying power and could enforce its desires. It quickly began carrying the banners of a strange power called Teenland, creating its own folklore and elevating its own heroes. The early shape of its rebellion was adolescent, if not infantile, and its gripes were immature—certainly by comparison with the protest rock of Bob Dylan and his successors.

With the emergence of Presley, the words "teen" and "teenage" became war cries. From 1956 on, there was a succession of songs like "Teen Age Crush" (Tommy Sands), "A Teenager's Romance" (Ricky Nelson), "Ballad of a Teenage Queen" (Johnny Cash) and "Sweet Little Sixteen" (Chuck Berry).

Songs of this period abounded in the styles and symbols of young living. Julius LaRosa sang of "Lipstick and Candy" and "Rubber Sole Shoes" while George Hamilton IV warbled about

36

"A Rose and a Baby Ruth." In 1957 there were songs about "Short Shorts" (Royal Teens) and "A White Sport Coat and a Pink Carnation" (Marty Robbins), followed in 1958 and 1959 by songs about "Queen of the Hop" (Bobby Darin) and "Bobby Sox to Stockings" (Frankie Avalon). During these years, Simon & Garfunkel, then still in secondary school and known as Tom and Jerry, had a modest and forgotten hit in "Hey, Schoolgirl." There were songs about teenage dances like "The Stroll" (Diamonds) and about teenage expressions like "All Shook Up" (Presley), "Raunchy" (Bill Justis) and "Rumble" (Link Wray).

But even this lightweight fare was superior to a large number of songs in which lyrics were sacrificed to the demand for a driving dance beat. In these teen and r&b tunes, an easy mark for critical condemnation, there was little or no verbal content. Words, and not merely nonsense syllables, were used for their sound. Rhythm was the content.

Humorous songs were rare. The teenage song cosmos seemed weighted down with problems. Unrequited love was one. It took a young-generation turn as the frustration of the young boy in love with an older girl, (and *vice versa*) became a frequent theme: "Born Too Late" (Poni-Tails) and "Diana" (Paul Anka). Parental domination, fault-finding and lack of understanding were others, as in "Yakety Yak," "Why Don't They Understand?" and "Get a Job." The problem of the ugly duckling was treated in a number of songs, but in none so moving as "Charlie Brown." Loneliness was a frequent theme, as in Dion's "Lonely Teenager" and Paul Anka's "I'm a Lonely Boy."

One of the first teenage idols to emerge after Presley was a young man whose white buckskins became symbolic of the image he sought to create in contrast with Elvis' blue suedes. Although Pat Boone recorded r&b songs, as did virtually all Dot artists, his renditions were whiter than white. When he cut Fats Domino's big hit in 1955, he changed "Ain't It a Shame" to "Ain't That A Shame." Other bestsellers like "Tutti Frutti" and "At My Front Door" were buckskin versions, the former

37

of a hit disk by Little Richard on Specialty, the west coast r&b label, and the latter of a hit by the El Doradoes on Vee Jay, a Chicago r&b label. The year 1955 saw *Rebel Without a Cause* and the rise of the James Dean alienation syndrome. But Pat Boone, married to his high school sweetheart, father of a baby girl and a student at Columbia University, stepped forth as a symbol of youthful optimism, purity and wholesomeness.

As the years rolled on, Boone never deviated from this image, and racked up a sale of disks and hit albums second only to Presley. Not too long after he became a record seller, he undertook the added function of guiding teenagers in the path of righteousness. His book *Twixt Twelve and Twenty* became the top nonfiction bestseller of 1959. "The Pat Boone Press Manual" enumerated the following as guideposts for maturity: the Bible, the Golden Rule, cleanliness is next to godliness, and sound financial practices. Frank Sinatra is supposed to have said: "I'd like my son to be like Pat—until he was three years old."

The image of the All-American Boy, applauded by parents and ministers, helped win Boone a seven-picture, million-dollar movie contract, and in 1956, his own TV program, *The Pat Boone Chevy Show*. The respect he commanded among teenagers has carried over to the present, so that today, as a granddaddy of rock, he has become the epitome of daytime TV interviewers. When Myrna Loy appeared recently on his show and he asked which leading men "were the most fun to do love scenes with?" Miss Loy's mouth fell agape, and she said: "Well, I certainly never expected that question of you."

Boone still has an outdoor face that suggests humility and solid patriotism. Of his film work, he has said: "I would never do anything with a story in which the moral doesn't have an uplifting influence. Leave the moody 'adults only' films to somebody else." His catalogue of over forty active LPs includes a number of religious albums: *He Leadeth Me, My God and I* and *How Great Thou Art*. On his TV show, he continues to wear white sneakers, white loafers or the famous white bucks.

In 1957 Ricky Nelson, then just sixteen, gave his first solo performance on the stage of Hamilton High School in Los Angeles. In April of that year, he made his TV debut on a program called *Ozzie and Harriet*. Those who were disposed to doubt his talent, since O & H were his father and mother, had to cope with statistics: before the end of the year, he was on bestseller charts with "Be Bop Baby" and "A Teenager's Romance" and in 1958–59 had hit records in "Believe What You Say," "I Got a Feeling," "Poor Little Fool" and "Never Be Anyone Else But You." Nelson early sensed (or was skilfully guided by press agents) that he must eliminate the possible enmity that might be engendered by his favored position. And so he always presented himself as "just another teenager" and stressed his concern, as the song titles above suggest, with sincerity. "If it's not, you know, sincere, it's not too good. In a song, I hate to hear lingo. . . . I like a song that tells a story without meaningless words." Like Boone, he projected an image of the good boy at home, living gracefully and lovingly with his solid parents. What he sold has been characterized as "sincere sex." Before long, it helped him sell 6 million disks.

The image of the less secure youngster appeared on the teen scene with a young Canadian of Lebanese descent. At the beginning of his teens, rather than the end, Paul Anka startled show business with "Diana," which he wrote and recorded, followed quickly by "(I'm Just a) Lonely Boy," which he surely was not by then, "You Are My Destiny" and the arching melody of "Put Your Head on My Shoulder." Anka's tremendous appeal was in his vivacity and extreme youthfulness, the latter concealing a precociously sharp business mind. If one is to accept the claim of psychologists that adolescent girls fear and worry about sex at the same time that they are curious, then Anka perhaps attracted them because he was so unprepossessing as to offer no threat at all. By the 1960s, he had been a hit singer for so many years that he had to go looking for the adult audiences that frequented the Copa in New York, which he has been doing without the sensational impact he had hoped for.

A teenage idol who made the transition rather easily was Bobby Darin, who came on the recording scene in 1958 with "Splish Splash," the hit song he co-authored about a young man who forgot that he had company and came out of a relaxed tub all naked. Presley was humble and sexy. Boone and Nelson were humble but sexless. Darin was neither humble nor sexless. He was brash, egotistical and arrogantly self-confident. He began emulating Sinatra early and drew a large press for a time by stirring up controversy both with and about Sinatra. His background explained his audacity in part. Born Walden Robert Cassotto in 1936, he was the son of a cabinetmaker and convicted racketeer who died in jail before Bobby was born. His mother, of old Yankee stock, had been in vaudeville (billed as "the girl with a thousand voices") and, after his birth, tried to support him by teaching retarded children. But the family was on home relief, and he had periodic bouts with rheumatic fever. Although he is still unable to read music—he is musically self-taught—he can play piano, drums, vibes, banjo and guitar, and he has written the scores for several movies.

He had been knocking around Broadway for five years when Connie Francis' manager got him a Decca recording contract. It proved nonrewarding, as did his first seven records on Atco. The eighth, "Splish Splash," sold over a million. His succeeding disk, "Mack the Knife" by Kurt Weill and Bertolt Brecht, not only was a winner, but gained him an adult following. Darin was one of the few teenage idols who made the transition easily and quickly, assisted by comic George Burns, who became friend, father substitute and sponsor of his nightclub act. Darin early manifested a large measure of cynicism, more adult than juvenile. "The kids have phony heroes," he told an *Esquire* writer, not long after he was chosen Best New Artist of 1959 and received a Grammy for Best Vocal Performance (Male). "They have no individuality. They don't know who's leading them. I feel for them, but I'm not going to lead, Charlie. You call the roll of commercial guys, put me first."

He was soon appearing in movies, winning a Best Actor citation from the Hollywood Press Association for his portrayal of a sadistic American fascist in *Pressure Point* and an Oscar nomination for his role as the mentally ill corporal in *Captain Newman, M.D.* (1964). He has appeared in more than ten movies, written many motion picture title songs and the complete scores for *Lively Set* and *That Funny Feeling*. At the Copa, he has broken all attendance records, including those set by Sammy Davis, Jr. and Frank Sinatra. In eleven years, he has sold more than 2 million LPs and over 15 million singles, and he has had seven songs in the Top Ten.

"I can only do things naturally," he once told a director, who suggested that he learn stagecraft. "Anything technical interferes with my love of what I'm doing." Like other statements of his, this sounds strangely reminiscent of what Sinatra has said on many occasions when he refused to rehearse or redo scenes. Darin has remained what doubtless contributed to making him a teenage idol: arrogant, self-confident and brash. Adults thought of him as obnoxious, which did not hurt his appeal. Although he is much more suave today, having been married to a movie teenage queen and fathered a child, he remains cocky and outspoken.

From the City of Brotherly Love came two singers who were frequently cited as instances of the period's "synthetic singers," or as they were sometimes more bluntly characterized, "no-talent" singers who became recording stars through the ingenuity of recording engineers. Both singers exemplified a theory held at that time by music biz pros—that teenagers did not appreciate polish and perfection, suspected those qualities, and flocked to those who were, like themselves, awkward, inept and not particularly·gifted. Frankie Avalon who came to the fore in 1958, had so little voice he was hardly audible in personal appearances and danced so little that he fulfilled the prescription of ineptness. But he had a high, shining pompadour of wavy hair, soulful eyes, sallow complexion and a baby, almost feminine face. He wore silk suits and, like Pat Boone, white buckskins. He followed a precept of breathless humility. His manner impressed press people as gentle, immature, if not a bit frightened. His first hit was "Dede Dinah," written by Bob Marcucci and Pete De Angelis, his mentors at Chancellor Records. Succeeding songs revealed no special outlook, though all dealt with baby love, as in "Venus" (1959), who was so far above him.

Of Fabian, Avalon's Philadelphia associate and part-protégé, it was once said: "No-talents fell in love with their own image." Having scored with Avalon, ex-waiter Bob Marcucci set about creating a new idol in Fabian, whom he had spotted one morning on a South Philadelphia doorstep, and whose looks appealed to him. Marcucci hired voice teachers for the fourteen-year-old, who had never sung a note in his life. They told him he was wasting his money. But Marcucci refused to give up and made a recording with his "find." It "bombed"—was an abject flop. However, in personal appearances, the Fabian charisma excited other teenagers.

Perhaps Avalon and Fabian would not have made it were it not for the assistance of a Philadelphia disk jockey described by *Life* as a man who could "make almost any record." Dick Clark was then the genial ringmaster of a daily TV show on the ABC network. *The American Bandstand* was one of the first, and doubtless the most successful, of the shows in which teenagers "danced apart" to recordings and heard their favorite r 'n' r artists "lip sync" to new and hit records. When Clark celebrated his birthday in December, 1958, among those who came to Philadelphia bearing good wishes were Avalon, Bobby Darin, Pat Boone, Sal Mineo, Danny and the Juniors, Little Anthony and Connie Francis—a veritable array of the aristocracy of teen record stars and an indication of the power of the platter spinner with the Arrow-collar profile to launch new hits.

By Christmas, 1958, "Turn Me Loose" became a bestseller,

followed in 1959 by "Tiger." Within the year of his discovery, Fabian had a screen contract. Although he received only $35,000 for his chore in Twentieth Century-Fox's *Hound Dog Man*, his records of the title tune and "This Friendly World" were substantial sellers. On the screen, Fabian sang no better than on disks and displayed the same adolescent awkwardness and nervous fumbling that ostensibly made the girls want to mother him. He himself made the most candid disclosure of his appeal when he told an interviewer: "Maybe I would never have made it if I could sing."

To the non-singers who became teenage singing idols in 1957–59 should be added a youngster who had the same feminine quality as Fabian and Avalon, but who really could act. That Sal Mineo could not sing, despite the electronic gimmicks and enveloping accompaniment employed on his records, was apparent in "Start Movin' " and "Lasting Love," two recordings that made noise in 1957. But there was one short-lived non-singer who actually had a # 1 record. It was a "fluke," as they say in the business, but it was also a testimonial to the power of repeated appearance on TV. The nonsinger was Edward Byrnes, who played a jive-talking parking lot attendant on *77 Sunset Strip* and who attracted teenage interest because of his compulsive habit of combing his hair. Although most of the singing on "Kookie, Kookie (Lend Me Your Comb)" was done by Connie Stevens, it was obviously Byrnes' TV image that sold the disk. An analyst of the appeal of the non-singers suggested that teenagers were buying "inept sex." While this epithet might have applied to some of the non-singers, it surely lacked applicability to the more suave brand of sex exuded by Byrnes and his comb.

The wartime population shift that saw many Negroes migrate to northern factory towns, thereby creating a market for ghetto r&b, also found many southern whites heading north and bringing with them a taste for c&w. It was not surprising, then, that pop charts of this period were invaded by c&w singers like Don Gibson, Jim Reeves, Webb Pierce, Ray Price and young Bobby

Helms ("My Special Angel"). At least one country duo made a special appeal to teenagers. The Everly Brothers, born in Kentucky and raised in Knoxville, Tennessee, were a decisive influence on The Beatles. They had a delicate nasal sound, somewhat feminine in texture. Although they were recorded by a New York company, Cadence Records, their songs were almost all the work of a Nashville-based writing team, Felice and Boudleaux Bryant. (Both Everly boys later proved themselves capable writers, with Phil, the younger, accounting for "Gee, But I'm Lonely," recorded by Pat Boone, and Don writing " 'Til I Kissed You," a song the brothers recorded in 1959.)

All of their hits from "Bye, Bye, Love," their first record and a smash in 1957, through "Take a Message to Mary" in 1959, were the work of the Bryants in collaboration or by Boudleaux alone. Unquestionably the most daring song recorded by the lads was their second hit of 1957, "Wake Up, Little Susie," in which it was apparent that Little Susie had slept in her young lover's company much beyond the time when she should have been home. But their sound was so innocently youthful—as The Beatles' was in their early records—that no censorship problems were encountered.

The light, bright, young sound also, perhaps, accounted for the effortless success of "Party Doll," a song that brought Buddy Knox to public notice. Knox was one of a group of singers that came out of the Texas-New Mexico complex. The most influential were Buddy Holly and the Crickets, who made their first recordings at the Norman Petty Recording Studio in faraway Clovis, New Mexico, and then landed on the Coral label, a Decca subsidiary. There is a Buddy Holly cult as there is a James Dean cult, and for a similar reason. After scoring with "That'll Be the Day" (1957) and "Peggy Sue" (1958), Holly's burnished, new career was dramatically cut short by an airplane accident in which the entire group was killed. His impact is apparent even today in a rock group out of Northern England that calls itself The Hollies, and in repackaged LPs that continue to be issued.

44

Although feminine-sounding boys were an important phalanx of teenage rock, few girls were successful as singers. Understandably so, since the record buyers were mainly girls. The major exception was Connie Francis of Brooklyn, New York, and Bloomfield, New Jersey, whose first hit on MGM Records was a revival of the oldie "Who's Sorry Now?" Miss Francis took command of the teenage market in 1958 with "Stupid Cupid," an ebullient rocker written by Howard Greenfield (music) and Neil Sedaka (words). Miss Francis was able to move into the film scene with *Where the Boys Are*, into the international market with recordings in different languages and, because of her versatility, into the adult LP market. Although she is still under thirty, she has over forty active LPs and is reputed to have sold over 50 million records.

Neil Sedaka, a student of classical piano from the time he was eight (he had gone to Juilliard on a piano scholarship) and a record seller from the age of seventeen (1958), was not able to make the transition. His first record, "The Diary," sold almost a million RCA Victor disks. During the succeeding five years, he had teenage hits in "Calendar Girl," "Little Devil," "Happy Birthday," "Sweet Sixteen" and "Breakin' Up Is Hard To Do," all songs written in collaboration with Howard Greenfield. Sedaka and his partner were part of a large stable of writing performers developed by Aldon Music, a young firm that set the pattern in the early 1960s for the independent recording-publishing-managing combines that now are characteristic of the rock scene both here and abroad. A partnership of Al Nevins, former guitarist with The Three Suns, and Don Kirshner, ex-manager of Bobby Darin, Aldon Music was sold for several million dollars to Screen Gems-Columbia, the present owners. At its sale in 1964, the company was just five years old.

Tom Morgan, who made a study of teenage idols for *Esquire* in 1960, concluded that it was a generation "with nothing to say," that it made virtues of "conformity, mediocrity and sincerity" and that it was interested in "safe-sex heroes" (in which classification most white singing idols seemed to fit). He added:

"All that seems real about teenage self-expression and the safe-sex heroes is their dedication to unreality, to songs of watered-down, self-pitying-blues-that-aren't-blues, and to aimless hostility." All these observations were valid in terms of the singers mentioned thus far. It is clear that the generation had not yet defined its enemies, except for parents, and that it was rebellious without causes. But would Morgan's conclusion have been the same had his survey included Jerry Lee Lewis, who approached Negro frenzy in songs like "Great Balls of Fire" and "Whole Lotta Shakin' Goin' On." And suppose he had included Negro singing sensations of the day in his scrutiny? After all, the record sellers of the period included "unsafe"-sex singers like Jackie Wilson and Chuck Willis. Would he have concluded that teenagers take refuge in a "pseudo-world that is spoiled and banal and hypererotic" had he considered such blue-suede singers as Chuck Berry, Little Richard, Clyde McPhatter, and such groups as The Clovers, The Drifters and the highly successful Coasters? It may well be that Negro singers began to gain acceptance in white markets because teenage ballads were so insipid and white teenage singers were so gutless. Of course, the Negro singers who gained acceptance were generally the whitest of the black—like Fats Domino, Chuck Berry and Johnny Mathis.

In 1955 a Negro group called The Platters, who had a number of r&b hits on the King label, moved over to Mercury and quickly invaded pop charts with two successive hits, "The Great Pretender" and "Only You." While the latter was a melodic ballad, given impact and intensity by the group's sound, the former tapped a vein of great appeal to teenagers: the torment of the individual who knows he is unworthy of the admiration he receives, and the inner insecurity of the outwardly accomplished. Of several groups on Atlantic Records that began to attract white audiences, The Clovers, The Drifters and The Coasters, the last mentioned made the strongest appeal. Originally known as The Robins—the names of birds were for a time most popular with Negro singing groups—and recorded by a Los Angeles label (Spark), they landed on Atlantic when Jerry Leiber and Mike Stoller sold the company and joined Atlantic as writer-producers in 1956.

The Coasters scored, not only because their records had a big, danceable beat, but because they sounded adolescent themes. "Searchin'" and "Young Blood" of 1957 were a build-up for the 1958 smash "Yakety Yak" and "Charlie Brown" in 1959. "Yak" brilliantly portrays the tension between parents and youngsters over fun versus chores. In driving, raucous voices, the group mimicks elders ordering them about and tongue-lashing them for goofing off. Adolescent resentment reaches its peak in the title phrase, repeated mincingly and almost in passing at the end of each verse.

Both as a record and song, "Yakety Yak" was a significant departure. Brushing aside a convention of the music business which favored the frequent repetition of a title at the top of a song, they made their title an exclamatory mark at the end. Moreover, since the title became a comment on what went before, it gave the record the dramatic character of dialogue in a play. This was an anticipation of a style that became quite important in rock with The Beatles and others.

"Charlie Brown," another song that employed this theatrical device, was funnier than "Yakety Yak." Obviously inspired by the well-known cartoon character, it told of Charlie's schoolboy transgressions, from loitering in the halls to writing on the walls and calling the English teacher "Daddy-O." And always there was that nasal voice with the confused air plaintively asking: "Why is everybody always pickin' on me?"

Among Negro soloists, two recording artists made a special effort to deal with teenage themes. On the Specialty label out of Hollywood, Little Richard scored with a series of young songs beginning with "Tutti Frutti" in 1955. Co-writer of this tune, which was covered by Pat Boone, Richard Penniman was also responsible for "Long Tall Sally," a favorite of British rock groups in the 1960s. Chuck Berry on Chess, who also exerted a strong influence on the British, was even more perceptive in uncovering subjects with teenage appeal. Beginning with "Mabelline" in 1955, he wrote and recorded "Roll Over Beethoven" (a Beatles' hit in 1964), "Rock and Roll Music," "School Days (Ring! Ring! Goes the Bell)," "Johnny B. Goode," "Sweet Little Sixteen," and, in 1959, "Almost Grown."

Among the blue-suede crowd, romance and love frequently took a physical shape, and their sound, regardless of lyrics, was inescapably sexy. This was true of Al Hibbler, who had a warm, yearning sound in blue ballads like "After the Lights Go Down Low" (1956); Clyde McPhatter, who was a shouter in declarative songs like "Without Love (There Is Nothing)" and the million-copy disk "A Lover's Question"; Lloyd Price, who started on the west coast Specialty label and quickly moved to ABC-Paramount where he had pop bestsellers in "You've Got Personality" and "Stagger Lee," an up-dated blues; and Jackie Wilson a Detroit screamer in the ecstatic groove of James Brown. Curiously, three of Wilson's bestsellers in 1958-59, "Lonely Teardrops," "To Be Loved" and "I'll Be Satisfied," were written by a trio that included Berry Gordy, later the creator of the Motown Sound.

The expanding market for Negro artists among teenage record buyers also brought to the fore "cafe au lait" stylists like Roy Hamilton, who possessed a big-preacher quality but hit pop charts with show tunes; Sam Cooke, whose abortive and later soulful career started with the pretty, succulent sound of "You Send Me"; and Brook Benton, who made the biggest dent in the pop market with songs in which he projected, not without a sly sense of humor, the image of the sexually domineering and egotistical male—"It's Just a Matter of Time," "Kiddio," "Thank You, Pretty Baby."

In short, while the blue-suede group presented a more realistic and visceral approach to love, it did not help clarify the churnings, confusions or direction of the younger generation.

48

This fact is made clear by an examination of the work of the most successful and original writing team of the period. Lieber and Stoller, who came originally from Baltimore but met in Los Angeles, first attracted attention in 1955 with a song called "Black Denim Trousers and Motorcycle Boots." To them, it was a takeoff on the coast motorcycle gangs, notably portrayed in the Marlon Brando film *The Wild Ones*. However, the song was taken seriously by the Harley-Davidson crowd and their followers, and became an enormous hit for The Cheers and Les Baxter. Lieber and Stoller came east shortly thereafter—they were both just twenty-one—and, except for Presley, wrote almost exclusively for Negro artists, some of whose recordings they supervised.

To Presley's list of hits, they contributed "Hound Dog," "Don't" and several of the songs, including the title tune, of his film *Jailhouse Rock*. For Ruth Brown, an Atlantic star of the late 1940s, they wrote "Lucky Lips" and "I Want To Do More," standard r&b ballads. As they became more effective in handling idiomatic Negro humor and styling, they produced "Fool's Fall in Love" for The Drifters. For The Coasters, in addition to "Yak" and "Brown," they wrote "Along Came Jones" and "Poison Ivy," the lattter a song that delighted adolescent listeners with its punning title. Although their more original songs, like those in the latter group, sold in the million copy class, it was "Hound Dog" that accounted for the largest sale, over 5 million disks.

Compared with the rock hits of the mid-60s, even the more original Lieber-Stoller songs are rather superficial. There is no criticism of or attack on adult values, but simply a sardonic, sometimes trenchant documentation of the conflict between generations. Siding with the youngsters, they were asking, as George Hamilton IV did in a 1958 bestseller, "Why Don't They Understand?" or humorously underscoring the plight of the adolescent underdog, who triumphed when his cheap car beat the Caddie in "Beep, Beep," a 1958 hit for The Playmates. Teenage songs of the 1955–59 era were little more than petty gripes against the adult world, or efforts to peer into some of the forbidden areas where adults had placed large "Keep Out" signs: namely, sex. The songs were omens of a youthful uprising in the making. The onslaught came later with Bob Dylan and The Beatles.

5 BOB DYLAN : *From Protest*

to Folk Rock

In 1959 a curious thing happened in pop music. The famous Mormon Tabernacle Choir of Salt Lake City had a bestselling record. The song had once been a hymn known as "Say, Brother, Will You Meet Me?" In the Civil War era, opponents of slavery had sung it as "John Brown's Body." It was best known as "Battle Hymn of the Republic," or "Glory, Glory, Hallelujah," the words sung by the Tabernacle Choir. In a backward glance, this occurrence acquires some special significance, particularly when one realizes that the name chosen that year for a new, standard-type western TV show was *The Rebel.* James Dean, one of the younger generation's idols, had already established that it was made up of "rebels without a cause." By 1959 it was evident that traditional tensions between adolescents and adults were crystallizing into basic value differences. The alienated were in the process of finding a cause for their rebellion.

In the preceding year, a group called The Kingston Trio had adapted and recorded a Blue Ridge mountain song about a Civil War veteran hanged for the murder of his faithless sweetheart. The tremendous success of "Tom Dooley" was the harbinger

51

of a folk revival. The youngsters who had grown up on rockabilly and teenage songs were now in college. They were beginning to re-examine the past as a means of probing their dissatisfaction with the present. "Collegians want songs that deal with what's going on in the world," *Variety* observed. Others noted that there was a search for roots, and that young people, disturbed by the insecurity and confusion of the times, were harking back to the stability and simplicity of folk values.

In 1961 a restless young man, who was soon to act as spokesman for part of his generation, left his midwestern habitat and journeyed to New York to commune with Woody Guthrie, a great folk poet of the depression generation. Author of "This Land Is Your Land," sometimes called the anthem of American folksingers, and of "So Long, It's Been Good To Know You," anthem of the dispossessed Dust Bowl farmers, Guthrie lay incurably ill in a hospital. (In a mood of depression, Guthrie had himself once journeyed east to draw strength from another folksinger, Huddie Ledbetter, the son of an ex-slave and known as Leadbelly.) Bob Dylan, who was then described as a cross between a beatnik and a choirboy, was deeply influenced by the "talkin' blues" style of the man to whose bedside he came.

Events moved apace for the twenty-year-old who from his early teens had been running away from his home in Hibbing, Minnesota, and who had found no answers to his troubling questions in a year of vagrant college work. Within weeks of his appearance at Gerde's Folk City, a Greenwich Village showcase for new talent, he was in a Columbia Records studio, strumming an acoustic guitar, playing a wheezing harmonica, and talking his own songs with a nasal twang. He was a crude performer, affectedly crude in the eyes of many. But listeners and reviewers were impressed by the originality of his poetry. The lyrics of his songs were early characterized as *poems*, leading later critics to credit him with inspiring the surprisingly widespread interest in poetry among the young.

The fact is that Dylan was writing "psychedelic" poetry long before the word came into common use. To some critics, the pile-up of imagery in which his songs abounded was prolixity, lack of discipline, inability to distinguish between the essential and the superfluous. For Dylan, who did not bother to discuss his esthetics, it was a calculated effort to achieve what later became known in rock as "sensory overload." Taking a cue from the poet whose first name he appropriated, Dylan Thomas, he achieved this, not through a vertiginous interplay of flashing lights, weaving color patterns and ear-shattering sound, but through a cascade of poetic images. "I'm gonna write a symphony with words," he said at one point. "There will be one song in one key and another in another key. Everything will be happening all at once."

Dylan's canonization came little more than a year after the March, 1962, appearance of his first record album. It occurred at the Newport Folk Festival, later the scene of his fall from grace. Four things were responsible: a song, two sets of singers, and the time. The song was "Blowin' in the Wind." The artists were Joan Baez, the First Lady of Folk, and Peter, Paul and Mary, who had made a # 1 chart song of the Dylan song. And the time was marked by tremendous growth of the civil rights movement, particularly on college campuses.

"Blowin' in the Wind" has been called "the civil-rights anthem" and "the famous integration song." It became that by usage. But the lyrics are really not that specific. Movingly and poetically, they inveigh against complacency, indifference, noninvolvement. On college campuses, plagued for years by the buzzards of apathy and fear loosed by McCarthyism, Dylan's words came as a clarion call. The troubling search of young people for positive ideas and a cause with which they could identify was over. Active involvement began to supersede cool spectatorism. The nationwide campaign against racial inequality became the rallying point, and more and more collegians became Freedom Riders.

If the Newport Folk Festival of 1963 had an unspoken theme,

it was one of brotherhood and racial equality. The appearance of the Freedom Singers, each of whose members had been jailed for civil-rights activities, stirred feelings that went beyond the musical import of their singing. Emotions ran higher for Dylan's on-stage stint. And in the closing minutes of the Festival when many singers locked hands and sang "We Shall Overcome," there were spontaneous calls for Dylan, whose appearance on the stage led to an ovation and the singing by the artists and the audience of "Blowin' in the Wind."

But as he was lionized and idolized in 1963, two years later, he was booed as a sell-out. At the Folk Festival in 1965, he performed, not to the accompaniment of his acoustic guitar and mouth-harmonica, but to the amplified electrical instruments of the Butterfield Blues Band. When Dylan himself appeared on-stage carrying an electric guitar, voices rose in disbelief and protest. When the sounds of disapproval could not be heard over the overpowering decibels of screeching electric organ, bass and guitars, the audience took to throwing pillows and other objects onto the stage. Dylan left the platform in tears. Only when the M.C. gave assurances that Dylan would return with his "pure" folk instruments was order restored. The idol had committed the unpardonable sin of wedding big message material to the big beat of electrified rock. Staunch partisans of folk, the college crowd then dismissed rock as infantile and beneath its intellectual level.

Although similar manifestations of displeasure and hostility were made by audiences at Forest Hills and at other Dylan concert appearances, the sales of his newly released single and LP showed no lessening of record-buyer enthusiasm. In fact, the rocking single "Like a Rolling Stone" became one of Dylan's biggest disks, as did the LP *Bringing It All Back Home*. Whether folk purists approved or not, Dylan had launched a new genre of song, soon known as folk rock. To his folk following, he had added a large group of rock enthusiasts.

Now songs of protest began exploding all over the pop charts.

Suddenly, ordinary pop artists were inveighing against conformity. In "Home of the Brave," a husband-wife team (Cynthia Weill and Barry Mann), responsible for many chart songs, tackled the problem of youngsters being excluded from classes for failure to adhere to traditional hair styles: "Home of the brave, land of the free," they wrote, "Why won't you let him be what he wants to be." And Sonny and Cher, a married singing couple who were ejected from restaurants because of their odd clothes—he wore oppossum vests and she wore bell-bottom trousers with alternating, prisonlike strips of white and black—recorded "Laugh at Me": "Why do they care about the clothes I wear," they sang. "Then laugh at me/If that's the fare I have to pay to be free."

The power of the trend became clear when an unknown singer, Barry McGuire, zoomed to the top lists with "Eve of Destruction." Badly rhymed and ungrammatical, the song apparently voiced a sentiment deeply felt by young record-buyers. The writer of "Eve of Destruction," P. F. Sloan, was a nineteen-year-old devotee of The Beach Boys' Surf Sound. Yet in "Child of Our Times," he warned his generation to choose its views carefully, for "they'll try to make hypocrisy your heredity. . . ." Song after song now dealt with basic social and political issues confronting adults as well as young people. But it was the young—Tom Paxton, Phil Ochs and others—who spoke out against atomic warfare, the John Birch Society, segregation, Vietnam, and other controversial matters.

Variety was not in sympathy. In a review of a Dylan concert at Carnegie Hall, it noted that the future held nothing for him but complaints against the past and present, "complaints against warmongers, Nazis, poverty, injustice, commercial hootenanies, blacklisting, prize fighting, atom fallout, hard-hearted sweethearts, Fabian and selling and buying of soap." Reluctantly, it concluded that, unlike the generation that came from World War II seeking serenity and happiness, the Pearl Harbor generation "seems to be in bitter, vocal revolt against the world today." And *Cash Box*, the juke box weekly, announced not without amazement: "Dylan has clearly established that his brand of seemingly uncommercial music is in reality a commodity the public wants. Dylan cannot be divorced from the protest issues he sings about. Far more than any other folk singer today, he is a derivative of . . . a time he earnestly believes is corrupt."

Dylan, who was properly credited with projecting seething sentiments into timely thoughts and helping transform adolescent alienation into social involvement, had his own thoughts: "The only thing where it's happening is on the radio and records," he said. "That's where people hang out. It's not in book form, it's not on the stage." A commentator later observed that he had "helped shape the probability that contemporary music is becoming the literature of our time."

In 1965, after Dylan had committed his act of so-called apostasy, the big circulation publications discovered him. On one Sunday in December, the magazine sections of both *The New York Times* and *Herald Tribune* appeared with long, scholarly articles on the man one called "Public Writer No. 1." By then, a new American rock group called The Byrds had made a # 1 song of Dylan's "Mr. Tambourine Man," both here and in England. But what stirred New York's two major newspapers, and later *This Week*, *Playboy* and *The Saturday Evening Post* (whose July, 1966, cover he monopolized as the Rebel King of Rock 'n' Roll), was the discovery that college students regarded him as the most important contemporary poet in America. (The *Post* found him that rare case of a "composer who got more attention than the performers" who recorded his songs.)

A senior at one of the Ivy League colleges said: "We don't give a damn about Moses Herzog's *angst* or Norman Mailer's private fantasies. We're concerned with things like the threat of nuclear war, the civil-rights movement and the spreading blight of dishonesty, conformism and hypocrisy in the United States, especially in Washington. And Bob Dylan is the only

American writer dealing with these subjects in a way that makes sense to us. And, at the same time as modern poetry, we feel that his songs have a high literary quality." Members of the Poetic Establishment were supercilious about the results of the collegiate poll. Louis Simpson dismissed him as an "entertainer" and no poet at all—"American college students don't know anything about poetry." W. H. Auden apologized, when he was interviewed, for being unfamiliar with Dylan's work— "One has so frightfully much to read anyway." (Alan Lomax, the folk song scholar, had told *Look* in March, 1966: "He really is a poet, not a folk singer. If he's given time, he'll go down as a great poet of this time . . . unless he kills himself first.")

Two members of the pop song scene joined the sneering corps in letters to *Playboy*. Bobby Darin's was a put-on: "I have been a fan of Mr. Dylan's ever since *Gunsmoke* started, and next to Batman he is definitely my favorite saloon performer. . . . Anybody who would change his name from Zimmerman to Dylan is much more aware of theatrics than he would like to appear." Buck Owens, leading country singer and hitmaker, put Dylan down for his "weird tactics." In Owen's opinion, Dylan had "the mistaken opinion that the bigger the nonconformist one is, the bigger he can be in the entertainment world. . . . I have proved that one can climb to the top of his particular field and retain the respect of everyone."

By the time *The New York Times* noted that "because of Dylan, song hits now are about war, not love," the prophet of the change was addressing himself to other matters. *Another Side of Bob Dylan*, released in 1964, indicated in its very title that Dylan was turning away from the topical subjects that had preoccupied him in *The Freewheelin' Bob Dylan* and *The Times They Are A-Changin'*, his second and third LPs. Much of *Another Side* dealt with imbalances in his relationship with women. "It Ain't Me, Babe" returned to an earlier theme, the female who would not be satisfied with his heart but wanted his soul as well. And there were songs like "My Back Pages" in which he dismissed his earlier political absolutes as the myopia of premature old age: "I'm younger than that now. . . ."

In *Bringing It All Back Home,* his succeeding album, an implicit bohemianism and self-centered individualism became explicit. While this LP preceded the Newport and Forest Hills uproars, it clearly indicated where Dylan was at. (Tom Paxton, the protest folk writer, was to say: "Where it's at is a synonym for *rich.*") Dylan had been on a sensation-making tour of mod England where his records were bigger than in his native land. He had been impressed by The Beatles' beat, as they had been challenged by his kaleidoscopic imagery. They traded influences. And he was taken by The Rolling Stones' unbuttoned eroticism and violent wallop. Out of the interplay came folk rock, which occupied one side of the LP. Using a five-piece rock group and playing electric guitar, Dylan sang "Subterranean Homesick Blues," his twangy nasality obscured in part by the amplification. He was still sensitive to the world's confusions, but he was now needling the masters of the world rather than denouncing them, as he had done in the simplistic "Masters of War."

The other side of *Back Home* was old-style Dylan, but with a difference. The outlaw was no longer the restless seeker roaming American highways and poolrooms, but an explorer of strange, inner worlds—"the smoke-rings of my mind . . . the foggy ruins of time," dream worlds that one could reach through "Mr. Tambourine Man." It took a bit of time before the Establishment discovered what hippie bohemians sensed and Greenwich Village acidheads knew: that the tambourine man was a pusher of drugs who used a tambourine to peddle his wares—it was turned wrong-side up when it was not safe to make a sale.

If Dylan was now at odds with folk purists, he also found no bond with the hippies. The purists failed to see that rock, like folk, was a music of alienation, perhaps because its protest side (before Dylan and The Beatles) was on a teen level—anti-authority rather than anti-Establishment, anti-middle age rather

than anti-middle class, anti-repression rather than anti-the ac-
quisitive society. Viewing Rock as moronic music imposed on
the young for selfish exploitation by the music business, tradi-
tionalists saw Dylan's affiliation as a massive betrayal. As for
Dylan, even though "Mr. Tambourine Man" became the unofficial anthem of the hippies, he could find no answer in their
culture. One does not have to give credence to his put-down
of drugs in "Memphis Blues Again" or his comments about
LSD ("It's for mad, hateful people") to realize that their concepts were too naive, too absolute—as in flower power—and too
communal for him.

Highway 61 Revisited, released in November, 1965, was an
expression of a man at odds with his followers, resentful of
some, angered by others, and a wanderer once again. It opened
with "Like a Rolling Stone," a record that had become a # 1
single for him—his other songs had reached the top on disks
by other artists—and that seemed directed against a faithless
love whom he castigated as a streetwalker. He took a pot shot
at those who were not keeping pace with him in "Ballad of a
Thin Man." "Something is happening," he sneered, "but you
don't know what it is, do you, Mr. Jones?" It was not difficult
to equate the mythical gentleman with the purists who had
driven him off the stage at Newport, and who failed to understand that rock was, as a writer in *Commentary* realized, "a
bottoms-up as well as top-down movement," a spontaneous
expression of new artist-listener sensibility as well as a hard sell
by record companies.

In August, 1966, Dylan was in a motorcycle accident—he
almost made a prophet of Alan Lomax—which kept him out
of action for more than a year. Some thought the accident was
a cover for dropping out of sight and finding his creative bear-
ings. There were rumors that he was planning to move to another record company, and he himself admitted afterward that
he did not record because of some "confusion" about his Columbia contract. Just before the accident, Columbia released a

double album *Blonde on Blonde,* which he recorded in Nashville with country-rock musicians. He told of how he wrote out the songs in the studio while the musicians sat and played cards. Devoid of topical material, *Blonde* consisted of a series of still-life snapshots of the sensory world around him. It seemed a response to the pop culture concepts of underground artists like Andy Warhol, who said: "If you want to understand me, look at my surface." A point of contact with earlier Dylan was in his attitude toward women, who still came through—even though he was married and had a son—as unreliable and impossibly demanding.

The release of *John Wesley Harding* in February, 1968, eighteen months after his brush with death, became something of an anticlimax only because it followed a public appearance at a Carnegie Hall posthumous musical tribute to the late Woody Guthrie, Dylan's early idol. Nevertheless, *Harding* became the subject of excited, widespread comment. The album had more than its quota of Dylan surprises. Fans did not know what to expect since it came after the new trend toward super albums launched by The Beatles with *Sgt. Pepper,* pursued by The Rolling Stones in *Their Satanic Majesties Request* and developed by the new Beach Boys in *Smiley Smile,* the last mentioned, an LP whose recording cost had mounted to over $50,000. The Stones had invested in an ultraexpensive 3-D cover for their super while The Beatles had employed a fifty-piece orchestra to play one chord. Dylan used three Nashville musicians to accompany him and an inexpensive Polaroid shot for the jacket.

To those who had been pained by his use of electric rock instruments, the sound of *Harding* was sheer bliss: Dylan played an acoustic guitar and his wheezing harmonica. And the songs were musically in the country and English ballad tradition, revealing the influence, not of Guthrie or The Beatles, but of Hank Williams, the Nashville singer-writer who was known as the Hillbilly Shakespeare. More than one reviewer agreed with Robert Shelton, folk critic of *The New York Times,* who characterized "I'll Be Your Baby Tonight" as a "sprightly visitation from Hank Williams," although a *Newsweek* writer thought it embodied an amusing play on love words that applied as easily to son-and-mother as to lovers.

In his approach to women, as to the craft of songwriting, most critics noted a marked advance. Tenderness had superseded the cynical, non-love attitude. And brevity of expression had replaced surrealistic prolixity. The album also had a unity rare in most of his LPs. Like the outlaw after whom the album was named—Dylan added a terminal "g" to John Wesley Hardin to compensate, many a reviewer observed, for all the "g's" he had elided in his pure folk period—he was concerned with, and viewed through the eyes of the alienated, the outsider, the underprivileged: drifters, hobos, thieves, immigrants, saints. His outlook was compassionate. He did not accuse or attack, as in his earliest LPs. He did not act above it all, as in his later work. He was trying to discover where he belonged, and to discriminate between illusion and truth. "Don't mistake paradise," he sang in "Ballad of Frankie Lee and Judas Priest," "for that home across the road." For the first time, too, he dealt with his own mortality in "All Along the Watchtower," hardly a surprising development considering the motorcycle accident.

Dylan continues to have his detractors, many of them the result of his obscurantism both as a person and a poet. Commentators are extremely conscious of his constant attempts to hide and distort his world, past and present, as in the phony tales about his family background. Even though he has admitted to his laziness as a writer, the *Harding* album brings into question a once-relevant brickbat of a *Commentary* critic: "The Robert Burns of Folk-rock displays a surly indifference to both coherence and communication, using words as if they were brickbats or rotten eggs." Most observers of the rock scene would agree with Ellen Willis, who wrote more recently in *Commentary*: "As composer, interpreter, most of all as lyricist, Dylan has made a revolution. He expanded folk idiom into a rich, figurative language, grafted literary and philosophic subtleties onto protest songs, revitalized folk vision by rejecting proletarian and ethnic sentimentality, then all but destroyed pure folk as a contemporary form by merging it with pop." Richard Goldstein, another youthful analyst, has said: "Today, he is Shakespeare and Judy Garland to my generation. We trust what he tells us." And another under-thirty writer in *KRLA Beat*, the publication of a Hollywood rock radio station, has said: "Dylan seems to be the hereditary genius of the immortals speaking with the tongue of here and now. . . ."

Without minimizing Dylan's talents, one must acknowledge the workings of an extremely sharp public relations mind in the shaping of his charisma and influence. From the transparent mystery in which he shrouded his background, the contradictory statements he customarily makes about himself, and his well publicized pilgrimage to the bedside of dying Woody Guthrie, to the accident that removed him from the recording scene during contract negotiations and a drop in his creative energies, Dylan has been artful in arousing public interest in himself and his doings. At the time that Columbia released the long-awaited *Harding* album after his recovery, the underground buzzed with news of a tape he cut during the recuperative period in his Woodstock home. Somehow, copies of the tape showed up in England as well as here—and soon there were numerous recordings of the new songs he had written and not recorded himself. To his credit, let it be noted that these included "Wheels of Fire," the hit title tune of the last album by The Cream.

Folk rock is a genre, not a form, and embraces several types of material and styles of writing. It includes protest rock, the blending of the folk revival started by the Kingston Trio with teenage rock 'n' roll that began with Elvis Presley. It also includes attitude rock, that more individualistic form of rebellion into which some protesters have lapsed. It is characterized by poetic expression, convoluted and rich in imagery, but can also be as blues-simple as "Ode to Billie Joe." Say "folk 'n' roll," and you get a sense of its breadth. Like folk, it is urban, not rural—now, not yesterday. As dance music, it rocks and is amplified.

Perhaps the first group to whom it was applied, after Dylan achieved the fusion, was the group that flew to the top of the charts with a Dylan song. Among the five who originally composed The Byrds, leader and twelve-string guitarist Jim McGuinn studied at Chicago's Old Towne School of Folk Music and toured with the Chad Mitchell Trio. Songster Gene Clark came from Tipton, Missouri, to work with the New Christy Minstrels. Drummer Michael Clarke and rhythm guitarist David Crosby both starved for years in folk coffee houses. A viewing of *A Hard Day's Night*, The Beatles' film, blew the minds of McGuinn and Crosby, and led to the realization that rock did not have to be dull, monotonous and humorless. Formed in August, 1964, The Byrds had a Columbia contract by January, 1965, and a # 1 record in "Mr. Tambourine Man" by the spring.

So swift was their ascent that when they opened at Ciro's in Hollywood in March, 1965, they were nervous, awkward, and really had no act. Nevertheless, their sound caught on with west coast hippies, presaging the rise of San Francisco as the capital of Psychedelia. By the time they paid a visit to England, where The Beatles embraced them as Dylan had at Ciro's, they had hit the top of British pop charts. Their sound was a mixture. The ringing twelve-string guitar of McGuinn suggested folk. Chris Hillman's bass had a bluegrass drive; he had forsaken his orientation on the mandolin. David Crosby's amplified rhythm guitar and Mike Clarke's drums added rock leverage.

Although their repertoire included many Dylan songs—"Baby Blue," "Back Pages," "Chimes of Freedom," "The Times They Are A-Changin'" among others—they turned for their August, 1965, single to a Pete Seeger song. "Turn! Turn! Turn!" was a melodically lovely adaptation of the words *To Everything There Is a Season* from the biblical book of Ecclesiastes. "Turn! Turn! Turn!" was an even faster flight for The Byrds than their first

63

disk and zoomed to the top so rapidly that they had two # 1 disks within a nine-months period. On their return to Ciro's in June, 1965, the club that once was the swank night spot of Hollywood's movie colony had changed its name to It's Boss. When The Byrds opened that fall at The Crescendo, once a swinging jazz club, it was called The Trip.

The hippie appeal of their first disk now became a dominant note in succeeding chart records. "Eight Miles High," which went to the top in England and the United States, seemed on the face of it to be a dreamlike description of a flying visit to London. But censors soon detected images that seemed merely incongruous to ordinary listeners ("small faces unbound . . . some just shapeless forms . . .") but which had psychedelic import for those on "acid" trips. These overtones became overt in "Mr. Spaceman" and "Five 'D' (Fifth Dimension)" both written by Jim McGuinn, with references like "floating and never hit bottom, and keep falling through just relaxed . . ." and "Joy innocently is just being quiet and fell it all around you. . . ."

By the time The Byrds were reduced to a quartet, McGuinn was immersed in the avant-garde styling of saxist John Coltrane, and guitarist David Crosby was experimenting with the sitar and Indian ragas—two developments evident in their 1967 LP *Younger Than Yesterday*. In describing their music, McGuinn has said: "The sound of the airplane in the Forties was a rrrooooooooooaaaahhhhh sound, and Sinatra and other people sang with that sort of overtone. Now we've got the kkrrrruusssss-ssssshhhhh jet sound, and the kids are singing up in there now. It's the mechanical noises of the era. The sounds are different and so the music is different."

When The Byrds were being denounced in *Variety* and by the McLendon chain of radio stations for contribuitng to pop music's moral crisis, The Lovin' Spoonful were caught up in the clamor. The bible of show biz intimated that the group got its tag from junkie jargon, from the spoon used for liquefying heroin powder. It was June, 1966, and the group's manager hurried to disabuse *Variety* of its unwarranted assumption: "For centuries," he wrote, "mothers all over the world have given their children a spoonful of sugar to help the medicine down. Even Mary Poppins did it. In the southern states of America, this spoonful of sugar-water was known as a 'lovin' spoonful.' Mississippi John Hurt, the great Delta blues artist, recorded a song called "Coffee Blues" in the 1920's. . . . The repetitive lyric of this song is, 'I love my baby by the lovin' spoonful. . . .' In 1965 John Sebastian, Joe Butler, Steve Boone and Zal Yanovsky . . . four good musicians with a good knowledge of American folk music . . . selected the most memorable phrase of one of their favorite songs. . . ."

Not unlike The Byrds, The Lovin' Spoonful is the product of diverse influences. Steve Boone, who plays guitar, bass and piano, comes from North Carolina of an Irish Catholic mother and a Protestant father. Guitarist Zalman Yanovsky is a Toronto Jew who lived on a kibbutz in Israel when he was sixteen. The most creative force in the group, John Sebastian, is the son of the famous virtuoso harmonica player whose name he bears. He began studying guitar when he heard Elvis Presley. After his father appeared on a TV show with Lightnin' Hopkins, young Sebastian developed what he has characterized as "this very purist attitude." He describes his subsequent path as follows: "I was bluesy. Then I started listening to what was comin' outta Nashville. All those cats played real good. . . . Then I began to hear music overlapping. You couldn't tell if it was blues or rock 'n' roll or jazz or what. That's when I started to write. . . . I love rock 'n' roll. It's beautiful. . . . But there's nothing frantic about what we play—or about any of us."

Perhaps the most successful of the group's hits is "Summer in the City," an urban folk song with a rock beat and a musical sweep that includes automobile horns, pneumatic drills and other sounds of the city. The early songs of Sebastian like "Do You Believe in Magic" and the group's first disks reveal the influence of r&b. But their approach is more musical and the

65

voices are sweeter and lighter, although a record like "Did You Ever Have To Make Up Your Mind" includes the typical spoken bass voice of many r&b disks. There is also a strong blues strain, countrified in "Wild About My Lovin'," modern in "Didn't Want To Have To Do It," and old-timey in "Night Owl Blues," which displays Sebastian's mastery of harmonica blues styling. No protest, no psychedelia as in The Byrds, but superior and sophisticated musicianship rooted in folk-country-and-blues—that is The Lovin' Spoonful.

Two different types of protest appear in several other aritsts covered by the umbrella of folk rock. Simon & Garfunkel ex-emplify what I have called attitude rock. Janis Ian, who attracted notice by her sensitive approach to social and parental problems, has moved in the direction of attitude rock. Arlo Guthrie stands forth as a protester with a rich sense of humor. But Phil Ochs, who was a doctrinaire protester at the beginning, has recently followed in Dylan's footsteps.

Of the four, Simon & Garfunkel stand out musically. But their sound is neither bluesy nor country like that of The Lovin' Spoonful. It is more frequently baroque than anything else. Paul Simon, the songwriter of the duo, is more allusive and literary than Miss Ian, Ochs or Guthrie. "Dangling Conversation" is typical in its use of images of noncommunication: "You read your Emily Dickinson, and I my Robert Frost. . . ." The break-down of understanding and the inability of men to communi-cate with each other verbally or emotionally are two of Simon's favorite themes—the latter expressively developed in "Sounds of Silence," the duo's first # 1 record: "People writing songs that voices never shared. . . ." ("Sounds of Silence" started out as an urban folk song and only made it when a rock background was dubbed in.) In "He Was My Brother" and "A Church Is Burning," Simon early displayed a concern about the violence being visited upon those seeking freedom and trying to bring it to others. "The future is now, and it's time to take a stand," he wrote in the latter. But Simon is constantly troubled by the impermanence and pain of love:

Hello, Hello, Hello, Hello
Goodbye, Goodbye, Goodbye, Goodbye
That's all there is
And the leaves that are green turn to brown.[1]

And in "I Am a Rock": "If I never loved I never would have cried/I am a Rock, I am an Island. . . . I touch no one and no one touches me/I am a rock, I am an Island/And a rock can feel no pain/And an island never cries."

But obviously Simon does feel pain, pain that approaches trauma, because he is also tormented by an overpowering fear of death, the ultimate alienation. But he is so suspicious even of friendship that darkness remains his "old friend." And so he writes delicate verses to gentle melodies, trying to destroy the psychological barriers that separate people from each other and engender fear, hatred, violence and indifference.

One of Simon's more recent undertakings was the score of *The Graduate*, a film that rated as one of the best of 1967 and garnered an Oscar for Mike Nichols' direction. The soundtrack LP climbed to # 1 in 1968, became a Gold Record, reawakened interest in *Parsley, Sage, Rosemary and Thyme*, their preceding LP, which climbed back into the Top Ten and became a Gold Album, and made the duo so hot that *Bookends*, their succeeding LP, became a Gold Record on its release. In the late spring of 1968, when "Mrs. Robinson" from *The Graduate* was the # 1 single in the country, S & G had three LPs among the country's top five bestsellers, an achievement equalled only by Herb Alpert and the Tiajuana Brass.

For Paul Simon as a songwriter, *Bookends* represents a deeper penetration of earlier themes and subjects. "Save the Life of My Child" is concerned with suicide, a matter he had touched in such songs as "A Most Peculiar Man" and the fine adaptation of E. A. Robinson's poem "Richard Cory." In "Overs," he deals once again with the apathetic complacency into which alienated

---

[1] "Leaves That Are Green" by Paul Simon © 1965 Charing Cross Music. Used with permission of the publisher.

lovers drift, remaining together even though they "might as well be apart." A sense of melancholia and futility pervades the collection and the emotions are wistfully recollected in a remembrance of things that could have been and never were. However, in "Silent Night: Seven O'Clock News," his approach is dramatic rather than merely philosophical. Electronic women's screams are heard in the background of the suicide song. And in "Old Friends," a song that deals with old age, another persistent Simon theme, we hear the actual voices of old people recorded in two homes for the aged. There is some indication, too, that Simon is moving away from the internalized approach of the earlier LPs. In "America" he takes a bus trip in which a search for the meaning of the country—and his discovery that it may lie in endless motion—becomes symbolic of his desire to get out of himself and make fruitful contact with the outside world.

Janis Ian was a sixteen-year old student at the High School of Music and Art in New York City when radio station KRLA of Los Angeles ran a trade-paper ad that read: "In the past, we have taken pride in displaying the courage and honesty to broadcast controversial material of social and artistic significance. We are embarrassed, however, by a recent timidity in not playing a remarkable record which deserves to be heard. . . . Now, with thanks to Leonard Bernstein for leading the way . . . and with apologies for our 'cop-out,' KRLA presents 'Society's Child.' " How many other stations by-passed the Janis Ian disk is not known. But despite the Establishment cop-out, the record proved one of the outstanding of 1967.

Young Miss Ian's song dealt with interracial dating. In moving terms, it told of the white girl pressured by parental and social disapproval to end her friendship with a Negro boy. Released in September, 1966, the disk immediately encountered censorship problems. A disk jockey tipsheet issued in Hollywood warned: "Magnificently done, but will probably never see the light of day. Too bad." Later in the month, Robert Shelton documented the quiet suppression of the disk in a *New York*

Times article. It took almost six months before the ban was broken through CBS-TV and Bernstein's exposure of it nationally.

Although Miss Ian entered the record market several years after Dylan's turn from protest, it was evident that the hang-up of youngsters with the inequities of contemporary society would continue to find expression in folk rock. Miss Ian's debut album on Verve Folkways consisted of twelve tracks of unremitting complaint against the adult world, some of it quite sarcastic:

> *She's in a frenzy*
> *For her children to leave,*
> *So she can be free.*
> *What a drag it must be*
> *Feeling wanted. . . .*

Miss Ian described her songs as "people sketches" rather than protest. She quickly displayed a maturity beyond her years. "I can't stay in the same old 'hate your parents' bag," she announced, and called her succeeding album *For All the Seasons of Your Mind.* Although she argued that "grown-ups only listen if you're saying what they want to hear," and stated that she wanted "adults to enter the world, to stay in the world . . . they made . . ." she felt that she had outgrown the songs in her first album.

Nevertheless, in "Shady Acres" she makes a devastating attack on elders who refuse to be bothered with aging parents and ship them off to senior citizen homes to await death. But she also fixes her acutely critical eye in "Honey, D'Ya Think" on the self-centered of her own generation. Even in "Society's Child" she did not excuse her age group for making an obedient acquiescence to older generation bigotry and cruelty. "A work of art" was the judgment of several critics on "Insanity Comes Quietly to the Structured Mind," a powerful vignette of a young girl preparing to commit suicide. Vexed by society's ills, Miss Ian is critical of those who cop-out, emotionally or morally.

She was not quite sixteen when she went one evening with folkster Reverend Gary Davis and his wife to the Gaslight in Greenwich Village. After Davis, who was performing at the cafe, brought her on-stage to do a number, the owner booked her. Word of mouth led to a visit by Verve executives and a recording contract. A performer of limited means and hardly a sexpot, Miss Ian has established a place for herself in the record scene through the power of her material. Hers is a triumph of matter over manner, of writing creativity over performance, of meaningful communication over showmanship.

Talented son of the most inspired and still the most prolific folk poet of our time, Arlo Guthrie was twenty when he made his concert debut at Carnegie Hall. At ten he had made an unscheduled appearance at Gerde's Folk City in Greenwich Village, brought on-stage by Cisco Houston, a folk performer who had worked with his father. At thirteen, when the Guthries were living at Howard Beach in Queens, he had met and liked Bob Dylan, who had come to their door to see Arlo's father, then dying of Huntington's chorea, an incurable disease of the nervous system. Arlo had dropped out of Rocky Mountain College in Billings, Montana, partly because he was ridiculed for his hippie ways. He still believed in what he called "traditional Americanism"—do what you want so long as you don't hurt anybody, or put someone up tight.

For years he had been performing in the bare-brick rooms of Greenwich Village coffee houses and in Rittenhouse Square Park, the Philadelphia equivalent of Washington Square Park. He had written "Ring-Around-a-Rosy Rag" to commemorate the arrest of a group of friends, who had been "busted" for playing the children's game in the Square. And his "Alice's Restaurant Massacre" had become an underground hit through a tape played by WBAI-FM. It was requested so frequently that the station had used it to raise funds, "Contribute and we'll play it." A talking blues of the type handled so skilfully by his father and imitatively by Bob Dylan, it was based on an actual incident.

While visiting The Back Room in Stockbridge, Massachusetts, a restaurant owned by Alice and Ray Brock, two close friends, he offered to dispose of accumulated garbage for them. Loading the refuse into the back of his jalopy, he then drove to the edge of town. As he was in the process of disposing of the stuff, he was caught by the Stockbridge chief of police and arrested for littering. The time was Thanksgiving, 1965, and the narrative takes us through a series of misadventures, including his subsequent appearance for his draft-induction physical in New York City. Asked in the course of the physical whether he had been rehabilitated since his arrest, Arlo replied: "You want to know if I'm moral enough to kill children and burn down villages after being arrested as a litterbug?"

By the time of the Carnegie concert in November, 1967, Arlo's underground reputation had surfaced. The turning point had come more quickly than he or anyone could have anticipated. At the Newport Folk Festival that summer, he had made an unpublicized appearance at an afternoon workshop open to hopeful amateurs. Twenty minutes of the deadly satire and humor of "Alice's Restaurant" so stirred the crowd that he was immediately added to the next afternoon's program on the Festival Field. The black-humored, melodically attractive blues brought cheers from an audience of four thousand. And so Arlo was invited to appear on the Festival's closing-night program. Now, ten thousand fans reacted with such fervor that all the major artists on the program, from Joan Baez to Pete Seeger, joined young Guthrie on stage in singing the chorus. In a large sense, the 1967 Folk Festival was Arlo's as the Festival of 1963 had been Dylan's.

The Carnegie Hall concert coincided with the release of his first Reprise album, *Alice's Restaurant*, which climbed into the Top Twenty, presaging a formidable future for Woody's son. "When you're talking about what people are thinking about," Arlo has said, "that's folk music." "Alice's Restaurant," which occupies all of side one, draws on the shaggy-dog humor of the little man absurdly trapped in circumstances beyond his control. Arlo's country accent, reminding one at times of Dylan, who used to remind one of Woody Guthrie, adds hayseed bitters to a narrative characterized by an over-thirty critic (Peter Reilly) in *Hi-Fi Stereo Review* as "one of the funniest, truest, most pointedly intelligent appraisals of our society that has come from anyone, old or young." By the time this book is in print, "Alice's Restaurant" may be a full-length feature film, a production of Hilliard Elkins and Arthur Penn, the director of *Bonnie and Clyde.* There has been talk of translating other rock albums into the film medium, an interesting development if it comes.

One of the topical folk writers who did not condemn Dylan for his turn to pop rock was Phil Ochs, a writer whose many protest songs include the tough condemnation of the Vietnam war voiced in "I Ain't Marching Anymore." Having written and recorded three albums of controversial material—much of which was treated as unsuitable radio fare by sensitive station managements—Ochs recently followed in Dylan's footsteps and moved toward rock. He now feels that the designation "protest singer" does not fit him, nor does he like it, since it conjures up an image (as he now sees it) of a nasal vocalist delivering dull melodies burdened with heavy lyrics. In a verse note that he wrote for his album *Pleasure of the Harbor*—a liner that is a montage of poetic images, convoluted, curiously punctuated and sometimes obscure—he addresses himself to his possible critics: "a vanguard of electricians a full village of tarts/ who say you must protest you must protest/ it is your diamond duty." And he replies: "ah but in such an ugly time the true protest is beauty," and he adds: "and the bleeding seer crawled from the ruins of the empire . . . he said, passion has led to chaos and now chaos will lead to order."

But obviously before it does, there must be a considerable change in the outlook and attitudes, not to say actions, of average people. In "Outside of a Small Circle of Friends," Ochs deals angrily with the callousness of people to the suffering of

Howlin' Wolf

Muddy Waters

B. B. King

Otis Spann

Chuck Berry

Bo Diddley

Fats Domino

Little Richard

Buddy Holly and the Crickets

Bill Haley

Jerry Lee Lewis

Elvis Presley

Bobby Darin (left)

Johnny Cash

Pat Boone

Frankie Avalon

Paul
Anka

The Everly Brothers

Fabian

Bob Dylan

Connie Francis

Bob Dylan

The Beatles

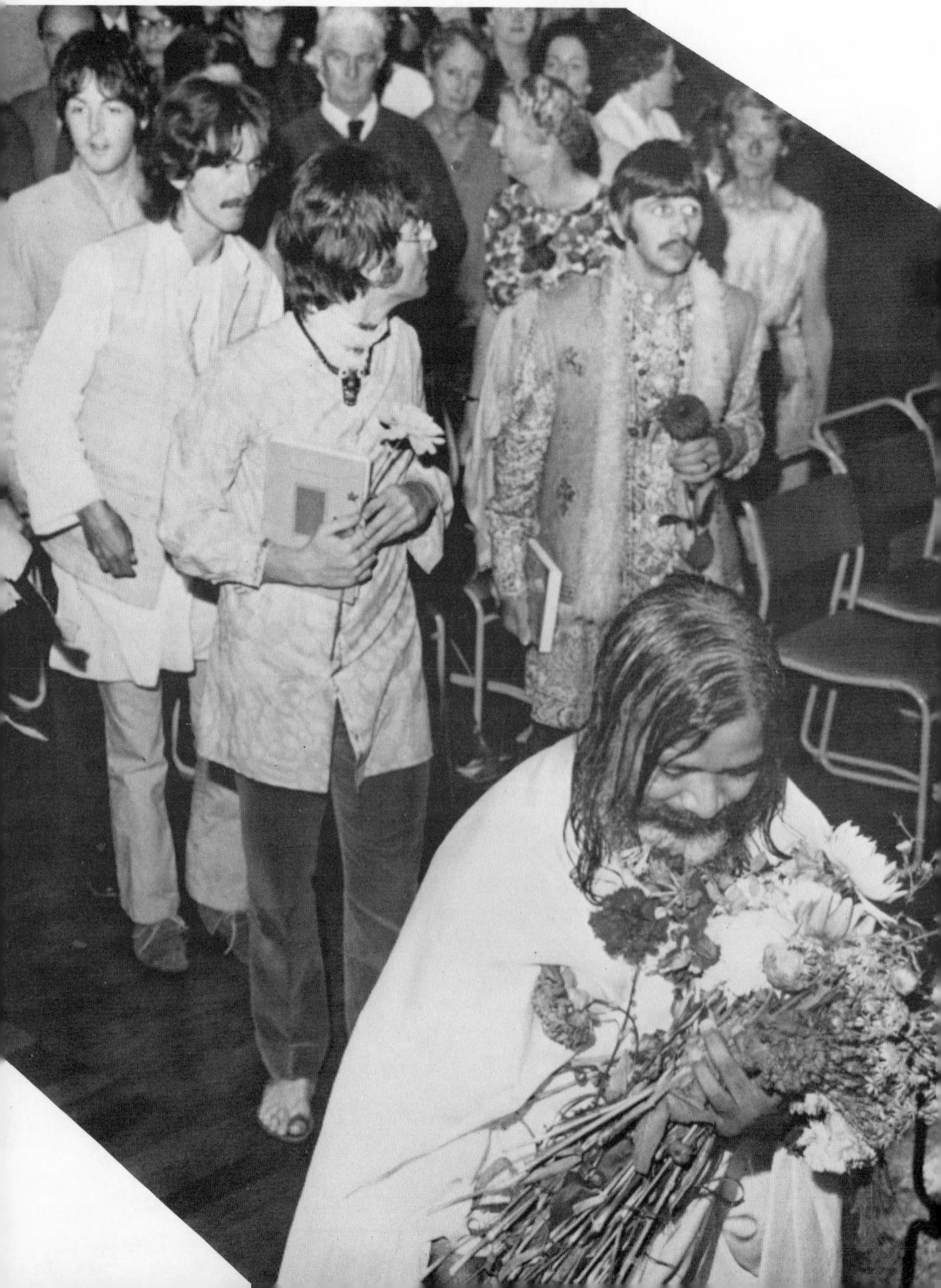

The Rolling Stones

Tom Jones

Mick Jagger

The Byrds

The Dave Clark Five

Eric Burdon and The Animals

Herman's Hermits

**Gerry and the
Pacemakers**

Chad and Jeremy

others: the citizens who wouldn't interrupt a game of Monopoly to call the cops for a woman being molested on the street; the drivers who wouldn't get out in the rain to help occupants of a car teetering on the edge of the rain-slick highway; and so on. Ochs still has a tendency to overwrite in the manner of early Dylan. But his use of a ricky-tick piano, playing a jouncy ragtime accompaniment to the angry narrative of apathy ("Demonstrations are a drag"), suggests an imaginative sharpening of his sense of satire and the economical effect.

Of the green-eyed, Glasgow-born visionary who writes songs under the name of Donovan Phillips Leitch and records as Donovan, Phil Ochs has said: "He's a fantastic presence. . . . He is one of the few writers whose aesthetic is his own person." When Donovan appeared at the Cow Palace in San Francisco, it was not too long after a Beatles' concert at which a number of young girls were injured and the group itself became worried that a full-scale riot was in the making. Of Donovan's concert, *Variety* wrote: "Such is the balladeer's personal charisma that one might have heard a petal fall here during a fragile air like 'Lullaby of Spring.' Between numbers a procession of teeny-boppers flowed quietly to the stage to make offerings of blossoms, bells and beads at Donovan's bare feet. . . . There was no screeching or screaming, no frantic charges to outflank the rent-a-cops. . . . The guards were thoroughly confused."

Having followed The Beatles in their turn from drugs to the transcendental meditation system of Maharishi Mahesh Yogi, Donovan comes barefoot on stage, clothed in floor-length robes, hung with beads and embroidered in green and gold. "He sees things," Judy Collins has said. "He doesn't tell you about the world. He creates it." And Donovan himself has said: "Pop is the perfect religious vehicle. It's as if God had . . . seen the ugliness that was being created and chose pop to be the great force for love and beauty." A writer in *Eye* has said: "The Beatles are the jokers and the conjuremen of pop; Bob Dylan is the magnificent psycopathic cowboy; the Stones are the cloak-and-dagger men; Brian Wilson is the mad scientist . . . and Donovan is the good fairy."

It was a slightly different songster that one encountered at the time of Dylan's "apostasy." At the Newport Folk Festival at which Dylan was booed, Joan Baez who had played a large role in the canonization of Dylan, appeared on-stage not with her tainted saint but with Donovan. The lad who was born of working-class parents in 1946, reared in the mountainous Gorbals area of Scotland and too indigent to complete art college, was then writing songs like "Ballad of a Crystal Man": "You fill your glasses with the wine of murdered Negroes. . . . Vietnam, your latest game,/ You're playing with your blackest queen. . . ." He still admires "beautiful people with something to say," but now feels that "the word *message* is for the older generation to use. The young just nod their heads 'I understand' inside themselves. . . . The words tell the story and the music makes it fly or soar like the sea."

Donovan's change of direction has taken a highly poetic and archaic turn. Instead of delving into personal emotional problems as Dylan has, he has taken flight on the wings of fantasy, becoming more exotic and quixotic. *Mellow Yellow*, a Gold Record LP, and *Sunshine Superman* both pursue the raga-sitar-tabla bit, but also contain contrasting elements of Dixieland and symphonic celli. *Sunshine Superman* is "dedicated to the bearer of the eastern gift" and projects the search for love in a fairy-tale wonderland. Opening with a collapsed love affair, it ends with Celeste, "my name for the lady . . . who weaves our fates on a silver loom in the silent room of eternal love."

In "a gift from a flower to a garden"—all the album's titles are in lower case—Donovan continues in the baroque, fey, poet-troubadour direction he has taken, except that the influence of Indian philosophy is more prominent. A photograph on the back cover of the LP shows him clasping the hand of the Maharishi Mahesh Yogi, The Beatles' guru, who is symbolically holding a flower. There are jazz elements in songs like "ship-along sam" and "sun," but the raga sound is dominant. The lower-case styling is doubtless prompted by the extreme humility Donovan affects. Signing an explanatory note on the album cover "Thy humble servant," he calls upon every youth "to stop the use of *all* Drugs and heed the Quest to seek the sun."

A super album, *a gift* contains two LPs in a box, complete lyrics and twelve original drawings in a portfolio. Donovan types "Phonograph the First," as he calls it, "music for my age group, an age which is gently entering marriage." He bequeaths the second record, which begins with the bawling of a newborn baby, to the children. "I wish only to enhance and beautify the days of youth," he states. "I honestly believe my generation is a blessed one and that we will tend to these newborn ones, so fresh from God's lips," filling their days "with fairies and elves and pussys and paints, with laughter and song and the gentle influence of Mother Nature."

In keeping with his intention, Donovan offers a muted, sweet-sounding type of rock. The beat is always present, enhanced by the pointedly rhythmic accents of his phrasing. But it is subdued. The music is frequently little more than monotonous chant, delivered to the accompaniment of bell-like organ and hollow flute. When it works for the rock Tolkien—it does not in his clumsy setting of Shakespeare's "Under the Greenwood Tree"—it has the trancelike magic of incantation. Donovan's voice has a burr and a buzz, and it is full of fuzz, but it has an appealing, sometimes mesmeric, sometimes childlike quality.

An American artist who echoes Donovan's optimism about the beginning of a new world is Richie Havens. Operating in the folk-blues idiom, he is like Donovan suffused with a feeling of love for life and people. In *Something Else Again*, his debut LP on Verve, there are several songs with socio-political orientation. "The Klan" recalls "Strange Fruit," the antilynching song of the Billie Holiday era. "Maggie's Farm," a Bob Dylan song, satirizes the death of the Horatio Alger syndrome and older generation shibboleths about hard work and wealth. But like Dylan, Havens is beyond politics and concerned, like Donovan, with affirming the beauty of the world and of freedom of the spirit.

Another American artist who is part of the muted rock scene is songwriter Tim Hardin, a descendant of the outlaw whose name (plus "g") supplied the title of Dylan's post-accident album. Considered by many the finest white singer of blues in the country, he is widely admired by other performers. "Hardin can take the rhythm-and-blues idiom," Phil Ochs has said, "and handle its guttural intonations without any unnatural stress. His voice has enough depth and feeling to simulate the sweet lyrical sounds of a string instrument." And Ochs concludes: "If such a form as folk rock does exist, the nuances and phrasing of his voice easily make him the master interpreter."

A number of Hardin's songs have been recorded by so many other artists, both here and abroad, that they already have the stature of standards. These include "Misty Roses," "You Upset the Grace of Living When You Lie," "The Lady Comes from Baltimore" and, to be sure, "If I Were a Carpenter." The latter achieved the unusual distinction of being a hit disk twice within a fifteen-month period, once for Bobby Darin and, more recently, for the Four Tops. Born and raised in Oregon by parents who were both trained musicians—his mother was concert-mistress of the Portland Civic Symphony—he was resoundingly received at the Newport Folk Festival of 1966. Although his debut album *Tim Hardin* appeared about the same time, he did not give his first New York concert until the spring of 1968. "The program was virtually whispered," Robert Shelton reported in *The New York Times*, "with the focus on the subtle and introverted world of bittersweet sadness of which he generally writes." All his songs are personal rather than political, with a strong strain of romanticism and little didacticism or surrealism.

Hardin's record output has been small. The first two on Verve and the third on Atlantic are all unsatisfactory to him, and he has recently joined the Columbia roster. Though rock audiences respond to him, he likes to think of himself as a jazz or folk artist. His influence among singers and writers is much greater than his own stature as a performer would suggest. John Sebastian played harmonica in Hardin's band when Tim was breaking in many years ago at the Night Owl Cafe in Greenwich Village and Sebastian is to be heard on the *Tim Hardin* LP. "I influenced his style," Hardin states bluntly. Others hear Hardin in the style of The Lovin' Spoonful as well as other rock groups. Despite Hardin's own understated singing style, there is an unmistakable intensity about his work as a performer and writer, perhaps accounting for an in-group adulation which may yet be reflected in public acceptance.

"Each generation finds its own artistic expression," an *Eye* reviewer observed. "Twenty years ago it was the novel; Norman Mailer, Truman Capote, Gore Vidal and James Baldwin, all under thirty, had all published startling novels by the end of 1948. This generation, grown up absurd, is forging its own values and legend in song. Dylan, John Lennon, Janis Ian—and now Arlo Guthrie—are doing with guitars what F. Scott Fitzgerald, J. D. Salinger and Jack Kerouac did with typewriters." Doubtless, the best documentation of this assertion is not the songsters mentioned, but a new artist on Columbia Records.

Leonard Cohen is a young Canadian who has written two novels *The Favorite Game* and *Beautiful Losers* and four volumes of poetry: *Spice Box of Earth, Let Us Compare Mythologies, Flowers for Hitler* and *Parasites of Heaven*. Although he had an established niche in the literary world, he obviously found that that's not where it was at. And so he took up a guitar and set some of his poems to music. In the summer of 1967, he made appearances at the Maraposa Folk Festival in Canada and the Folk Festival at Newport. At a later date, he went down to Nashville and recorded ten of his songs, including the surrealistic "Suzanne," which Judy Collins and Noel Harrison have done better. And yet his debut album, released in April, 1968, impressed most reviewers as an earnest effort to express himself in song and not merely as an attempt to capitalize on a craze.

Because of the genuinely poetic character of his work, Cohen was inevitably compared with Dylan, who suffered not at all. For Mr. Cohen's music tends to be monotonous and his lyrics, ambiguous. Like Dylan and most folksters, he is an alienated young man. But the brand of soft rock he sells lacks bite. Whatever the limitations of his performance or of his world-weary outlook, the spell of rock and folk rock on an increasing number of literary people is unquestionable.

In turn, an increasing number of young songwriters are pursuing the chansonnier tradition, long a phase of French songwriting and made attractive here by the growing popularity of Jacques Brel. In the songs of Rod McKuen, John Hartford, Joni Mitchell, Laura Nyro, Van Dyke Parks and Jim Webb, among others, we find examples of sung poetry rather than words-and-music—lyrics, in short, that can stand the challenging isolation of the printed page.

That rock must inevitably therefore take a highbrow direction has been envisaged by many commentators. And so it has already. Among the spring 1968 album releases, there were a not inconsequential number that went beyond a simple song orientation and that emphasized poetic content or artistic approach. In two LPs, rock or raga rock was used as an expressive accompaniment to other media. *The National Gallery Performing Musical Interpretations of the Paintings of Paul Klee* presented "rock-art" treatments of ten canvases while in *Flowers of Evil*, Yvette Mimieux read the famous Baudelaire poems to a raga background created by Ali Akbar Khan. Other literary art-rock mixtures were to be found in the work of Pearls Before Swine, a New York rock group that took its title from the bible and that illustrated its debut LP with a poster by Hieronymous Bosch—also in the name of a new Los Angeles group that called itself Steppenwolf after the novel by Herman Hesse. An album with the mundane title *The Beat Goes On*, so named after a rock song by Sonny Bono of Sonny and Cher, incorporated the taped voices of world-famous figures like Roosevelt and Churchill as well as musical fragments from Beethoven and Mozart. The high seriousness is inescapable.

But by the summer of 1968, many of the under-thirty critics began to bewail the cerebral, poetic, superalbum, studio-shaped direction that rock had taken after *Sgt. Pepper*. Possibly this reaction was prompted by the intensity with which the older generation and particularly some of the professorial community —Prof. Richard Poirer of Rutgers, Prof. Benjamin DeMott of Amherst, Profs. F. W. Dupee and Albert Goldman of Columbia—suddenly began honoring rock as an art form.

Whatever the impetus, whereas artiness had previously been hailed, even when results hardly warranted it, now accolades were showered on performers who departed Lincoln Center for the Ryman Auditorium of Nashville, Tennessee. Among the celebrated Music City fellow-travellers were Buffy Sainte-Marie, who pointedly called her album *I'm Gonna Be a Country Girl Again*; the high-flying Byrds who appeared on the Grand Ole Opry and titled their new album *Sweetheart of the Rodeo*; and even the Rolling Stones whose *Beggar's Banquet* was greeted with huzzahs because of its c&w orientation. The group that seemed to benefit most from this shift in "what's in" was Dylan's own backup band whose debut LP *Music from Big Pink* was widely typed "an event," and whose nondescript name (The Band) was commended as "a slap at ornate titles." (Curiously, the younger group of c&w writers, men like John Hartford and Billy Edd Wheeler, were then moving in precisely the opposite direction—toward a pop synthesis. Eschewing the saccharine, lachrymose, three-chord ballads so dear to the nasal school of country singers, they displayed interest in a new realism, fresh forms and sophisticated sounds.)

Another sign of the simplistic trend was the revival and reissue of recordings by early rockabilly and r&b artists, a development that took shape in Europe but seemed by the summer of 1968 to be growing apace in the United States.

6 THE BEATLES : *Raga,*
Rib and Baroque Rock

In December, 1967, *Newsweek* asked thirty-eight of its campus correspondents to conduct a survey of the new heroes on college campuses. The idols they found were not any of the world's political leaders, or even any of the formerly popular figures like authors Salinger and Tolkien. "The most popular non-ideological idols," according to the consensus, "were The Beatles, particularly John Lennon, and their record *Sgt. Pepper's Lonely Hearts Club Band.*"

Sgt. Pepper has been characterized by the Dean of Chapel at Stanford University as a record that "lays bare the stark loneliness and terror of these lonely times," a theme reminiscent of T. S. Eliot's highly allusive poem *The Wasteland,* and like Eliot's for his generation, expressive of the charged feelings of the young generation. The Beatles seemed, in fact, to summarize the Now generation, expressing its distrust of the Establishment and the adult world, its disbelief in traditional gods and goods, and its despairing gaiety about life in an indifferent society.

But the British group were the idols of their performing peers as well as their listeners. "They're untouchable," said Cass Elliott of The Mamas and The Papas. "No matter how hard anybody tries," said one of our most successful young producers, "no matter how good they are, almost everything we do is a cop on The Beatles." And Ned Rorem, a distinguished American composer of art songs, has said: "The Beatles are colleagues of mine, speaking the same language with different accents." To Mr. Rorem, "She's Leaving Home" "is equal to any song that Schubert ever wrote." In short, the significance of the group, artistically, socially and psychologically, approaches, if it does not transcend, their remarkable achievement as record sellers.

Of that achievement, it can be said that they have sold more wax in a shorter period of time, had a longer run of consecutive hits, and excited more hysteria than either Presley, a forerunner, or Sinatra, swooning idol of the parent generation. "I Want To Hold Your Hand," their first American hit, has now passed the five-million mark. According to Capitol Records, within fifteen months of their first appearance here in 1964, they had sold over 30 million records in the United States alone. By September, 1966, two and a half years after their Ed Sullivan debut, eleven of their singles had been certified as Gold Records by the Record Industry Association of America. Within three months of its release, *Sgt. Pepper* attracted 2.5 million buyers, suggesting that the group's hold on the record-buying public has not noticeably diminished.

Born in Liverpool of working-class parents, they gravitated toward music because the cold port city of the late 1950s was much like New Orleans at the turn of the century. Sailors and longshoremen made it a tough, nightlights metropolis, with hundreds of cellar clubs, shebeens and dives that gave employment to rock 'n' roll bands. Among Liverpudlians, these were known as "beat groups," from which, as from "beatnik," stems the name and the spelling by which they eventually became known. John Lennon, who was half-heartedly studying art at a local institute when he met McCartney and Harrison, then lackadaisical students at Liverpool Institute, is generally credited with coining the name.

In 1960 The Silver Beatles, as they then called themselves,

81

took off for Hamburg. The Indra Club, a strip joint on the Reeperbahn in the city's red-light district, had offered them $5 a week more than the $15 they had each been collecting at The Cavern, a Liverpool dive. The group was then composed of the three drop-outs plus Paul Best on drums. (After The Beatles hit, a record company issued an LP *The Best of the Beatles*, a deceptive title but not illegitimate since it featured the drummer whom Ringo succeeded.) At the time, the group was just another of the more than three hundred rock 'n' roll beatnik bands working around Liverpool—a situation emphasized by the number of names with which they experimented. Among these were The Cavemen, The Moondogs, The Moonshiners, and during the period in which Anglicized Kentucky Bluegrass became popular, The Quarrymen Skiffle Group. While in Hamburg, they recorded for an offbeat label with Best on drums. The disk, now a collector's item, documents their indebtedness to Presley rockabilly and Everly Brothers harmonies. (They once called themselves The Foreverly Brothers.)

Late in 1961 they were discovered by the elegant young man who guided their affairs so successfully until his accidental death in 1967. Brian Epstein became interested in them when customers came into his father's department store asking for Beatle records. He was then in charge of the record-radio-TV division. (One of the titles they had recorded for Tollie Records was "Twist and Shout," an imitation of an American recording by The Isley Brothers and an effort to capitalize on the then burgeoning twist craze.) Epstein undertook to manage the group at a percentage that gave him a larger share than each Beatle received. Designing a pseudo-choirboy outfit—deep white collars over collarless, lapel-less jackets—to replace their beatnik get-ups, he took them to London where he tried to interest British Decca in recording them. Electrical Musical Industries (EMI) was more receptive, and "Love Me Do," which sold respectably but not phenomenally, made its appearance late in 1962. It was at this time, partly at the behest of EMI executives, that Ringo replaced Best on drums. In October, 1962, they made their debut on television, an occurrence that later led Granada TV to claim credit for their discovery.

The pace of developments now became jetlike. By April, 1963, they had their first British Gold Record in "She Loves You." Beatlemania was sweeping not only England but the Continent as well. Between April and December, they made thirteen appearances on British TV, played a riotous engagement at the Palladium (London's still operative Palace Theatre), and received the nod from Princess Margaret and the Queen Mother at a Royal Command Performance. The recognition from the royal family came in November, by which time their odd hairdos, charming irreverence, un-British brashness and iconoclastic humor had won a hysterical following among the young. At the Command Performance, Beatle John announced: "The people in the cheap seats can clap. The rest of you, just rattle your jewelry."

Parliament was less ready to embrace The Beatles than the royal family, who had had over a century of experience in joining the enemy to save the Empire. A member arose at one session to protest the number of British bobbies that were being taken from their appointed rounds to guard the group. But the Prime Minister soon termed them Britain's secret weapon to keep the pound stable, and Barclay's, England's largest bank, conceded that they were contributing significantly in the maintenance of the nation's balance of payments through their overseas sales.

Despite the lionization of the group in England and the frenzied reaction of youngsters throughout the Continent, the American record business displayed no great interest in their disks. Their first chart song, "Love Me Do" made its first appearance abroad on November 10, 1962. Nevertheless, all through 1963, their recordings went begging, as Capitol, EMI's American affiliate, did not exercise its first-refusal option. When The Beatles finally broke in the United States in 1964, their disks were available on four different labels. The break seemed an overnight occurrence. The *Billboard* of January 11, 1964, did not list a single British group or artist in its Hot 100. One week later, a song called "I Want To Hold Your Hand" leaped to the # 45 position. A week later, it was # 1. Within weeks, Vee Jay of Chicago was selling "From Me to You" and "Please Please Me." Swan of Philadelphia was marketting "She Loves Me," while MGM dug "My Bonnie," an early disk, out of its files. It was an unusual situation in record business, but it worked greatly to The Beatles' advantage. They had four singles on bestseller charts at one time, a most rare development for any artist. Their air play was so tremendous that a company without any Beatle releases complained: "Stations are playing our records like spot commercials between Beatle tunes."

The first Beatles invasion of the United States occurred in February, 1964, when they played Carnegie Hall and made their American TV debut on the Sullivan show. Magazines anticipated their coming with lavish spreads. Writing from London, Frederick Lewis observed: "They are working class, and their roots and attitudes are firmly of the North of England. Because of their success, they can act as spokesman for the new, noisy anti-Establishment generation which is becoming a force in British life. In their uncompromising Northernness, they are linked with actors like Albert Finney . . . and with novelists like Alan Sillitoe and John Braine."

Possibly their most attractive personal feature to American newsmen and audiences was their mocking depreciation of themselves. "All this nonsense about a Liverpool Sound," Paul McCartney said, "it doesn't exist, not really. It's a load of rubbish." And John Lennon added: "Well, it's fun, of course. We're having a fab time. But it can't last long." Like The Beatles themselves, writer Lewis made one underestimate. "Their rise," he stated, "marks the end of American domination of popular music in Britain." He could well have said: the end of American domination of popular music in America. Of the Liverpool

Sound, whose existence McCartney shrewdly questioned, Lewis observed: "Its significance is that it is a raspberry blown in the direction of London."

As The Beatles stepped out of their plane at Kennedy Airport on February 7, their first LP, *Meet The Beatles*, occupied the # 1 position on bestseller charts. A squad of 120 policemen battled 5,000 rampaging teenagers to save the lads from affectionate mayhem, causing newspapers to observe that their tumultuous reception "topped that given General Douglas MacArthur when he returned from Korea." After several rehearsals, Ray Bloch, orchestra leader on the Sullivan show, prophesied that the group "wouldn't last longer than a year." Although the show garnered a record Nielsen rating—three of every four sets in the New York area were tuned to the group—TV reviewers were quite blasé. "The boys hardly did for daughter," wrote *The New York Times* commentator, "what Elvis Presley did for her older sister or Frank Sinatra for mother." Sneering at "the pretext of a connection with the world of music," Jack Gould labelled their appearance "a sedate anticlimax."

Acknowledging their appeal as symbols of adolescent rebellion against adult society, Dr. Joyce Brothers, a newspaper and TV psychologist, found another facet in their popularity: "mannerisms which almost seem a shade on the feminine side." To her, none of the Beatles was an obvious, rugged he-man symbol, making them attractive to adolescent girls still a bit frightened of sex. A WMCA disk jockey, Joe O'Brien, thought that The Beatles made rock respectable in that they gave adults an image of the music they could accept—white, well-groomed, well-spoken, even charming. To Bob Dylan's manager, their main contribution was—"They proved it was all right to be white."

The coverage of the Carnegie Hall concert was less extensive than the stories of the hysterical crowds of girls that besieged the Plaza Hotel where the group was staying. However, Louis Biancolli, long a concert critic, was symptomatic of the many who believed that Beatle power was fundamentally nonmusical.

"Their effect is like mass hypnosis followed by mass night-mare," Biancolli wrote. "I never heard anything like what went on around me. I've read about the bacchantes and corybantes in wild Greek rites screaming insensately. They were antique squares compared to these teenage maenads." As for the music, he was ready to scream, "Quick, Henry, the flit!"

The incessant screaming, which made it impossible for the group to be heard, was a phenomenon that dismayed most adults. Obviously, the sequences depicting it in the first Beatles film *A Hard Day's Night* were hardly exaggerated. "They have on occasion sung silently," Earl Wilson claimed, "gesturing and moving their lips but making no sound . . . and due to the screaming of the little girls, the audience never knew the difference."

After Music's Gold Bugs departed for a riotous reception at London airport, American analysts tried in a backward glance to uncover the secret of their impact on the young. The most clinical analysis was given by Vance Packard, author of *The Hidden Persuaders*, who listed five ingredients. (1) *Identifying symbol*: the overlong hair. (2) *Rebelliousness*: not as rough-necks but as "lovable, almost cuddly, imps" who excited the mothering instinct in girls. (3) *Freshness*: exuberance, clean-liness, joyfulness and humor were in; surliness, sloppiness, self-pity and pomposity were out. (4) *Carrying device*: their odd name. (5) *Time factor*: they were an expression of England "bursting out of its inhibitions." But like the conductor of the Sullivan show, Packard felt that their popularity would be short-lived: they were not offensive enough to grown-ups and their appeal depended much on the visual. "If I were in the business," he concluded, "of manufacturing mophead Beatle wigs, I would worry."

Packard's disregard of The Beatles as a performing musical group was characteristic of most analyses of their popularity. A New York high school student put it succinctly when he said: "They're great—not much talent, but they handle themselves well." And Noel Coward said: "I've met them. Delightful lads. Absolutely no talent." In a sense this was inevitable since they overpowered people with their refreshing directness and disarming humor and constantly minimized their so-called talent. John said, "We're kidding you, we're kidding ourselves, we're kidding everybody. We don't take anything seriously except the money." By way of revealing the secret of their songwriting, Paul wrote: "'There are two things John and I always do when we're going to sit down and write a song. First of all we sit down. Then we think about writing a song." And even George Harrison, who was silent through press conferences and whom Lennon called The Bloody Sphinx, wrote of their musical ambitions: "Well, of course, I'd like to hear John sing in tune. . . . And I'd also like to become a really good guitar player." In short, compared to most performers, they handled themselves with such flippancy and frivolity that they seemed more a triumph of manner over music. Let it be added that, sparked by John Lennon, they sounded a new note in teenage song and conduct: for protest and diatribe, particularly as popularized by Dylan, they substituted the art of the put-on and the humorous put-down. Moreover, they were pro-adolescent without being anti-adult. In their put-down of the parent world, there was neither hatred nor hostility. Their targets were conditions and values, not the rulers.

By the summer of 1966 Capitol Records estimated that they had sold twenty million singles and as many LPs in the United States alone. Nevertheless, they continued to be regarded as folk heroes rather than performer-writers, and they were constantly written up for their social rather than musico-lyrical impact. When *The Saturday Evening Post* queried two American composers about the group, Aaron Copland confessed that he liked Beatlesong and said: "It has an unanalyzable charm. . . . It will definitely mark the period of the Sixties." But Richard Rodgers stated: "I find it monotonous. . . . I can't make any sense out of them. I don't think there's anything creative or original about it. It's just loud. I think their music won't last." By then, Lennon & McCartney had written the hauntingly beautiful ballad "Yesterday"—their gentle performance by a string octet was to launch baroque rock—and the equally lovely "Michelle." In some of their songs, like "Nowhere Man," "Paperback Writer" and particularly "Eleanor Rigby" with its desolating theme of lonely and wasted lives, their irreverence had turned to social criticism. Though *The Post* acknowledged that they were regarded by some—Leonard Bernstein, for example—as among the most talented songwriters of the day, and though it noted that their songs were being widely recorded by singers as diverse as Peggy Lee, Duke Ellington, and The Kingston Trio, it nevertheless left readers with the impression that theirs was (in bold type) "the art of adequate music." And it used a typical bit of Beatle self-depreciation to do this. From a press conference in Japan, it cited the following colloquy: "*Q*. How do you rate your music? A. We're not good musicians. Just adequate. *Q*. Then why are you so popular? A. Maybe people like adequate music."

It was not until 1967 when the emotional furor had simmered down that the considerable esthetic contribution of the group came to be properly evaluated. A retrospective appreciation by young Richard Goldstein, whose perceptive articles stirred other critics to take a serious view of rock, contributed to popular recognition of Beatle artistry. "They are creating the most original, expressive and musically interesting sounds in pop music," *Time* acknowledged in a lengthy cover story. "They are leading an evolution in which the best of current post-rock sounds are becoming something that pop music has never been: an art form."

Noting that The Beatles had not lost "any of the genial anarchism with which they helped revolutionize the life style of young people in Britain," *Time* announced that they had moved onto a higher artistic plateau with their new album, *Sgt. Pepper's Lonely Hearts Club Band*. This was the group's first complete

88

in-studio production, the result of months of dedicated, and costly, experimentaion at the electronic control board. With typical Beatle-ish humor, the cover of the album made it clear that this work was a departure. It depicted a large crowd, composed of known and unknown people—movie stars, authors, comics, dancers, singers, including Bob Dylan and themselves— all standing at a grave on which was spelled out "The Beatles." Among the plants growing around the grave were quantities of marihuana, an indication that they had outgrown another phase of their existence. By then, they had become celebrated disciples of Maharashi Mahesh Yogi, an Indian mystic who taught transcendental meditation.

The contrast between *Sgt. Pepper* and early Lennon & McCartney is marked. Although there was much talk at the beginning of a Mersey beat and a Liverpool Sound, Paul was not spoofing when he denied knowing what they were. These were not, as Richard Goldstein has said, "a reworking of the rock-blues tradition." While The Beatles were familiar with the disks of r&b singers of the 50s and recorded a number of Chuck Berry songs, including "Roll Over Beethoven" and "Rock and Roll Music," their kinship was with *country* rock not blues rock. When Paul talked of their influences, he recalled the excitement he experienced on hearing Bill Haley's "Rock Around the Clock," a rockabilly number. George Harrison named country guitarists Chet Atkins and Duane Eddy as idols of his youth. And even Chuck Berry is regarded by many as a country singer who happened to be Negro, in the vein of Joe Tex and Charlie Pride. *Variety* was on the right track when it cited the opinion of those who said of the Mersey Sound: "Mullarkey, The Beatles are dishing up a rock and roll style that was current in this country ten years ago and that is still typical of such groups as the Everly Brothers." Of course, The Beatles parted company with the rockabilly crowd in the tongue-in-cheek sexlessness of songs like "I Want To Hold Your Hand" and "And I Love Her."

Before long, emergent folk rock, mainly in the person and

work of Bob Dylan, gave a new edge to their writing, directing their anti-Establishment churnings into antibourgeois channels. Out of this came the condemnation of hack commercialism in "Paperback Writer," the experimentation with drugs and drug imagery in "Day Tripper" and "Yellow Submarine," and the deeply felt castigation of an indifferent world in "Eleanor Rigby."

By the spring of 1965, The Beatles had begun experimenting with new musical ideas. This development became evident in the mockingly titled *Rubber Soul*—the market was then flooded with pseudosoul artists and albums—an LP on which Paul played fuzz bass, George Martin, their record producer, played harmonium, and Ringo performed on Hammond organ. The most important innovation was in "Norwegian Wood," a track which found George Harrison tackling the sitar after a course of study with India's master sitarist, Ravi Shankar. While "Norwegian Wood" displays psychedelic influence in its use of trancelike musical background and ambiguous, dreamlike imagery, its significance is in the impulse it gave to what became known as raga rock—also in the tremendous audience it created for Ravi Shankar and other Indian musicians. ("Norwegian Wood" also made it clear that The Beatles were the Restoration poets of rock, wittily instead of sensually sexy: "I once had a girl/Or should I say/ She once had me. . . .")

While *Revolver*, the LP released in the summer of 1966, displayed advances in raga rock ("Love You To") and psychedelic rock ("Yellow Submarine"), it revealed that The Beatles were still moving into new areas, musically and lyrically. In its electronic distortion and harmonic dissonance, "Tomorrow Never Knows" showed that the group was not unfamiliar with Cage, Stockhausen and other exponents of electronic, tape and aleatory music. The expanded resources added to rock were further exploited in a remarkable single, "Strawberry Fields Forever." Here, the atonality achieved by electronic gimmickry proved a staggering accompaniment to a song of apathy and alienation.

"Living is easy with closed eyes," they sang. "It's all right, that is, I think it's not too bad. . . . But it's all wrong, that is, I think I disagree." Terminal rasps and roars suggest what a confusing mess the whole world is in.

"Strawberry Fields" summarized the new mood of the Now generation in the same way as Simon & Garfunkel's "Sounds of Silence." In 1967, despite the activism and sacrifices of the Freedom Riders, the South was rampant with new anti-Negro violence and northern communities were fighting school integration. Despite mounting protest, the war in Vietnam continued to escalate and American casualties continued to mount. A chilling wind of apathy was blowing once again through the colleges, which only a year earlier had been vibrant with political activity. Young people were turning on, freaking out, blowing their minds with drugs, escaping into the communal dives of hippieland, lapsing into the lackadaisical bohemianism of the teeny-boppers. As "Blowin' in the Wind" sounded the tocsin of social protest, so "Strawberry Fields" confirmed the flight from action, the frustration of noninvolvement.

Despite its innovations, *Revolver* did not elicit unanimous acclaim. Conceding that the songs were "brilliant and witty, pointed and barbed, and silly and fun to listen to," *Hi-Fi Stereo Review* found the performance tiresome and concluded: "They are finally as hip, as revolutionary, as new and urgent, as Elvis Presley in his ten-year-old gold lamé suit." Critic Richard Goldstein was in total disagreeement, and in a lengthy appreciation, hailed *Revolver* as an illustration of The Beatles' capacity for growth. However, he became a minority voice in his manifest disappointment over *Sgt. Pepper*, which he characterized as "an album of special effects, dazzling but ultimately fraudulent." At a later date, he conceded that the LP broke many molds and became a pacesetter for future rock albums. It was clearly the first of the superalbums, the most impressive of the studio rock LPs till then, and the work that initiated the burgeoning vogue of integrated albums. By the time that Goldstein acknowledged this legacy (in a spring of 1968 review of *Bookends*, a new Simon & Garfunkel LP), he also attributed to *Sgt. Pepper* the novel use of the orchestra "to illustrate the text"—a device that had earlier been skilfully employed by The Lovin' Spoonful in "Summer in the City" and by other rock groups.

But even in his original put-down, Goldstein saluted the final track of *Sgt. Pepper*'s flip side as a "historic pop event." Whether "A Day in the Life" warranted this hyperbole or not, it is one of Lennon & McCartney's most effective satires, musically and lyrically, of the terrible futility of the average man's existence, the search for the nothingness of drugged dreams, and the utter alienation of men. In this track of *Sgt. Pepper*, the intense absorption in production about which Mr. Goldstein complains, becomes a creative force: instrumentation, orchestration and electronics are all employed graphically to project the shattering atonality of contemporary existence.

Between *Revolver* and *Sgt. Pepper*, musical and literary admirers of The Beatles seemed to become as hysterical as their fans. This may have happened because the artists were not content to sit on their laurels and their millions but dared to adventure and change. Comments of both the musical and literary establishment became shrill with hyperbole. There was a constant search for hidden meanings and an unwillingness to hear put-ons and put-downs as they were intended. Richard Goldstein made a deflating comparison of "She's Leaving Home," a mock-operatic treatment of the provincial lass leaving home—she's got everything that money can buy except happiness—with the sombre and tragic "Eleanor Rigby," a song with an entirely different dimension.

The same inability to take the humor of "All You Need Is Love" at its value characterized a lengthy review that appeared in *The New York Times*. Here, again, though Tom Phillips sensed the song's slapstick quality, he refused to believe that it was "merely a sabotage on the Love Generation," and managed to conclude, after the kind of twisting and turning characteristic of academic treatises, that "while this song is profound, it's not at all solemn." An editor of *Partisan Review* reached higher in the realm of critical absurdity: "Far from being satiric in any way," wrote Richard Poirer, "the song gathers into itself the musical expression of the 'need' for love as it has accumulated through decades of popular music." Mr. Poirer's panegyric, incidentally, was an unremitting rave that ran to twenty-one polysyllabic pages. Titled *Learning from The Beatles* in a proper spirit of parental humility, it was an exercise, sprinkled with references to Shakespeare, Joyce, Pope and T. S. Eliot, in the most ponderous intellectualization to which pop song has ever been subjected. It reached its ludicrous summit in his comment on the Beatle parody of a song like "Rio Rita": "Not everyone their age," he praised, "is capable of seeing the odd wonder of a meter maid—after all, a meter maid's a meter maid; fewer still would be moved to a song of praise like "Lovely Rita" ('When it gets dark I tow your heart away'); and only a Beatle could be expected, when seeing her with a bag across her shoulder, to have the historically enlivened vision that 'made her look a little like a military man.' "

Having overstated the achievement, it was to be expected that the canonizers would turn on the saints they had created. The condemnation came sooner than one could have anticipated. Richard Goldstein performed such a complete act of dismemberment on *Magical Mystery Tour*, the LP following *Sgt. Pepper*, that *The New York Times* received a flood of angry letters. Rex Reed's review in *Hi-Fi Stereo Review* was peppered with words like "repulsive," "revolting," "creepy" and "stagnant," and concluded by dismissing the album as "phony, pretentious, overcooked tripe."

On the other hand, a reviewer in the *Saturday Review* thought *Magical Mystery Tour* "easily their best album" and characterized their description of their acquired Hindu philosophy and its application to everyday life as "distinguished." Ned Rorem, who once again could not resist making comparisons with Schubert, now found a self-contained creativity which led to comparisons with Stravinsky. He lamented our becoming "so hung on what they Mean, we can no longer hear what they're performing," and concluded that they represented "the most invigorating music" of our era.

It was inevitable, of course, that they should become controversial. But their contribution is so substantial that it hardly requires intellectualization or overstatement. They have led rock into new musical channels, promoting an interest in new instruments, new styles, new forms and new sounds that have given rise to baroque rock, raga rock, electronic rock, and possibly aleatory rock. If Bob Dylan brought high seriousness to rock, applaud The Beatles for adding high and low humor to it. No more than John Lennon has to apologize for his book *In His Own Write*, which the British publisher described as "funny Lewis Carroll jabberwocky with a slight tinge of William Burrough's *Naked Lunch* and an almost Joycean word play," is it necessary for Beatle admirers to read Deep Meaning into their mastery of the art of the Put-On and the Put-Down.

7 THE BRITISH INVASION

The Beatles had hardly landed in the United States for their first personal appearance in February, 1964, than *Variety* announced, "Britannia Rules Airwaves," and noted: "The advent of the group now has shattered the steady, day-to-day domination of made-in-America music here and abroad." By the end of 1964, it was estimated that British rock groups had sold singles and albums in the United States to the cash-register tune of $76,000,000.

As The Beatles deplaned in London after their rocking two-week reception in America, another British group took off from Tottenham. The Dave Clark Five (DC-5) had then displaced their countrymen from the top of British charts with "Glad All Over." After a performance on the Sullivan show, the DC-5 took off for a personal appearance tour. This proved so successful that all five members of the group were badly injured by over-enthusiastic fans. When they returned six months later for a fifty-five-day tour, their contracts stipulated that they were to be given the protection of 100 security guards in addition to local police. On this tour, they grossed from $10,000 to $15,000 a night, and carted away between half a million and three-quarters of a million dollars.

Despite their continuing success, the DC-5 has none of the charisma of their potent predecessors. "Glad All Over," which became a Gold Record LP, is characteristic of a style, colorless but appealing. The group projects an image of unspoiled friendliness, offering music that is amicably and joyfully rhythmic. Their songs are without profundity, but clean-cut, and their sound is without electricity, but clean-cut. Clark has said: "Records are for enjoyment; there's no message in our music; it's just for fun." But apparently the fun is infectious, for the group has had a succession of record hits, including such # 1 songs as "Over and Over." It has made more than a dozen appearances on the Sullivan show, a rare occurrence. The DC-5's *Greatest Hits* also became a certified Gold Record with sales in excess of one million dollars. And the total sales of their more than a dozen albums are estimated at over 15 million copies in the United States alone.

The group displays no uneasiness about finding its repertoire outside its own members, even though drummer Dave Clark and organist–lead singer Mike Smith are responsible for many of their hits. Smith has a hoarse voice and can sing black when a Detroit song like "Do You Love Me" or a Fats Domino hit like "Blueberry Hill" requires it. The group also has a Nashville sound. Whether and how long their simple danceability and glad-all-over eclecticism can survive in the increasingly complex rock scene is anybody's guess. American youngsters have progressed far beyond the 1964 feeling of anything-British-is-great.

The third group to invade American pop was controversial from the start. Whether teenagers sought a counterbalance to The Beatles, or the group itself determined only an opposite set of characteristics would be competitive, The Rolling Stones overwhelmed and outraged where The Beatles charmed. *Variety* reflected the Establishment reaction to the group that took its name from a Muddy Waters blues, when it castigated them for "tapping a Freudian vein of savagery and malignancy in their parlay of frantic guitars and drums, wild vocals, bumps, grinds and twitches." And the British Establishment voiced its disapproval, if it did not display a large measure of vindictiveness, as *The London Times* charged, when three of the Stones received severe jail sentences on drug charges. *The Times* was quite vehement that leaderman Mick Jagger had been victimized because he was a symbol of decadence to the middle-brow world, of youthful customs resented by adults. They noted that the Italian pep pills, whose possession had netted him a jail sentence, had been approved by Jagger's physician; that had the doctor written a prescription, Jagger would have been in the clear; and that a first offense, even of a more serious nature, frequently drew a probationary warning.

But the very qualities that antagonized adults found enthusiastic response among the young. The Stones came charging on the scene like Angry Young Men and tackled sex with a vehemence that quickly put them in line for the title of the group parents hate most. Although they had a good seller in "Tell Me," their first big American hit was "Satisfaction," a song that became controversial after it became # 1 when someone dug under Mick Jagger's hard black sound and uncovered references to seduction. Many radio stations clamped down on the side while others continued playing it, but with the questionable stanza deleted. A subsequent hit "Let's Spend the Night Together" also ran into censorship problems—older generation people seemed to forget an oldie that went, "To spend one night with you/In our old rendezvous/That's my desire"—and Jagger was compelled to substitute "some time" for "the night" when The Stones appeared on the Sullivan show. His feeling manifested itself in the lascivious leer with which he delivered the euphemism.

The discontent voiced by The Stones was more basic and comprehensive than a dissatisfaction with adult reticence about sex. They were savagely negative, in early albums like *Aftermath*, about Establishment values in general. But the adulation they attracted from under-thirty publications like *Crawdaddy* was based on more absolute matters: their mastery of structure, the rock power of their lyrics, the attractiveness of their melodies, and their virtuoso musicianship. "Having a brand new Rolling Stones album in your hands," Paul Williams, editor of *Crawdaddy* has said, "is like being a virgin on the brink."

The peak of veneration came with *Their Satanic Majesties Request*, the album that followed The Beatles' *Sgt. Pepper*. By then rock was the scene of a sweepstakes in which the groups who could afford it, and some who couldn't, were spending prodigious sums of money and time on new LPs. It was reported that The Beach Boys' *Smiley Smile* LP cost over $50,000 in studio time and musicians' fees. Now, word came that the cover of The Stones' album, a 3-dimensional color print, in which their heads moved magically, cost $25,000 alone. One 8-minute track, which took untold hours of studio time to prepare, was described as a "pocket opera of a disoriented world, a perfectly articulated jet-stream of sound which vacuums out of the air everything from pure melodies, to fragments of conversation, screams, volcanic rumblings, mad ornithological croakings, Stravinsky karate-chords, turning itself rhythmically inside out like a wind sock. . . ." In short, The Stones had gone the *Sgt. Pepper* route of electronic, exotic, music-hall and dramatic rock.

To many critics, however, the significance of the album lay in its positive outlook. The Stones had gone lyrical. "In Another Land" and "She's a Rainbow" were love lyrics and melodies with an appealing Oriental sound, and showed a tremendous expansion of instrumental resources and devices. Songs like "Citadel," "The Lantern" and "2,000 Light Years From Home," which led to characterizations of the LP as a science-fiction album, employed an eerie interplay of distances and sounds. *Newsweek* reflected the excitement of most critics: "The revolutionary excellence of work like the Stones' and the Beatles', together with the incredible extent of their popularity, has just about become the most amazing cultural fact of our time."

However, by the time that *Beggar's Banquet* was cut in August, 1968, the under-thirty critical contingent decided that *Satanic Majesties Request* was a disaster and that the group had foolishly fallen into the *Sgt. Pepper* trap of artiness. A return to the unencumbered drive and excitement of "Satisfaction" (with a bit of country air blowing through many of the numbers), *Beggar's Banquet* was hailed as a "comeback." And the editor of *Rolling Stone* saluted the album as marking a historical moment in rock—"the final end of all the pretentious, nonmusical, boring, insignificant, self-conscious and worthless stuff that has been tolerated during the past year.

Three other English groups early accounted for chart-climbers in American pop. By April, 1964, a disk by a duo named Peter and Gordon was # 1 on British record charts. While The Beatles might have been displeased, the development brought pleasure to Lennon & McCartney as the writers of the hit "A World Without Love." The crossing of interests becomes clear when we learn that Peter's surname is Asher, which happens to be the surname of the Jane who frequently accompanied Paul Mc-Cartney. Gordon is Gordon Waller, like Asher the son of a London physician. The two met at a private school, began singing together at local coffee bars and folk clubs and eventually secured an engagement at London's Pickwick Club. At that point, they stopped scaling the high wall surrounding their school (to get out for gigs after the nine o'clock curfew) and dropped out altogether.

Signed by EMI as a result of their Pickwick engagement, they were # 1 on American charts with "A World Without Love" by June, 1964. In succession, they had hits in "Nobody I Know" and "I Don't Want To See You Again," both written by the two Beatles, and in "I Go to Pieces," a screamer by Del Shannon, an American writer-performer. A nonwriting team, they possess a pair of vigorous, versatile voices. *In London for Tea*, a recent LP, demonstrates their mastery of country material ("Red,

99

Cream and Velvet" and "Please Help Me I'm Falling"), folk rock ("London at Night") and blue-eyed soul (covers of American r&b hits. "I'm Your Puppet" and "Stop, Look and Listen"). They also have an album of film tunes (*Lady Godiva*). The one with glasses smiles and wears a tie in cover photographs. The other wears a white business shirt open at the collar. Both are shaggy-haired but look like a pleasant pair of Eton school boys. They sing for their generation but display no antagonism toward the older one. Like the Dave Clark Five, they reveal no contact with the new developments in sound, instruments, harmony and electronics. But their versatility has given them six successful albums.

Chad and Jeremy was another duo that began peppering American charts with hit records from 1964 on. Writers of "What Do You Want with Me?", they turned to other writers, English and American, for "Summer Song" and "Before and After." Although they both now reside in the Los Angeles area, they come from solid English backgrounds. Chad Stuart of Durham attended local schools to become an accomplished pianist and guitarist, eventually landing at a school of speech and drama in London where he met Jeremy Clyde. A graduate of Eton, Jeremy spent time with the Scottish Dundee Repertory Theatre, appeared in a London musical and still has thespian ambitions.

They work at the muted and pretty side of rock, producing a combination of raga and baroque rock, and their songs are full of delicately satirical smiles. They have a point of view, understated though it may be, as the cover of a recent LP reveals: "Chad's dog Roger," a caption reads, "ate the entire score of 'Ballad of the Green Berets,' which otherwise would have been assured a place of honour in this album." Of course. *Of Cabbages and Kings,* as the LP is titled, reveals their adventuring spirit. One side is composed mostly of songs by Clyde. "Family Way," which ends with the cries of a baby, anticipated but premature, takes a gentle swipe at middle-class morality and pretensions.

The opening song, "Rest In Peace," reminiscent of *Spoon River Anthology*, is more caustic in its cameo biographies of frustrated and unfruitful lives. It is the work of Chad, who seems to wield a sharper scalpel than his associate and who is responsible for most of side 2. *The Progress Suite*, as it is called, is an ambitious instrumental composition in five movements whose program and partial text—Editorial and Epilogue by Jeremy—deals with the decline of Western civilization. Baroque sounds predominate in a preponderantly woodwind-and-strings instrumentation. Chad can be heard playing guitar, banjo, harpsichord, organ, tack piano, ukelin and sitar. His own comment on the album cover: "Big deal." The *Suite* falls pleasantly on the ears, is rife with interesting rhythms and arresting nonmusical sounds, and suggests that they believe a man's reach should exceed his grasp, or what's music for? They are reaching gracefully and promisingly.

The third group that made an early impression on American listeners, Gerry and the Pacemakers, takes us back to the hometown of The Beatles. Gerard Marsden, responsible for such 1964 chart songs as "It's Gonna Be All Right," "How Do You Do It?" "Don't Let the Sun Catch You Crying" and "Ferry Cross the Mersey," not only grew up in Liverpool, but also played The Cavern, the smoky cellar that formerly gave employment to The Beatles. *Ferry Cross the Mersey* was the title of a British film in which Gerry and his group appeared.

Two other British groups of recognized significance in American rock—Herman's Hermits and The Animals—offer a study in violent contrasts. Herman's Hermits, who did not ride in on the big Beatle wave, have been called "the Boy Scouts of rock" and "everybody's choirboys." Although the group was formed in 1964 at a youth club in Manchester, it did not begin hitting the Top Ten until early in 1965 when it scored with "Mrs. Brown, You've Got a Lovely Daughter." They have since become known for "I'm Henry the VIII, I Am," "There's a Kind of Hush All Over the World Today" and "No Milk Today," the last-mentioned a song that has swept the world. Herman is not really Herman, but Peter Noone, the proper son of a proper Manchester accountant. In 1966 he was voted one of the Ten Best Dressed Men by the association of British clothing manufacturers, who doubtless approved the group's wholesome image. Looking like an amiable, well-bred English schoolboy—Noone started as an actor and has not given up acting ambitions—Herman sings in a young, soft, at times almost feminine voice. Much of the group's material comes from the English music-hall tradition. But their sound is country-and-western, more country than western.

The pens and pianos of other writers have accounted for most of their hits. But Herman's own "Take Love, Give Love" suggests the well-adjusted, well-balanced outlook of the group, a point of view given more bite in "This Door Swings Both Ways." "I dislike hippies," Noone has said, "I don't like people who go about shouting and wearing badges. . . . I know I can't sing Negro music and I don't need to, or want to." This square stance in the middle of the road has netted the Hermits a flock of # 1 disks and eight bestselling LPs.

Turning to the group led by Eric Burdon is like walking out of a tidy ice-cream parlor into a noisy, brawling saloon. The Animals were originally known as the Alan Price Combo, but their freewheeling antics provoked comparisons with animals. The name stuck and their style has changed little, save that they are now known as Eric Burdon and the New Animals, and Alan Price heads his own new combo. Not inappropriately, the first Animals hit was a British reworking of "House of the Rising Sun," the famous folk ballad about a red-light establishment. They dig Chuck Berry, with whom they have toured, John Lee Hooker and other pioneer bluesmen. Their guitars, as well as Burdon's vocals, have a blues-directed rather than blues-inflected sound. Some refer to the sound as British soul, but this is misleading unless you think of it as a whiter shade of blue-eyed soul. In most ways, the group is a triumph of manner over substance, and more exciting visually than aurally. And yet their exuberant, bad-boy, let's-talk-about-sex style, akin to that of the early Stones who were stronger musically even then, has won them a large following. They have had nine fast-selling albums, many of them with subtitles like *Animal Tracks, Animalism* and *Animalization.* Burdon is a musical adventurer who has flung himself into new developments. But as in "When I Was Young," a chart song that pointlessly exploited a bozouki motif, there is no real integration of sound and substance, and the group-made lyrics have flaws as well as vitality. Mark it down to the intensity of Burdon, and the excitability of the other members of the group, all of whom hail from Newcastle in County Durham, a mining area in the North of England where the inhabitants have little use for the clean look and prize the tough, independent, uninhibited kind of man.

In a recent album, *Winds of Change,* the readiness to explore new worlds of sound is apparent in the use of ragas, electric violins, and other exotic instruments. But the lyric content remains predictably animal: "Yes, I Am Experienced," "It's All Meat," "Hotel Hell" and "Paint It Black" are some of the titles. The last mentioned went to # 1.

When the Bee Gees' recording of "New York Mining Disaster —1941" became a hit, Richard Goldstein wrote in *The New York Times,* "The rock revolution is history now; the Bee Gees are its children." Considering that little more than three years separated the American record debut of the new group—May, 1967—from the advent of The Beatles, to whom they are constantly likened, it is startling to think of them as "children." But the fact is that they were part of a second wave of British invaders. Actually, the group has as much right to be called Australian as English. Though three of them, the Gibbs brothers, Barry, Robin and Maurice, were born in Manchester, they spent their formative musical years in Australia, where the family migrated in 1958. During the eight succeeding years, the three brothers, known as the Bee Gees, developed into one of the hottest Aussie groups, with a TV show of their own, a Festival Records contract from 1963 on, and successive # 1 hits in 1965 and 1966, which they themselves wrote.

When they left Sydney in February, 1967, to return to England, "Spicks and Specks" was # 1 on Australia's national charts. In short order, they acquired a top-notch manager as well as two additional musicians in Colin Peterson on drums and Vince Melouney on guitar, both Australians. The release of the "Mining Disaster" disk brought immediate outcries of Beatle imitation. The tragic tale reminded many of "Eleanor Rigby" by its understated narrative: "Don't go talking too loud," said the miner facing death. "You'll cause a landslide." The singing was also reminiscent of The Beatles in its gentle, underplayed, undramatic style. Then the group came out with the single on which "To Love Somebody" was backed with "Close Another Door." Now the similarity was gone, for these two sides were not folk rock or rockabilly, but tough r&b, and the orchestral backing had the many-layered density of a Righteous Brothers wall-of-sound disk.

Another second-wave British group is The Hollies, whose reputation in England, on the Continent and even in Israel and India, long antedated their debut in America. Their first single, "Carrie-Ann," exploited a Trinidad steel band sound and their first LP, *Evolution,* suggested Herman's Hermits, with whom they toured and appeared in a CBS-TV documentary on rock. Although they were North of Englanders, they exhibited none of the uninhibited violence and sensuality manifested by a neighboring group, The Animals. Three of the five, Graham Nash (leader and rhythm guitarist), Allan Clarke (lead singer) and Tony Hicks (lead guitarist), account for the songs they sing. These lack the poetry and distinction of the Bee Gees' material, just as their performance provides pleasure without challenge. Nevertheless, they placed in the Top Ten of *Billboard*'s Top Groups for 1967 along with the *Billboard*'s Beatles, while Herman's Hermits came in at # 12, the Rolling Stones at # 14 and the Tremeloes ("Here Comes My Baby") at # 18. The British windstorm had dwindled to a mild breeze, as only five British groups appeared in a list of twenty-five.

In truth, since 1967 an increasing number of successful British groups are not scoring so quickly or so well on American charts.

Among these is The Incredible String Band. Once a duo consisting of Robin Williamson and Clive Palmer—they joined forces in 1965 and performed in Palmer's Incredible Folk Club in Glasgow—and later a trio that included Michael Heron, the Band is now a duo once again, made up of Williamson and Heron. Their title is only partly misleading. Between them, they perform engagingly on enough instruments to sound like an eighteen-piece band. Their instrumental proficiency involves such exotic devices (for us) as gimbri, oud, sitar, drahani, tamboura and finger cymbals, and (for them) penny whistle and banjo. In 1965 they placed two albums at the very top of British folk charts: their debut LP in March and *The 5,000 Spirits or the Layers of the Onion* in August.

Although their original repertoire was heavily weighted with jug band tunes and Uncle Dave Mason songs (of Grand Ole Opry fame), their first Elektra disk revealed an interest in the sounds washing into British rock from the Far and Middle East. Their second LP and *The Hangman's Daughter*, their third, were marked by a continuing inventive and innovative spirit that caused many British critics to compare them to The Beatles. Like other rock groups responding to Indian philosophy, they express awe at the phenomenon of life and emphasize the organic connection between all things. Mystical at times, they also are heirs of the pantheism of British poet William Wordsworth. Though they made an appearance at the Newport Folk Festival in 1967, their impact on American record-buyers is uneven.

The Seekers of "Georgy Girl" fame are another British, really Australian, group that have yet to find a dedicated American following. Like The Lovin' Spoonful, much of their repertoire is composed of rewrites of old blues. Unlike the Spoonful, they do not include a talented songwriter like John Sebastian, and turn for their repertoire to songs of their contemporaries: Pete Seeger's and The Byrds' "Turn! Turn! Turn!," Simon & Garfunkel's "Some Day, One Day," Bob Dylan's "The Times They Are A-Changin'."

Three other groups of the second wave stand forth as representatives of hard rock and, in varying measure, of the rage-and-frustration syndrome. At the Monterey Pop Festival in June, 1967, The Who ignited smoke bombs, overturned their drums and crumpled a guitar while the Jimi Hendrix Experience climaxed their appearance by setting Hendrix's guitar on fire. Although The Cream is doubtless the wildest-looking of the three new British groups, it burns with an inner fire, stoked by the hot coals of pioneer blues.

The arrogance of the name bespeaks the virtuosity of the threesome who make up The Cream. Drummer Ginger Baker, with his long red hair waving wildly, is master of the demanding style of playing around, against and with the beat, not on it. Bassist Jack Bruce, who once worked with the Mann Manfred group and John Mayall's Blues Breakers, wails the vocals with the same ferocity that marks guitarist Eric Clapton's tough blues style. Most admired of the three, Clapton admits that it is not easy to be white, English and bluesy. "You're a blues person," he has said, "only when you're playing. But Negro bluesmen live the blues environment, eat soul food. Even hearing them talk can be like hearing the blues. Rock is like a battery that must always go back to blues to get recharged." Despite the admission, listeners hear lines and chords in Clapton's playing that have the authenticity of Muddy Waters and B. B. King blues styling. Both in *Fresh Cream*, their first album, and in *Disraeli Gears*, the group pursues a technique of simultaneous improvisation in which all three are continuously manipulating the basic melody of a piece. There is no soloist and no accompanist. There is no foreground and no background. All three are soloists and up front, producing an enveloping sheet of sound characteristic of the New Thing in jazz. Their motto: "Forget the message, forget the lyrics, just play."

In July, 1968, The Cream had three albums in the Top Fifty bestsellers. *Disraeli Gears* and *Wheels of Fire*, both Gold Records, were then in the Top Ten, with the latter holding the # 1 spot for weeks. "I just want to perform contemporary blues," said guitarist Eric Clapton, who had gone from the

Yardbirds to John Mayall's Blues Breakers and then to The Cream. Commenting on the demands of success, he added: "You got really hung up and try to write pop songs or create a pop image."

The Who has also worked at eliminating the traditional pecking order among its members. In a number of records, like "My Generation," for example, they have established a sound parity between singer Roger Daltrey and the accompanying guitar-bass-drum trio. Experimentation and showmanship distinguish The Who, rather than quality of material or performance. Keith Moon drums so ferociously that his sticks splinter. Peter Townshend rams his guitar into its amplifier and produces a roaring, overpowering feedback. Although unusual packaging and the single hit "Happy Jack" contributed greatly to the rise of the group, a talent for satire displayed in the song "A Quick One While He's Away" added to the impact of *Sell Out*. One side of the LP was a spoof of Top Forty radio programming, with typical blaring ads appearing between tunes.

Unquestionably, the most inspired of these three groups is that headed by Jimi Hendrix, who has been called the Black Elvis and the Cassius Clay of pop. He is included in the second British wave only because, though American-born and -reared, he had to go to England to receive recognition. A native of Seattle, Washington, he was expelled from Garfield High School allegedly because he held hands with a white girl in art class. Having learned guitar by listening to Muddy Waters records, he pursued the route of the black musician, playing segregated clubs in Nashville, hanging around Harlem bandstands, and touring with r&b bands backing Negro headliners. "Like once with Little Richard," he recalls. "Me and another guy got fancy shirts 'cause we were tired of wearing the uniform. Richard called a meeting. 'I am Little Richard, the king,' he said, 'King of Rock and Rhythm. I am the only one allowed to be pretty. Take off those shirts.' Man, it was all like that. Bad pay, lousy living, and getting burned."

Hendrix credits Dylan with turning him on. "Not the words

or his guitar," he says, "but as a way to get myself together. A cat like that can do it to you. Race, that was okay. In the Village, people were more friendly than in Harlem where it's all cold and mean. Your own people hurt you more." It was early 1966 when, as Jimmy James, he played the Cafe Wha in Greenwich Village with his own group, the Blue Flames. This was when he began to write songs and developed what he describes as his "rock-blues-funky-freak sound." But it was in England, where he emigrated at the suggestion of the ex-bassist of The Animals, that Hendrix found himself and became part of the In-crowd of British musicians.

Forming a trio that included two young English musicians—Mitch Mitchell on drums and Noel Redding on bass—the Jimi Hendrix Experience quickly scored with "Hey Joe," which climbed to the Top Ten, and with "Purple Haze." Paul Mc-Cartney arranged for the group to be invited to the Monterey Pop Festival in June, 1967. The tour that followed, despite the notices that his violent performance drew, was unsuccessful compared with audience excitement during his second American tour in February-March, 1968. His three nights at the Fillmore in San Francisco were the biggest in the auditorium's history. By then, his virtuosity and weird showmanship had become legendary. He could play the guitar by plucking the strings with his teeth. In a pose reminiscent of honking tenor saxists in r&b bands of the 40s, he would throw himself on his back and wildly play the instrument as he held it upright on his belly. Using no hands at all, he would make the instrument wail dissonantly through masterful use of the wah-wah pedal. While audiences were magnetized by these exhibitions, many critics were not. Peter Reilly remarked amusingly in *Hi-Fi Stereo Review* that Hendrix's frenzied biting of his guitar often made Reilly wish "it would bite him back."

Reilly and others were troubled by the volume at which the group performed. Of Noel Redding's bass, Tom Phillips wrote in *The New York Times*, "It sounds like a cello bowed with a hacksaw and fed through a bullhorn." But the adult world also took umbrage at the frankly erotic character of Hendrix's material and presentation. *Are You Experienced?* was the title of his first LP. It included songs like "Foxy Lady" and "Let Me Stand Next to Your Fire." The second LP, *Axis: Bold As Love*, leaped quickly into the Top Ten. During his first American tour, the D.A.R. drew attention to the markedly erotic character of his stage performances and was successful in blocking an appearance he was to make with the Monkees.

"People who put down our performance," he has said, "they're people who can't use their eyes and ears at the same time. . . . Man, it's the music. That's what comes first." Whether he admits his sexuality or not, Hendrix has also said: "I'm the one that's got to die when it's time for me to die, so let me live my life the way I want to. . . . I want to see and hear everything." The libertarian outlook, the violence of his presentation, the challenging eroticism—all have made him a hard competitor of James Brown, except that he is apparently able to overwhelm white audiences as well as black.

A second-wave group that has not gone beyond its one-hit status is Procol Harum. It merits mention if only because "A Whiter Shade of Pale" was chosen Single of the Year in *Melody Maker's* 1967 Reader's Poll, outdistancing even Lennon & McCartney's "Strawberry Fields," and because in this country, it climbed to # 5 as a hit single. A curious combination of a blues melody superimposed on a recognized Bach organ background, "Pale" embodied lyrics with a weird, enigmatic quality. It is said that the name of the group means "beyond these things," an image that it tried to preserve when organist Matthew Fisher, in a performance at San Francisco's Winterland, appeared in a monk's black, hooded habit. The cover of the LP titled after the hit single was an Aubrey Beardsleyesque black-and-white drawing that emphasized the group's feeling for Gothic terror. However, the substitution of Robin Trower for the original lead guitarist reinforces the blues orientation of organist Fisher and vocalist-pianist-songwriter Gary Brooker. While the baroque-blues sound of "Pale" was unique, the failure of follow-up singles suggests that Procol Harum may yet have to rely on the lasting power of the blues.

The second British wave also includes a number of solo singers, female as well as male. With the exception of Petula Clark, all have been deeply influenced by American Negro artists. Miss Clark is, strictly speaking, not second-wave since she blasted into the rock scene in 1964. But then again, she is not really a rock singer even though she won the NARAS award that year for "Best Rock and Roll Recording." And she surely is not under thirty, even though she has the face and sound of a perennial teenager. Petula began recording in the era when the "belters"—singers like Frankie Laine, Johnnie Ray, Teresa Brewer and Georgia Gibbs—superseded the crooners and tender balladeers. She is still a belter today, and in 1964 she had the good fortune to record one of the best rock songs ever written—Tony Hatch's ebullient "Downtown." Mr. Hatch and a number of other talented young writers have managed to supply her with material that has kept her disks spinning and selling in the rock market.

Dusty Springfield also made her first solo disk in 1964—"I Only Want to Be With you"—but her real impact in the American market came later. Born Mary Isobel Catherine O'Brien in Hampstead, near London, in 1941, she derives her name from the Springfields, a group with which she sang from 1960 on until she stepped out on her own. A laundry assistant, record sales-girl and department-store clerk before she became a singer, she is an individualist with a lively sense of humor. Queried as to what she wanted out of life, she replied: "All the Twentieth Century-Fox musicals, so I can sit in bed and watch what I want by pushing a button." She plays spoons as well as piano and guitar, but "only Woolworth spoons." In 1967 she sang "The Look of Love" in *Casino Royale*, a Bacharach-David song that was nominated for the Academy Award. She is fond of offbeat leather clothes, which offers a hint as to the quality of her voice: husky, tough and sharp-edged.

While Dusty's 1967 hit was in the running for the Oscar, another British star complained bitterly that her million-copy hit "To Sir, With Love" was not. Of the three ladies under discussion, Marie McDonald McLaughlin Lawris, known as Lulu, is really second-wave, really rock, and under thirty. Daughter of a Bridgeton butcher, she became interested in singing as a result of the Kay Starr and Teresa Brewer 78 r.p.m.'s her father brought home. She was still in school when a record she made of "Shout" sailed into the British Top Ten. At fifteen, while singing at Glasgow's Le Phonographie Club, she acquired her present manager, Marian Massey, and her nickname. "She's a lulu of a singer," Miss Massey said when she heard her. Green-eyed like Dusty, but a redhead rather than a blonde, she prizes soul in singing. *To Sir, With Love* was the first film in which she played and sang. She runs around with The Beatles whom she has joined in their antidrug search for inner peace and relaxation-through-meditation.

It was a film, or rather a song about the characters in a film, "The Ballad of Bonnie and Clyde," that made Georgie Fame a Top Ten singer in American charts in 1968. Born Clive Powell in Lancashire in 1943, he was a Jerry Lee Lewis fan in his early teens and by seventeen, a member of the Blue Flames, a vocal group backing hit-singer Billy Fury. For a period of time, he played piano with a jazz group that performed at a club in London's Soho district. As a result of a single that sneaked into American charts in 1964 ("Yeh, Yeh"), he appeared on several American TV rock shows—*Hullabaloo* and *Shindig*—and toured Britain with Tamla-Motown artists in 1965. The following year, he was voted Top British Blues Artist and Top Male Jazz Singer in the *Melody Maker* poll. He placed second as Jazz Organist. The impact of his disk of "Bonnie and Clyde" led to his singing the title song in an Elizabeth Taylor–Richard Burton film, and to his touring with the Count Basie Orchestra.

Tom Jones—his full name is Thomas Jones Woodward—has said that he became interested in show business "the moment I realized how heavy a hod was." Born in a mining region of South Wales, he early played drums in working men's clubs and sang in the chapel choir. Although his father and uncle were miners, he was a brick-carrier for several years, a fact which may account for his massive build. His breakthrough came in 1965 with the hit "It's Not Unusual," followed soon by the title song of the film *What's New Pussycoat?* and a country ballad "Green Green Grass of Home." He has appeared many times on the Sullivan show and played the Copa, using a repertoire that consists mainly of American songs.

"I've been fascinated by American music since I was a kid," he explains. "Especially Negro music and country music. Country music is very big in Britain. The songs have a lot of feeling and meaning and . . . are always about life." Backed by a Welsh quartet, The Squires, he delivers in a style that reminds one of Frankie Laine, though he has a bigger and richer baritone, and he has a sound that is Negro enough to put him in the British contingent of blue-eyed soul.

While British artists continued to invade the American entertainment scene and record charts, by August, 1968, Henry Pleasants observed in his monthly letter from London: "The flow of musical influence outward from America . . . now continues as pervasively as ever." Writing in *HiFi/Stereo Review*, Mr. Pleasants noted that the most important elements of that influence were r&b, urban blues, and soul, and expressed his amazement at the "almost flawless approximation" of black sound achieved even by British cockneys. Not only was blue-eyed soul a marked trend, but the English record market was highly receptive to reissues of early American rockabilly and r&b disks.

8 SOUL : *Blue-eyed and Black*

Out of the boil of emotions generated by the current civil rights and integration movement, "soul" emerged in the 60s not only as a concept of Negro identity but of muscial expressiveness. The emotions were complex: a new pride in Negritude, escalating in some quarters to black nationalism; a feeling of disillusionment at the frustratingly slow progress of school desegregation, despite the Supreme Court decision of 1954; mounting anger at the white man's continuing efforts to restrict the Negro to second-class citizenship; resentment that the goods available in our consumer economy and so tantalizingly hawked on TV are economically out of his reach. All these emotions led to an intensification of the attitudes of discontent, hostility and rebelliousness that had been building among Negroes for several centuries. The emotions exploded in the rioting, burnings and lootings that began in Los Angeles' Watts district in 1965 and that have continued through subsequent summers in other American cities with large Negro ghettoes. In these communities, white merchants have tried to prevent the destruction and looting of their establishments by painting "Soul Brother" on store windows.

"Soul is sass, man," said Negro writer Claude Brown. "Soul is arrogance. . . . Soul is walkin' down the street in a way that says, 'This is me, muh-fuh!' Soul is that nigger whore comin' along . . . ja . . . ja . . . ja, and walkin' like she's sayin', 'Here it is, baby. Come an' git it.' Soul is being true to yourself, to what is *you.* . . . Soul is that uninhibited, no, *extremely* uninhibited self-expression that goes into practically every Negro endeavor. . . . And there's swagger in it, man. It's exhibitionism, and it's effortless. . . ."

Some years ago, the man known as the Father of the Blues described them as the music of deprivation and the Negro race. "Like the spirituals," said W. C. Handy, "the blues . . . involve our history, where we came from and what we experienced. . . . The blues came from nothingness, from want, from desire." "Soul" is the blues of the 60s—an expression of a people imbued not merely with giant needs and desires but with a determination to win Freedom Now. It stems from the chain-gang song, the field holler, the spiritual chant, the gospel shout, the blues cry, the r&b bellow—but has been amplified by the electrical intensities of the rocking 60s. Part of the so-called "revolution of rising expectations," it is provocative, unrestrained, and runs to extremities on any level of experience—social, religious, political or sexual. Musically speaking, soul is the first "form" of Negro music that has penetrated the pop market and entered it on the Negro's terms.

Like Gaul, the world of soul may be divided into three parts: *authentic,* or the gospel-blues tradition in the civil-rights era; *blue-eyed,* meaning white performers who sing black, like the Righteous Brothers and Mitch Ryder; and *sophisticated*—probably a better term would be black pop—meaning black performers who sing white, like Nancy Wilson, Johnny Mathis, Brook Benton, and at times, Dionne Warwick and Diana Ross of The Supremes. At least three sounds enter into the sound of soul, each the product of a different record company situated in a different city: the Detroit or Motown Sound, the Atlantic Sound and the Memphis Sound. In addition, there are several artists of such commanding stature that they require consideration as individual shapers of soul: Ray Charles, James Brown, Nina Simone, Lou Rawls and the late Otis Redding.

The pre-eminent figure of all is Ray Charles, who was the living embodiment of soul long before it became a dominant factor in pop, and whose primary role in forming the style is unquestioned. Blind from his childhood, early orphaned, and a drug addict from his teens, he was compelled to depend on others, some of whom continue to abuse his trust to this day. "On the road, the man hasn't a soul to lean on," one of his sidemen has said. "It's no wonder he's restless, suspicious, often irritable, and so desperately committed to his music. Oh, he likes to laugh and he gets his kicks. But the music is the only way he gets full release."

Although he has perfect pitch, Charles learned music through Braille, a painfully slow process involving a prodigious use of memory. Eventually, he mastered not only piano, saxophone and trumpet, but even the complex art of arranging. By the time he was seventeen, he was on the road as a professional musician, playing in r&b as well as hillbilly bands. He worked and starved in many Florida and Tennessee towns. "I've known the worst kind of despair," he has said. "I remember being paid once in a tin of jam. When I tried to open it in my hotel room, I was so tormented by hunger that I jabbed the can opener into the top too quickly, and everything inside fell on the floor."

Seattle, Washington, proved a turning point in Charles' life. His Maxim Trio, a jazz group modelled on the highly successful Nat "King" Cole Trio, became the first Negro combo to appear on a sponsored TV program in the northwest. Charles' singing style was then imitative Cole. However, by the time that Atlantic Records took over his contract with Swingtime Records, a west coast label, he had become a typical r&b shouter. Two years later, in 1954, he called his mentors at Atlantic with a new idea. They flew to Atlanta where they made a session that, in the words of an Atlantic executive, "marked the emergence of the Ray Charles we've been hearing ever since. What he had done was to fuse gospel and blues. For instance, instead of staying with the 12-bar blues changes, there were 8- and 16-bar patterns, as in gospel music." One of the tunes on the Atlanta date, and one of his first big hits—"I Got a Woman"—was a blues that he had audaciously created out of the gospel song "My Jesus Is All the World to Me." It was a bold move because separation of sacred and profane music is one of the fundamental tenets of Negro religious life. One sang gospel to celebrate the joys of the afterlife. Blues were to confront the miseries of this life. They were as far apart as heaven and hell.

Later Charles was to say: "Gospel music background is important to a jazz musician, for it draws out feeling. What you speak of as *soul* in jazz is *soul* in gospel music. The important thing in jazz is to feel your music, but *really* feel it and *believe* it—the way a gospel singer like Mahalia Jackson obviously feels and believes the music that she is singing with her whole body and soul."

But the epithet of approval in jazz, as late as 1957, was not soul but "funky." Pianist Horace Silver was the moving spirit behind the Negro jazzman's search for roots and a return to playing hard on the beat, with the uninhibited feeling of intensity inherent in the blues. The word "funky" may be of Flemish, Anglo-Saxon or Negro origin, and may have been taken out of a nonmusical context relating to the smell of smoke, fear or sex. But the style itself represented a backlash against cool jazz, with its glorification of unmetered rhythm, suppressed emotionalism and cerebral detachment.

The gap between "funky" and "soul" has been well described by pianist Ramsey Lewis. "I know some pianists," he has said, "where everything they play comes out, not with depth and feeling exactly, but downright funky. Now, when everything you do comes out funky, that's trying . . . that isn't really soulful." And he adds: "To me, Ray Charles is a soulful musician . . . all the time. Not the piano playing so much, but his singing. He makes me feel the story he's telling. And he does it in simple form . . . all the time. That's real soul."

Big Bill Broonzy, the bluesman who had been a preacher, once said of Charles: "He's mixin' the blues with spirituals. That's wrong. . . . He's got a good voice but it's a church voice. He should be singin' in church." The fact is that Charles displayed a tendency to mix categories almost from the start. Blessed with the warm, comforting voice of a preacher, he never was just an r&b screamer, just a jazz artist, or simply an impassioned gospel shouter. And he certainly was not just a country singer when, after his shift to the ABC label in 1961, he displayed a marked preference for Nashville songs, garnering a Gold single in "I Can't Stop Loving You" and a Gold LP in *Modern Sounds in Country Music.*

Charles' talent was so prodigious that he *possessed* material, regardless of classification. "I think Mahalia Jackson is the greatest," he said, at the time that record-buyers were overwhelmed by his song "What'd I Say." "But even in that field, just because they are singing gospel songs doesn't automatically make them good. Whether it's blues or gospel or classical music, there is good and bad. It has to be a fine song and the artist has to feel it, or it's no good."

"Feeling" is, of course, the nub of the matter. Apart from the man's charisma and the inescapable anguish in the hoarse voice, intensity of feeling is what makes for the genius of Ray Charles. As the struggle for Negro rights has grown more intense, Charles' own expressiveness has become more intense—a reaction not to politics but to the upsurge of emotion in the black community. What one hears in recent records is not just sincerity but conviction. Not just determination but aggression. Not just persuasion but possession. Projected in this way, soul becomes a quantity as well as a quality, a force as well as a mass, an accolade as well as an identification, and on the pop level, it is Ray Charles.

"His capacity to evoke reality—sensual pleasure as well as frustration—is the base of Charles' command of so many different kinds of listeners," critic Nat Hentoff has observed. "But Charles packs an added dimension of intensity because he communicates the vulnerability of a man who is aware that he has not been able to escape the demons of his past." In 1965 Charles made his most determined effort to escape some of these demons. He retired from personal appearances and entered a California clinic in an attempt to free himself of the drug habit. The twentieth anniversary of his career came during his temporary retirement. To mark the occasion, *Billboard* dedicated a special issue to *The Ray Charles Story*, the title also of an Atlantic album that has been characterized as "one of the most arresting musical and social documents in the history of American popular art." On the floor of the House of Representatives, the Honorable Charles S. Joelson of New York introduced a resolution honoring Charles which read in part: "The pain of his early life and the hardships he has overcome are part of the Ray Charles Sound."

When he came out of retirement, he made one of his memorable appearances at The Copacabana, a nightclub that for years had been out of bounds for performers who had records of narcotics arrests. He became the second performer in the club's history to eliminate the traditional line of Copa girls and to bring in his own show and band.

While Charles has been able to reach a white adult audience as well as rock record-buyers, James Brown's Soul is of a more primitive character that addresses itself primarily to Negro audiences and to the young, and even the very young. ("I have seen children fifteen months old," the late Syd Nathan of King Records told me, "who were standing quietly listening to records. All of a sudden, when James Brown comes on, they would start shaking their little backsides.") Charles' face, with the large, blacked-out glasses and clenched rows of white teeth, is a picture of acute suffering, and sometimes, strangely, of intense self-amusement. By contrast, James Brown's has a savage quality.

While Charles deals expressively with the euphoria and frustrations of love—"Drown in My Tears," "A Fool For You," "Hallelujah, I Love Her So"—Brown represents aggressive male sexuality. "When he does one of his slow drags, like 'It's A Man's World,'" Albert Goldman has observed, "the rapport between him and the girls reaches scandalous proportions. He shouts with killing sincerity, 'just be there when I get the notion!' and the screams come back from the house like an enormous trumpet section screeching in on the cue." Perhaps that is why Charles can play the Copa but Brown requires Madison Square Garden or Yankee Stadium. His audience is big, black, rock and demonstrative, exulting in the sentiments of his beautiful opening and closing ballad, "If I Ruled the World."

"Soul Brother Number One," as he is generally called, was born in Georgia sometime between 1930 and 1934. He refuses to pin the date down. Before he turned to singing, he picked cotton, shined shoes, danced in the streets for handouts and boxed. Since he became a singer, he has acquired two radio stations, a twin-engine Lear Jet, a fleet of cars (including a Mark III Continental, a Rolls and a Cadillac convertible) and a wardrobe said to number three hundred pairs of shoes and five hundred suits. He tries to persuade his soul brothers that all of this is within their reach. Whether they believe him or not, his charisma is so great that he is credited with stopping race riots in Boston and Washington, D.C. In both cities, after the assassination of the Reverend Martin Luther King, Jr., the mayors asked for his aid. Extended appearances on TV are said to have kept a large segment of the Negro population at home during the tense evenings. "You gotta fight with dignity," he told his viewers.

Just before he starred in a Soul Festival at Yankee Stadium in June, 1968, he became the first major performer of his race to entertain Negro troops in Vietnam. He confessed, not without discomfiture, that it had taken over a year before his offer to go had been accepted, also that he had been compelled to travel economy class and was permitted to take only eight members of his band although there were "plenty of empty seats on the plane." He adds: "I spent $3,500 of my own, but I want the black man to know that a black man could go and nothing could change his mind—I want this thought to go to the back of a white man's mind, too."

Since 1956 when he had his first big hit in "Please, Please, Please," Brown has been a steady bestseller and has seldom been off the charts. In 1967 he had six hot singles, which gave him a Top Ten position in *Billboard*'s annual survey of Male Artists, and a # 3 position among r&b Singles Artists. "Cold Sweat" went over the million mark, as in previous years "Prisoner of Love," "I Got You (I Feel Good)" and "I Want You So Bad" had done. In personal appearances, Brown is able to work up a frenzy that has provoked commentators to use the word "orgiastic" in describing his impact. Brown develops a number through a series of crescendoes—mounting steadily in volume, fervor and drive—until the rising tension demands the release of shouting and body movement. The physical side of love has seldom been projected with such excitement and power as Brown can command. *Raw Soul*, the title of one of his LPs, tells it like it is.

A Top Ten star from 1957 until his murder in 1964, Sam Cooke was a product of the gospel tradition as channelled through Little Richard and Jackie Wilson. He himself became the seminal influence on the late Otis Redding, who included "Shake" and many other Cooke hits in his repertoire. There are few Negro pop singers who do not reveal Cooke's influence, particularly in the handling of ballads. One cannot listen to Diana Ross, Dionne Warwick, Percy Sledge, or any of the more pop soul-stirrers without hearing the soft, resonant voice that captured the public with "You Send Me" and that developed into an instrument of unbearable intimacy and intensity.

Cooke was so deeply steeped in the gospel tradition that it took time for him to make his way into the pop scene. Son of a Chicago Baptist minister, he was a member—along with seven brothers and sisters—of his father's church choir. By nine, he was part of a family quartet known as The Singing Children that went from church to church performing for "free will offerings." Until his graduation from the Wendell Phillips High School, he and a brother performed as The Highway Q.C.'s, named after the Highway Baptist Church of Chicago. Once he fixed on singing as a career, he joined a gospel group known as The Soul Stirrers. After a time, when he felt that he was ready for a solo venture, he journeyed to Los Angeles. Specialty Records liked him but limited his repertoire to spirituals. Anxious to invade the pop market, he persuaded the company to let him record some pop tunes; but he could not persuade them to release these sides. (They probably felt that this would take him out of the gospel field without necessarily giving him a place in the pop market.) Eventually, his break came through a former Specialty executive who founded his own label and took Cooke with him. "You Send Me," his first release on Keen Records, sold 2.5 million and led to a short association with Capitol Records and a long-term contract with RCA Victor.

"If you have ever attended Baptist services," Cooke once said, "you know . . . you have to stir up the emotions of the congregation and literally lift them from their chairs. To do this you have to muster up all the sincerity in your body and project it to every solitary person in the church. This is precisely what I strive for every time I open my mouth to sing. . . ."

Nina Simone, who had her record start on King, has yet to attain the popularity enjoyed by Brown, Charles or Cooke. She first came to public notice in 1959 with a unique, jazz vocal-piano version of "I Love You, Porgy" from *Porgy and Bess*. Her more limited impact is, perhaps, due to her intensely individualistic style, a style that fits into no easy classification and that causes her to be listed in the Jazz section of the Schwann LP Catalogue. But it may also be due to Nina's tendency to speak her mind—to audiences as well as Mississippi governors.

"You're not giving one thing," she told her listeners, not too long ago at the Village Gate. "What bag are you in tonight?" John S. Wilson, reviewing the show in *The New York Times*, noted: "Any performance by Nina Simone is essentially a battle of wills—hers against the audience's—whatever she plays or sings is adapted to the atmosphere in which she finds herself."

A piano prodigy from the age of four in Tryon, North Carolina, she grew up in abject poverty, to which was added the excruciating burden of being "the most outstandingly talented little girl in town—and I was colored." A woman for whom her mother worked as a maid paid for her piano lessons. At the first recital she gave in the white library, "there was a big hassle," she recalls, "about where my mother and father sat. That hurt me." But her white piano teacher was so convinced of her talent that she raised a fund to send her to boarding school in Asheville and, for two years, to Juilliard in New York. When the funds ran out, she went back to her family, then living in Philadelphia. She gave piano lessons and served as accompanist at a local recording studio until an offer for a job in Atlantic City came along. She had never regarded herself as a singer. But her first job paid $90 and she was expected to sing—so sing she did.

Since the murder of the four little Birmingham girls in the bombing of a Sunday school, her songs have taken on a protest character and her style has become more and more intense. "All my life I've wanted to shout out my feeling of being imprisoned," she has said. "I've known about the silence that makes that prison, as any Negro does." Out of the anger and sense of outrage over the Birmingham murders came the vehement "Mississippi Goddam." Since then she has written "Four Women," a bitter satire in which skin color is related to the conditions and outlooks of four ladies. She has also set to music "Go Limp," a humorous lyric by Alex Comfort, in which a girl goes on a Freedom March, "with a brick in my handbag and a smile on my face/And barbed wire in my underwear to shut out the disgrace." "Backlash Blues," "Turning Point" and "Strange Fruit," the classic anti-lynching song, are now a basic part of her repertoire.

"Music gets me worked up," Eunice Waymon, alias Nina Simone, has said. (She changed her name when she first became an entertainer, lest her intensely religious mother be upset by her working in nightclubs.) "I can't sing a song without meaning it." And she cannot write a song without being intensely moved. The overpowering sincerity of her art is what forms Nina Simone's soul and prevents her from making even limited concessions that might enlarge her appeal to audiences. One of her most recent singles is "I Wish I Knew How It Felt To Be Free."

The youngest of the soul-makers is Lou Rawls, who was a Capitol recording artist for five years before he scored in 1966 with "Love Is a Hurtin' Thing," a contemporary blues. During those years, his albums revealed the many skeins that have gone into the fabric of his soul. An album of gospel songs, made with the Pilgrim Travelers, recalled the days when he had been part of the famous group and earlier, when he had sung in a church choir in Chicago. *Stormy Monday* and *Black and Blue*, two of his earliest LPs, reveal his blues roots, the latter a collection of traditional blues, and the former, an anthology recorded with jazz pianist, Les McCann. The collaboration also suggests Rawls' jazz orientation, a facet of his work honored with an award in *Down Beat's* 1963 Jazz Poll.

Although Rawls' approach is now more pop than that of the soul singers previously discussed, his blues orientation is unmistakable. Like bluesmen of old, he still breaks into monologues in the middle of songs. "Dead End Street" in *Too Much!*, a recent LP, is typical in the poignant humor of his spoken lines: when he was a child in Chicago, to go to sleep on cold, wintry nights, he had to get fully dressed! Rawls vividly remembers the deprivations of his early years and the hardships and isolation of his years as an artist on "the chitlin' circuit." These have left an acidity in his voice, which gives bite to his style and shows up in songs like "Yes, It Hurts (Doesn't It?)" and the ironic "It's An Uphill Climb to the Bottom." He does not have the warmth of Charles or the gritty hoarseness of Brown. He reminds one of big Joe Williams in the metallic clarity of his diction and, occasionally, of Billie Holiday in the curled, blue sound of his voice and the expressive articulation in the small corners. His accompaniment is frequently gospel-like, giving his delivery the declamatory quality of a southern revivalist preacher.

By contrast, one of the oldest of soul artists, and yet one of the newest, is Otis Spann, who has been called "the best blues piano player we have today" by the great Muddy Waters, and who emerged in 1968 as a soloist from the anonymity of fifteen years in the Waters band. Born in Jackson, Mississippi, in 1930, Spann migrated to Chicago in his teens, early adding the rawness of 1950s r&b to the warmth of downhome blues—both qualities that are audible in his debut LP *The Bottom of the Blues*. His life and career provide a strong link between the origins of soul and its contemporary impact. His mother was a blues-and-barrelhouse singer who once performed with Memphis Minnie. When he was eight, he won a $25 first prize singing Bessie Smith's "Back Water Blues" at an amateur night at the Alamo Theatre in Jackson. "My biggest inspiration," he has said, "was Coot Davis and Tommy Johnson, Leroy Carr and Big Maceo. [All bluesmen and writers of the 1930s.] Today it's Memphis Slim and the white boy, Paul Butterfield. He's very great, a good man with the blues. As a matter of fact, he came up just like we did. . . . That's important." And he adds: "The blues are like a feelin'. Singing and playing the blues is something you done did or heard tell about. I write a lot of blues . . . but not by music. I writes about what I do and what I've gone through. It's very important to live the blues. . . ."

Of the three cities contributing to the sound of soul today, the Memphis Sound is not only the most southerly, but also the closest to the roots and the least market-directed. It is the product of a cluster of artists who record for the Stax and Volt labels, distributed until recently by Atlantic Records of New York. These artists include Booker T. and the MG's (Memphis Group), who broke big with "Green Onions" (1962); Carla Thomas, daughter of a WDIA disk jockey, who had her first hit in "Gee Whiz" (1961); papa Rufus Thomas, who scored on his own with "Walking the Dog" (1963); Arthur Conley, a protege of the late Otis Redding, who produced "Sweet Soul Music," a million seller; Sam & Dave, the "Double Dynamite Duo" who earned a Gold Record in 1967 with "Soul Man"; and The Bar-Kays, a young instrumental group groomed by Booker T. and who were riding a hit LP, *Soul Finger,* when death claimed their lives in the plane crash that took Redding's.

The main architect of the Memphis Sound, Redding did not live to see himself # 1 on the charts. "(Sittin' on) The Dock of the Bay" hit the top after his tragic accident. But two months before his death at the age of twenty-six, the *Melody Maker,* an English trade paper, named him the World's # 1 Male Vocalist, a designation that had been monopolized by Elvis Presley during the preceding ten years. It was a title he could not command in his own country. Commenting on this recognition in *Rolling Stone,* the west coast rock publication, Ralph J. Gleason observed that the British Broadcasting Corporation had flown a TV documentary crew to Redding's Georgia ranch to tape an interview with him. He noted also that the national radio network of France had broadcast a Memphis show featuring Redding and other Stax-Volt recording stars. "Why has there never been any similar broadcast on U.S. TV or radio?" Gleason asked—and replied: "The answer is color." In short, despite Redding's affluence and influence, he was still an artist whom the rock audience had to see on "the chitlin' circuit." The son of a Baptist preacher, he was at his death in December, 1967, the owner not only of the twin-engine plane that brought

125

him to an untimely end, but of a three-hundred-acre farm near Macon, Georgia, where he raised prize-winning cattle and horses. He had bought these with the earnings from his remarkable talents as a songwriter, singer, record producer, talent scout and, recently, the manager of other artists.

Redding was one of the first artists cut by Jim Stewart, founder and owner of Stax-Volt, when the latter set up shop in the deserted Capitol Theatre in the heart of Memphis' Negro ghetto. Stewart, a former country fiddler, called his label Stax, forming the word from the first two letters of his surname and that of his sister, Estelle Axton, who runs Satellite Record Shop, their retail outlet. (Volt came later, "a shot out of the blue," in Stewart's words. Both labels were recently bought by Paramount Pictures for seven figures.) Redding was accompanied at the start by an eight-piece combo, not unlike the territorial r&b bands of the 1950s—save that an electric guitar, bass and organ were added to the traditional line-up of tenor and baritone saxes, trumpet, piano and drums. The musicians who played these instruments were soon recording as Booker T. and the MG's and accompanying virtually every Stax-Volt vocalist, a situation that helps give the Memphis Sound much of its identity.

By contrast with the Detroit Sound, the Memphis Sound has much Mississippi mud in it, the urgency of country blues and the sexual electricity imparted by rock instruments. It is also deeply rooted in gospel. Booker T. and the Bar-Kays both reflect the influence of earlier r&b bands in their use of repeated riff figuration, raucous reed and brass styling, and four-beat drive overlaid with strong boogiewoogie rhythms.

Redding was an "ecstasy singer" for whom visual contact added a mighty dimension. At the Monterey Pop Festival in 1967, he did not appear until close to 1:00 A.M., by which time the audience had heard enough to make it restless and listless. But he came out stomping, kicked the band off with four beats and had the crowd screaming within seconds. Like gospel shouters, he seemed "possessed"—but in a way that was contagious to audiences. Jazz critic Ralph J. Gleason, who heard Chuck Berry and Redding on successive nights in San Francisco, commented: "Redding's music is more McLuhanish than that of Berry. In person, everything he does is an all-out, powerhouse, total emotional explosion. He may start singing "Try a Little Tenderness" with tenderness, but it always ends up 'sock it to me, baby.' . . . He can work listeners into a frenzy more quickly than any night club performer of his time."

Growing up in Dawson and Macon, Georgia, Redding was deeply influenced by Little Richard, a native of Macon whose shouting style can be heard in *Pain in My Heart* (1963), Otis' first album. Redding had become a solo artist quite accidentally during the preceding year. Vocalist with a group known as Johnny Jenkins and the Pinetoppers, he had driven Jenkins to an Atlantic Records session in Memphis. During a portion of unused time, Jenkins allowed him to cut a tune he had written. "These Arms of Mine" became Redding's first single and led to his recording a group of soul ballads that earned him the name of "Mr. Pitiful" (after one of his hits). The Memphis date not only established a base of operation for him, but initiated his songwriting and producing collaboration with Steve Cropper, the exciting guitarist of the MG's. Redding attained his musical maturity in 1965 when the Rolling Stones paid tribute to him and other soul artists by recording a group of their hits in *Out of Our Heads*. In turn, he recorded the Stones' "Satisfaction," which featured the stomp beat that he regarded as a major feature of soul rhythm. It became his biggest hit until then.

In the year of his death, Redding had three LPs on bestseller charts, causing him to finish # 40 in *Billboard*'s tabulation of Top Album artists. Though he had six singles in the best-selling category, none of them reached high enough to give him more than a # 69 position among Top Singles Artists. But a song he wrote, "Respect," was a # 1 seller for soul sister Aretha Franklin.

Redding was keenly aware of his more limited acceptance and hoped that he might some day "fill the silent void left by Sam Cooke's death." It was a wish he might have realized. Soon after his death, he not only had a # 1 single but a retrospective *History of Otis Redding* climbed into the Top Ten as an album seller. In a moving commemorative article in *Eye*, Jon Landau concluded: "They will tell you that Wilson Pickett has style and that James Brown has sex. But Otis Redding had soul. He was truly the 'king of them all'!"

Berry Gordy, Jr., founder of Motown Record Corporation—Motown is a contraction of Motor Town—once defined the Detroit Sound as "rats, roaches, struggle, talent, guts, love." More recently, he has described it as "a happy sound, a big happy beat with a good strong bass. Tambourines give it a gospel flavor, but it doesn't have so much of that now." The earlier definition doubtless applied when Gordy wrote a song called "Way Over There," borrowed $700 from his family's credit union, and recorded it, with only limited success, by Smokey Robinson and the catlike Miracles. It began to apply less in the early 60s after The Miracles scored with "Shop Around" and even less after The Supremes crashed through in 1964 with "Where Did Our Love Go?" Since 1966 the Motown complex has included four separate companies—Jobete, the highly successful publishing operation; International Talent Management; Hitsville, USA, owner of the recording studios; and Motown Record Corp., which embraces five labels, Gordy, Tamla, VIP, Soul and Motown. The companies occupy seven brick bungalows, situated on both sides of a tree-lined boulevard in an integrated middle-class residential section of Detroit. Over a bungalow that Gordy used to live in, a bright white sign tells you that you are in *Hitsville, USA*. The Motown Sound now has, in the words of a recent critic, "a comparable glossiness at a comparable cost and commercial profit."

Having in the early years been excluded from the playlists of Top Forty stations like WABC in New York and WERE in

Cleveland, Gordy has for some time been concerned with records that would become pop breakouts. The soul he has developed is a combination of r&b and pop, a sound that is both black and white, a style that uses Negro writer-producers and employs the strings of the Detroit Symphony for record dates. Call it soul slicked up for white listeners, an amalgam of gospel rhythms, modern harmonies, soft melodies and bright lyrics.

The most successful of the Motown artists are The Supremes, a trio of girls who came out of a Detroit housing project and started singing together while they were attending high school. When they auditioned for Gordy, he advised them to finish school. They eventually cut nine records before a song by Eddie Holland, Lamont Dozier and Brian Holland (HDH) yielded a record that sold over 2 million copies. In addition to "Where Did Our Love Go?" HDH supplied the girls with such hits as "Baby Love," "Come See About Me," "Stop in the Name of Love," "Back in My Arms Again" and "You Can't Hurry Love." The girls established the unequalled record of having six consecutive Gold Records and, in England, were successful in ousting The Beatles from # 1. By the time their billing was changed to Diana Ross and The Supremes in the summer of 1967, they were also the first Motown artists to have played the Copa and Philharmonic Hall at Lincoln Center in New York and the Cocoanut Grove in Los Angeles.

The sound of the group, which now has a new girl singing top harmony, is in large part the velvet sound of lead-singer Diana Ross, who has said of her childhood: "We were six kids, three girls and three boys. We slept in the same room, three in a bed, with a kerosene jar lighted to keep the chintzes away. . . . I got a job after school at Hudson's department store as a bus girl . . . the first colored girl in the cafeteria basement." Diana does not sing. She purrs, producing a kittenish sound that has sex, tenderness and youth in it.

About the same time that the billing of The Supremes changed, a male group on Tamla, a sister label, became known as Smokey Robinson and The Miracles. It was the first group signed in 1958 when Gordy, then an auto worker and part-time songwriter, went into the record business. It was not until 1961, however, that they racked up their first Gold Record in "Shop Around," a song written by Gordy and Bill "Smokey" Robinson. Since then, Smokey has written numerous songs recorded by other artists. In 1965 and 1966, he received five awards for songs that yielded hit recordings. As the years have gone on, other members of The Miracles have contributed songs to the group's repertoire, among these, "What's So Good About Goodbye?," "I Gotta Dance To Keep from Crying," "Tracks of My Tears," "Whole Lot of Shakin' in My Heart" and "Everybody Gotta Pay Some Dues."

At least three other groups figure prominently in Motor City soul. The most seasoned performers are The Four Tops. Their first hit "Baby, I Need Your Loving," which they call their national anthem, came in 1964. Powerhouse voice of the group is Levi Stubbs, Jr., who can muster a striking emotionalism against the candy-sounding, blues harmonies of his three associates. Growing up in the musical as well as geographical environs of Chuck Berry, they stress choreographic precision in personal appearances to vie with their idol, who has been characterized as "the most choreographed singer" in the world.

The Temptations, another male group, do not include a single native Detroiter. Hailing from Alabama, Mississippi and Texarkana, Texas, they have a strong feeling for gospel, though they also impress in personal appearances with their intricate choreography. (The Motown complex includes a charm school for the girls and a course in choreography for all acts.) The Temptations' showmanship, including imitations of other groups, is potent enough to make them an effective Copa act. Their singing style is the delicate soul, characteristic of most Motown groups. "My Girl," a collaboration of Smokey Robinson and Ronald White of The Miracles, was their first Gold Record (1964–65). Despite their continuing success, in the summer of

1968 lead-singer David Ruffin left, or was ousted from, The Temptations. His explanation: he was dissatisfied with the patent leather product packaged by the group and wanted to get into the soul bag.

On the distaff side, Motown has a trio to compete with its own Supremes in Martha Reeves and the Vandellas. Lead-singer Reeves began her career as a secretary and managed through her contribution to an emergency recording situation, to interest Berry Gordy in her group. They actually hit before the Diana Ross group when "Come and Get These Memories," an HDH song, became a bestseller in 1963. That same year, they had "Heat Wave" by the same team, a song that has been recorded so frequently it is already a rock classic.

No account of Motown soul is complete without mention of young Stevie Wonder, who, after seven years as a successful Tamla artist, is today only nineteen years old. Blind from birth and proficient on piano, organ, drums and harmonica, Stevie first attracted attention with his disk of "I Call It Pretty Music" in 1962, which was followed by the two-sided hit version of "Fingertips." Although Motown has an integrated staff and record roster, its main contribution has been to the impetus it has given by its succcess to the vaulting ambitions of Negro singers, writers and record producers. This, too, is an aspect of soul.

There is no definable Atlantic (Harlem) Sound, as there is a Motown and Stax-Volt Sound, even though Atlantic is the company most responsible for bringing Negro song to white listeners. Atlantic's sound is more complex, more elusive and more professional, the product of a varied list of Negro artists and writers. Important samples are provided by Aretha Franklin, *Lady Soul* as a recent album types her, and by wicked Wilson Pickett.

Born in Memphis in the Bible-blues belt, Aretha Franklin is the daughter of a fiery Revivalist minister and swinging spiritualist who was convicted of failing to file federal tax returns

131

between 1959 and 1962. Her mother deserted the family when Aretha was six and died four years later, creating a void which Mahalia Jackson recently verbalized as, "the whole family wanted for love." Another famous gospel singer, James Cleveland, boarded in her father's household for a time and "showed me some real nice chords." Since still another inspired gospel shouter, Clara Ward, sang in her father's church, it is hardly surprising that Aretha early worked with the choir of her father's New Bethel Baptist Church in Detroit. It was Clara Ward, in fact, who formed her desire to become a singer. Aretha vividly remembers a funeral for an aunt at which Miss Ward, reverently singing "Peace in the Valley," was so overcome by feeling that she tore off her hat and flung it aside.

Shy and troubled, Aretha started her recording career at Columbia in 1960 through an audition disk that bewitched talent scout John Hammond. "I was afraid," Aretha has said of those years and of her personal appearances. "I sang to the floor a lot." Columbia tried gently and unsuccessfully to nudge Aretha in the satin soul and gray ballad direction of Nancy Wilson. It was confusing to her and to critics, some of whom evaluated her as a pop artist and inevitably came to the conclusion that her phrasing was sloppy and that her delivery "overpowered all meaning, all semblance of order and dignity." Only after she moved to Atlantic was she able to reach back into her past, and use her tremendous emotive power as a gospel singer; then she found her place on the American record scene. And a potent place it is! Her first Atlantic single, "I Never Loved a Man the Way I Love You," was that highly explosive combination of amatory fervor and gospel intensity that is an earmark of soul singing. Recorded in Muscle Shoals, Alabama, at the "ham hocks and collard greens" studios of Fame Records, the disk became an overnight smash. It was followed by a succession of hit singles, including "Baby I Love You" and "A Natural Woman." By this time it was clear that Aretha had discovered the right image for herself. She had taken the utter absence of inhibition characteristic of gospel song and made it, in Albert Goldman's fine *New York Times* phrase, "the greatest proclamation of sexual fulfillment since Molly Bloom's soliloquy." She had, in short, become a new, vibrant image of the emancipated woman of the 1960s—a sensual, ecstatic, shouting, female James Brown.

Her second album, *Aretha Arrives*, brought forth a chorus of critical panegyrics such as few LPs have received. Of a Rolling Stones' hit "I Can't Get No Satisfaction," included in this LP, a *New York Times* critic observed that she took the song's feeling of middle-class frustration and turned it into "discord . . . something more like the stuff that contributes to civil disobedience." (It should be noted that Aretha brought the song back to us after the Stones had taken it from Muddy Waters, an interesting crisscross of influences characteristic of rock today.) Of "That's Life," Frank Sinatra's tough attempt to make it in the r&b field, critic Peter Winkler contended that the song suddenly acquired flesh and blood when Aretha took over." He concluded, "I could rhapsodize over every song . . . everything is absolutely perfect." With five Gold Records to her credit, Aretha emerged as Top Female Vocalist of 1967 in *Billboard's* annual poll.

Wilson Pickett's journey in music followed the well-worn path of many soul artists. Born in Prattville, Alabama, he moved to Detroit in his teens and became involved in gospel singing, working for four years as a solo and group singer of church songs. In 1959 he became lead-singer of The Falcons, a group that helped him discover the world of r&b, and that was successful with "You're So Fine," a black ballad by one of its members. When Pickett left The Falcons after four years, it was to record for Lloyd Price's Double LL label, a Liberty subsidiary. A hit of his own authorship "It's Too Late" stirred Atlantic executives, who had known his work through The Falcons—they distributed their Lupine disk of "I Found a Love," a secularized gospel song—to add him to the New York label.

"Midnight Hour," a 1965 hit, emerged from a collaboration between Pickett and instrumentalists of the Stax-Volt complex. The following year, Pickett shifted his recording locus to the Muscle Shoals, Alabama, studios of Fame Records, where he used local musicians. Out of this collaboration came "Everybody Needs Somebody To Love," a hit originally for Solomon Burke, another Atlantic artist, and subsequently a Rolling Stones cover. "Land of 1,000 Dances," a bigger Pickett hit, exploited a device much used by Bo Diddley: a song written entirely on one chord. Pickett's peregrinations south suggest a studied effort to avoid the urbanization that came for him with "Funky Broadway," a city blues. But this is a tendency that few soul artists can escape.

Nevertheless, Pickett represents a frenzied type of soul. He is more raucous, hoarser and can screech with greater intensity than either Percy Sledge or Arthur Conley, two other strong Atlantic artists. And he can deliver with such force that his voice sounds like a whip snapping. Percy Sledge's style is well characterized by the title of a recent LP, *Warm and Tender Soul*. His reach stretches from the sensuousness of "You Send Me" to the gospel-preaching approach, full of gravel, of "Tell It Like It Is." Arthur Conley, whose star rose with "Sweet Soul Music," has a wide vibrato, a powerful choke quality and a ballad style in which he sounds almost feminine. He zoomed onto the record horizon with a revival of the r&b classic "Shake, Rattle and Roll." All of these artists project with a degree of animal intensity and gritty sincerity that are basic to soul. They sing of wordly problems with gospel fervor—Negro gospel fervor.

It is these qualities that attract the artists included under the heading of blue-eyed soul. This was a designation that came into being when a Negro group used it affectionately with reference to the duo known as the Righteous Brothers, "our blue-eyed soul brothers." A development of the 60s, it parallels a post-Civil War phenomenon, the minstrel show, in which white men donned black face and imitated Negro song, dance and humor, save that the minstrel approach was partly pejorative: there was a degree of mockery, burlesque and put-down in minstrel presentations. Today, the white men who sing black do so out of a high regard for Negro singing, and in an effort to capture the vitality, exuberance and emotional voltage of Negro music.

Although it was the influence of the British that helped bring r&b into the dominant position it now occupies in pop, rock 'n' roll was in its earliest manifestation—with Presley, Buddy Holly and Jerry Lee Lewis—Negro in its roots. And the Righteous Brothers, singing on the west coast Moonglow label in 1963, preceded the Stones in their Negro mimicry. Phil Spector, who produced Righteous Brothers' recordings, has said: "We deal with the younger generation, with people lacking identification, the disassociated kids who feel they don't belong, who are in that 'in-between' period. . . . Soul means yearning . . . the yearning to be free, to be needed, to be loved. Singers like The Beatles and the Righteous Brothers have caught this need."

"You should have seen his face drop," the general manager of station WWRL of New York said of Rocky G., a leading r&b disk jockey, "when he found out that the Brothers were not really Negroes." But so many other Negro jockeys had been playing the records of Bill Medley and Bob Hatfield that the Brothers had succeeded in breaching the Negro artist monopoly of Negro stations—and the road was paved for an influx of white artists on r&b playlists and charts. In 1965 the Brothers crashed such lists with "Unchained Melody" and with a number of LPs, such as *Right Now* and *You've Lost That Lovin' Feeling*. While their voices and phrasing were Negro, their records were not r&b. Spector developed an approach that came to be known as "wall-of-sound." It eschewed silence even for a hemidemisemi quaver, and relying on electric organ, sustained strings and booming echo, developed a dense carpet of sound.

By the time they recorded "Souled Out," an inadvertently apropos title, the Brothers had changed producers, and commentators were beginning to dismiss their work as ersatz soul.

Not too long afterward, the duo split up, with Bill Medley trying to make it on his own. At that point, they had worked together for nearly eight years and had sold nearly ten million records. Soon, Bobby Hatfield acquired a new partner in Jimmy Walker, and the name Righteous Brothers was once again visible on club marquees and on TV—not on disks because MGM still had two unreleased albums made by the original duo.

Bobby Hatfield admits that the Negro sound did not always prove advantageous. "A lot of rhythm and blues stations," he has said, "won't play Righteous Brothers records. They used to, but the records got yanked. 'Little Latin Lupe Lu' was getting a lot of air time—but once we went around to visit the stations and they found out we were white . . . that was it, man, that was it."

While "Crow Jim," as musicians type the reverse backlash of anti-Negro discrimination, also operated on the club scene, in Harlem, for example, and other Negro districts, the Righteous Brothers were able to gain bookings frequently closed to black performers. "Guys like Sam & Dave," Hatfield observed, "nobody's booking them into Las Vegas, and they're great! . . . Club owners and guys who book concerts prefer taking clean-cut looking buys, guys who look good, you know, rather than somebody else."

Among the white artists who may be classified under blue-eyed soul are Tom Jones, Tim Hardin, Spencer Davis, Mitch Ryder, The Young Rascals, Vanilla Fudge, The Soul Survivors, The Magnificent Men and The Box Tops of Memphis. Of these, Mitch Ryder and the Detroit Wheels have been picking up so much speed that they warrant special consideration. Ryder can screech and grunt as gutsily as James Brown. But he has a warmth rarely audible in Brown and a depth of feeling never approached by the Righteous Brothers. In 1957 Ryder heard a Little Richard record ("Keep A-Knockin'") that inflamed his imagination. A native of Detroit, he began sitting in with Negro acts that were the backbone of the Motown Sound—eventually stirring a word-of-mouth that led to his being signed by independent producer Bob Crewe (# 1 in *Billboard's* 1967 tabulation of Hot One Hundred Producers). Although Ryder has recorded and scored with a number of Crewe songs, including "Jenny Take A Ride" (a rewrite of "See See Rider"), "Little Latin Lupe Lu" and "Sock It to Me, Baby," he has a Ray Charles quality (including a more developed stutter) that gives him control of material in many areas. In *What Now My Love*, a recent LP, he demonstrates command of a wide variety of songs, from Chuck Berry's "Brown-Eyed Handsome Man" to the rock hit "Sally Go 'Round the Roses," from the Four Seasons' hit "I Make a Fool of Myself" to sophisticated, dramatic songs by French chansonniers Jacques Brel and Gilbert Becaud. Instead of employing the dense backgrounds of his early r&b-inflected disks, "What Now My Love" uses soft, spaced, thin and pretty musical accompaniment, affording Ryder an opportunity to display the emotional depth of his style. There are few singers today, soul or blue-eyed soul, who can deliver with his intense power, his hoarse clarity of diction and his driving, soulful appeal.

Paralleling blue-eyed soul in the vocal area is the emergence of young, white blues bands in the instrumental area. The Rock Revolution has brought reissues (and a revival) of the work of elder statesman like B. B. King, Son House, T-Bone Walker and Sonny Boy Williamson, and also of r&b kings like Chuck Berry, Howlin' Wolf, Bo Diddley and Muddy Waters. ("I had to come to you behind the Rolling Stones and The Beatles," Muddy Waters told an American college audience. "I had to go to England to get here.") Chess Records of Chicago, has not only reissued many old LP's but recently brought Muddy Waters, Bo Diddley and Howlin' Wolf into a studio to record a new album. On Chicago's South Side, new clubs are giving living space to these artists as well as a younger set of bluesmen. Many of the lesser knowns, like Junior Wells, J. B. Hutto, Otis Rush, Jimmy Shines and Johnny Young, can be heard in a three-volume Vanguard collection, cut live, and called *Chicago: The Blues Today*. Over-zealous record companies and recording studios have even begun advertising a Chicago sound. But though a number of groups like The American Breed, The Buckinghams, Paul Butterfield Blues Band and others have become nationally known and contributed chart songs ("Blend Me, Shape Me"), it would take a computer to uncover its characteristics.

Playing black is almost a religion with certain white youngsters striving to emulate Negro bluesmen. It was so with Danny Kalb and Steve Katz, two New York youngsters, who went to study with Dave Von Ronk of Jug Band fame, himself a devotee of folk blues. Out of the interplay came the quintet known as The Blues Project. Except for conventional drums, it was electrified, including even an electric flute that accounted for its most interesting number "Flute Thing." Boasting a repertoire of tunes associated with Muddy Waters, Chuck Berry, *et al.*, and pursuing an assimilated gospel-r&b-jazz approach, The Blues Project produced two attractive LPs, *Projections* and *Live at Town Hall*—and then disbanded.

A new group known as Blood, Sweat and Tears came into being as part-son of The Blues Project. It included organist Al Kooper and guitarist Steve Katz of the Project. Kooper, who organized the new combo, explained: "I wanted to bring a big band sound to a rock-and-roll group." The inspiration for the move apparently dated back to the big band of jazz trumpeter Maynard Ferguson. "In 1963," Kooper stated, "when Maynard was at Birdland, I never missed a night." (One of the trumpeters, Jerry Weiss, had in fact been a member of the Ferguson aggregation.) Kooper also believed that the string instrumentation of rock groups was inadequate for a 1968 emotional approach to the blues.

An octet instead of a quartet, Blood, Sweat and Tears became the first rock group to include a horn section, two trumpets, trombone and sax. While its repertoire emphasized the blues, arrangements in its debut album *Child Is Father to the Man* exhibited the mixed influence of Bach, Stravinsky, Bartok and The Beatles. The emergence of the group led to a *New York Times* headline: "Now Rock 'n' Rollers Are Wooing the Jazzmen." About the same time, the man who plays electric bass with Dizzy Gillespie speculated in the *Hit Parader*: "It's possible that in the next year or two, jazz and rock will be so close, you won't be able to distinguish between the two." To Michael Zwerin, jazz critic of the *Village Voice*, the emergence of the combo was "as important a milestone as Miles Davis' *Birth of the Cool* band in 1949 . . . and [proof] that, contrary to the nasty rumor, jazz is very much alive and kicking." Unfortunately, Kooper, who organized Blood, Sweat and Tears, left the group shortly after its first album was released—he became an A & R producer at Columbia Records—and changes were made in three of the horn men.

In Chicago a development paralleling the Blues Project transformation occurred with a seven-piece combo that started as the Paul Butterfield Blues Band. After a short time, guitarist Mike Bloomfield seceded and formed The Electric Flag, An American Music Band. "It's not a good name," he said, "but I called it The Electric Flag because a friend of mine copped one from an Elks Hall and gave it to us." (An electric flag is a device that has an electrically activated blower that keeps the flag waving.) An integrated octet, the combo has diverse influences blowing through it. Bloomfield was hooked at fifteen on Lightnin' Hopkins and John Lee Hooker. Organist Barry Goldberg worked with Dylan at Newport and manned the piano on Mitch Ryder's disk of "Sock It to Me, Baby." Overweight drummer Buddy Miles, who performs in a shirt made from an American flag, has played with Wilson Pickett and Otis Redding. The group has used a Moog Synthesizer in recording and Richie Havens on sitar. It also includes a three-man horn section, in which trumpeter Marcus Doubleday is partial to the music of Charles Ives and Bela Bartok.

139

Making its debut at the 1967 International Pop Music Festival at Monterey, the Flag caused such excitement that Columbia Records waved a contract in front of it. Its debut album *A Long Time Comin'* includes old blues like "Easy Rider," the famous Ma Rainey song, as well as "You Don't Realize," a Mike Bloomfield blues dedicated "with great respect," in the words cn the jacket, to the late Otis Redding. In his vocals, Bloomfield musters a gravel-choked screechiness that bears comparison with Mitch Ryder's blue-eyed soul and, at times, with James Brown's orgiastic soul. But critic Ralph J. Gleason of *Rolling Stone* has said: "They keep insisting that the name of their game is chitlins and collard greens, but it's actually chicken soup, baby, chicken soup." He urges: "Originality is the key. . . . Play your own soul, man, and stop this shuck."

The Paul Butterfield Blues Band, from which Bloomfield seceded, has in the meantime added a horn section to a personnel whose only original member, besides Butterfield, is guitarist Elvin Bishop. They play hard rock with a 1950s drive and orientation, with the result that some detractors put them down as white youths "rehashing a form that has been brought to perfection by its black originators." But some of the black originators—Otis Spann for one—reject this condemnation. They remember Butterfield as the white kid who early became hooked on Muddy Waters and who thereafter sat in at South Side Chicago clubs with bluesmen like Howlin' Wolf, Little Walter and Otis Rush. While he was a student at the University of Chicago, Butterfield formed a professional blues band that played regularly at the Blue Flame Lounge. By 1965 the Butterfield legend had spread so far that the group was invited, despite its electrical instrumentation, to the Newport Folk Festival.

Butterfield's drooping mustache may give him a Viva Zapata look. But he sounds Negro when he sings or talks—and though he has moved to San Francisco, he and his band still play the blues, Chicago style. His phrase is "blues overstated" but some reviewers describe it as "sound and soul . . . where folk, blues, rock and jazz unite." *The Resurrection of Pigboy Crashaw*, a 1968 album, emphasizes songs popularized by urban bluesmen like Otis Rush ("Double Trouble"), Bobby Bland ("I Pity the Fool") and Albert King ("Born Under a Bad Sign").

Los Angeles has its white blues bands, too, among which Canned Heat has been characterized by *Down Beat's* Pete Welding as "the best band of its type in the world today." It is not easy to discover the basis for this hyperbole either in the group's debut album on Liberty or the follow-up volume *Boogie with Canned Heat*. The group performs old country blues in a style imitative of the urban postwar bands of the 1950s, but without the drive that horns give either the original Negro r&b bands or the white blues bands that have recently added them. Since its first rehearsal in November, 1965, Canned Heat has seen a number of changes in personnel. What distinguishes the present group is that three of its members, vocalist Bob (The Bear) Hite, lead guitarist Henry Vestine and Al Wilson, who sings and plays guitar and harmonica, are all avid record collectors and discographers. Hite and Vestine collect prewar and postwar blues while Wilson is said to specialize in postwar disks. Apparently, collecting and listening have led to an unrestrainable urge to reproduce what they hear.

The white blues band movement even has a second generation. The Hollywood-based Dirty Blues Band acknowledges Paul Butterfield as the most immediate source of their inspiration. Being young and outspoken, they readily discuss problems which all white blues bands face. "In some instances we can relate more to a white audience," steel-guitarist Glenn Ross states, "than to a colored because the colored seemed somewhat prejudiced. . . . Some colored audiences actually resented the fact that we played their music. . . . The white kids don't actually like it. But they'll say they do because it's the groovy thing to do." The group also is conscious of another ambiguity—that of white musicians attempting to re-create music expressive of an entirely different milieu. Lead singer Rod "Ginger-man" Piazza's answer is, "I've had a lot of hard luck . . . I'm singing from what I feel myself." But critic Nat Hentoff's comment in *Hi-Fi Stereo Review* was, "It's not only that you can't go home again; you can't pretend to be from a place you've only visited."

Conscious of these paradoxes, some white blues bands attempt to add something of themselves to the repertoire and style: new voicings, modern chords and contemporary instrumentation. But John Mayall's Bluesbreakers eschew anything that is not ethnic blue. Mayall, who regards himself as a crusader for the *real* blues, is critical of rock as ersatz blues. But then again the Mayall group hails from Manchester, England, and has the zeal of the foreigner for an adopted tongue, and the high seriousness of the white purist for black music. Guitarist Peter Green, who replaced Eric Clapton in The Blues Breakers, has recently formed the Fleetwood Mac with another ex-Blues Breaker, bassist John McVie. Along with Ten Years After and the Savoy Browns, two other dedicated English bands, the Fleetwood Mac attempt to "live" the depressed music they play, seeking in the atmosphere of grubby clubs and halls, a substitute for the underprivileged existence of American blacks. But how do you find a substitute for the rootlessness and the lack of identity from which blacks have suffered and created for centuries?

It seems inescapable, however, that little of significance can emerge from the attempt slavishly to reproduce copies of the work of pioneer Negro r&b bands of the 1950s. The more exact the duplication, the less consequential the results, as a group of San Francisco combos (Turk Murphy, Bob Scobey and others) demonstrated some years ago when they struggled to reproduce the style and sound of pioneer New·Orleans and Dixieland jazz bands. If the white blues bands of today are to accomplish something more than jogging our memories, they must find a way of using the feeling, flavor and fervor of the blues to vitalize their own expressiveness. I am disposed to believe that this is an insoluble problem, especially if the white groups persist in affecting Negro accents and instrumental styles. Technical mastery is possible. But since the Negro's feelings are based on life in a ghetto and segregated society, how can any white musician do anything but imitate those feelings? Surely, sitting-in is not an equivalent of living-in.

Regardless of whether they produce anything beyond exciting dance music, which some of the groups have surely done, the blues bands have played a significant role in interesting the rock audience in a "new" sound—horns instead of strings, trumpets; trombones and saxes instead of guitars. In this respect, they should be credited with a seemingly growing interest in the Big Band sound. Witness the single disk on which a 65-piece band plays the instrumental theme of "MacArthur Park," the Don Ellis band and its *Electric Bath* LP, the 51-piece band on *The Wichita Train Whistle Sings,* and Van Dyke Parks' use of a 55-piece orchestra on *Song Cycle.*

The relationship of the blues bands to soul is tangential. While there is such a thing as a black sound, instrumentally and vocally, it is the feeling conveyed by the sound that makes it soulful or not. Johnny Mathis and Nancy Wilson both sound black, regardless of repertoire and styling, but neither is a soul singer. However, Dionne Warwick, whose repertoire is contemporary and frequently showy, does have soul. Born in East Orange, New Jersey, Miss Warwick played organ in church and sang in the choir. Later, she did background singing for The Drifters, an Atlantic quartet that itself started as a background group for Clyde McPhatter. If ever a singer was the visual embodiment of a voice—subtle, sensuous and feline—Miss Warwick is it. She purrs much like Diana Ross of The Supremes, but has more flute in her sound. Pretty in an exotic way, she has slanting eyes, high cheek bones and full upper lip over a pronounced overbite. Since her breakthrough with "Don't Make Me Over" in 1963, she has had a succession of hits, virtually all written by composer Burt Bacharach and lyricist Hal David, who also serve as her record producers. Miss Warwick's break came when Bacharach used a group called The Gospelaires to make a demo of the song for submission to The Shirelles, then recognized as the #,1 of satin soul artists. When he played the demo for the record company releasing The Shirelles, they expressed interest in the lead singer of The Gospelairs, who happened to be Miss Warwick.

Her hit disks of the past five years include "Walk On By," "Message to Michael," "Trains and Boats and Planes," "Alfie," "I Say a Little Prayer," "Valley of the Dolls" and "The Look of Love," an Academy Award nominee in 1968 as "Alfie" was in 1967. Bacharach, who arranges and conducts her sessions, has developed into one of the most inventive of rock composers, with perhaps the most original of harmonic concepts. Hal David's lyrics are literate and pop, so that Miss Warwick's style might be called pop soul. There is heat and excitement and wallop in her delivery. And though Miss Warwick has travelled a long road from the choir loft in which she once sang, the gospel feeling is not gone.

Amidst all this discussion of soul, it is interesting to note that 1968 saw a tidal upsurge of interest in rhythm-and-blues, and specifically, the r&b disks of the 1950s. Two record companies confirmed this development: Atlantic by issuing a four-volume *History of Rhythm & Blues*, really a cavalcade of its own hits from 1947 through 1960; and Columbia, by releasing *18 King Size Rhythm and Blues Hits*, a cavalcade of hit disks made by one of its small competitors, King Records of Cincinnati. But Arthur, the New York rock discotheque, also supplied evidence of the growing trend. In April, 1968, it announced that it was discarding all psychedelic disks and making r&b the exclusive house sound. "Psychedelic music is dying," announced the resident disk jockey, who played r&b disks four hours a night, before, between and after shows. "Even England is putting out its own brand of r&b." *The New Yorker* offered additional evidence: "The Mothers of Invention, noted for devastating Brechtian parodies of rock and roll," Ellen Willis reported, "are rumored to be recording original r&b tunes under the name of Reuben and the Jets. In England, where old rock records have become collector's items, boys are trading in their Edwardian furbelows for leather jackets and greasing down their Beatle cuts."

9 THE CALIFORNIA SOUND : *From Surfing*
to Psychedelic and Electronic

The California Sound went from one extreme to another—from "Be true to your school!" to "Let's freak out!", from the Surf Sound to fuzztone and feedback, from celebration of the open road to a search for strange inner experiences, from the thrill of speed to liberation through sensory overload, from the excitement of bodily motion to the explosiveness of mind-expanding drugs, and from the Beach Boys to the Mothers of Invention— a process in which the Boys themselves underwent an audible, if not visible, transformation.

Beach Boy music began, as music frequently tends to do in the rock era, as a do-it-yourself bit, and a family bit as well. Brian Wilson began jamming with a cousin, Mike Love, and a school chum, Al Jardine, eventually drawing in brother Carl on guitar and brother Dennis on drums. Living in Hawthorne, a few miles from Southern California beaches, with Dennis a rabid surfer and the surf fad taking off like a high-rise breaker, Brian and Mike first wrote "Surfin'." A modest chart-climber in 1962, it led to the name of Beach Boys, a Capitol recording contract, their big hit single of 1963 ("Surfin' U.S.A.") and a best-selling album. (Within four years, they had sold over sixteen million singles and received Gold Records for ten of their twelve album releases.)

Despite all the talk about a Surf Sound, it is difficult to discover its distinctive characteristics. It seemed to incorporate a modified walking boogie bass in a typical 12-bar blues, and a gentle afterbeat whose pattern was *rest/clap-clap/rest/clap*. The group was occasionally tagged the "bleach boys," perhaps as an inevitable reaction to their frank statement, "We're white and we sing white." Nevertheless, Chuck Berry's 1958 hit "Sweet Little Sixteen" was the basis of "Surfin' U.S.A." Those envious of the group's fast rise to stardom dismissed the Surf Sound as "pimple music." Apart from the group's sound, which included the inevitable falsetto (Brian Wilson's), what attracted was an image wedded to a wild craze. On stage, they appeared in slacks and candy-striped, short-sleeved shirts, visually projecting images of beaches, sea breezes and breakers. After the big kahoona of the surf craze had broken on shore, Brian took up hot rods ("Shut Down") and in 1964, motor scooters ("Little Honda").

The exhilarating sense of freedom, implicit in the outdoor tradition, reached its apex in a song that originated not on the coast but in Nashville. Roger Miller's "King of the Road" epitomized the feeling of supremacy that came from riding a giant wave or speeding down a highway. It became the biggest disk and song of 1965, winning awards for Miller as the best male vocalist and Best Country-and-Western Male singer. But the impetus for the tradition came from the coastal area where the Beach Boys' white backlash received solid support from a duo known as Jan and Dean. Blonde, white, Anglo-Saxon, middle-class and collegiate, Jan Berry and Dean Torrence espoused the same breezy cause as the Beach Boys. In fact, "Surf City," one of their hits, was the product of a collaboration between Jan and Brian Wilson. During 1963 and 1964, their LPs were titled *Take Linda Surfin'* and *Ride the Wild Surf*. And when interest swung from the beaches to the freeways, they recorded "Drag City" and "Dead Man's Curve."

Strangely, the Surf Sound as well as Hot-Rod Music embodied not only a glorification of fast living but a self-destructive feeling for dying fast. "Angry sea/Took my love from me," The Beach Boys had sung, "No surfin' today." Apparently, the only sense of loss was that one had to give up surfing for a day. After the automobile became a romantic symbol, they sang: "The last thing I remember, doc, I started to swerve/You won't come back from/Dead Man's Curve." Through 1964, the death wish, as psychologists term it, found full expression in songs like "The Last Kiss" and "Leader of the Pack," a hit for The Shirelles. Accidents and violent deaths on the highways occurred in both. The latter also added the provocative element of parental interference in a love affair. (The new totem of esoteric teenage cults, continuing the tradition of power through speed and defiance of death, is neither the surfboard nor the hot rod, but the motorcycle.)

Like many rock groups, the Beach Boys displayed a remarkable talent for growth and a compulsive sensitivity to competition. In 1966 when San Francisco was becoming the turned-on city and the home of psychedelia, they suddenly produced an album titled *Pet Sounds* and a single called "Good Vibrations." The single reportedly took more than six months of studio time, during which ninety hours or over 400,000 feet of magnetic tape were used. On its release, the resulting 3-minute, 35-second master—ten other completed takes were discarded—sold over a million copies in less than two months and garnered the group its only Gold single. It was a plunge into the crackling sea of electronics and the expression of a maturing outlook. The concern with a more permanent relationship than premarital sex ("Wouldn't It Be Nice?") and the realization that life goes on though a love affair ends ("God Only Knows") marked quite an advance over "We'll have fun, fun, fun/Till your daddy takes the T-Bird away."

148

In a subsequent LP, *Smiley Smile*, Brian Wilson led the group into more experimental areas of sound painting. The wailing theremin employed in "Good Vibrations" had its counterpart in weird effects achieved by tape manipulation in "She's Goin' Bald," a selection in which their intonations and phrasing took a Negro turn—"I blew my mind, I blew my cool." Though the album title was based on Indian wisdom ("The Smile that you send out returns to you"), some of the material was satirical. There was even the hint of a put-down in "Vegetables," which sounded like a reply to "Call Any Vegetable" by The Mothers of Invention. The Beach Boys had been the subject of some acid remarks by the Mothers, with a put-down reference to Wilson's song "Little Deuce Coupé" figuring in the collage on the cover of *Absolutely Free*.

Unless one is aware of Brian Wilson's obsessive tendency to tinker, it is difficult to understand why the opening track of *Smiley* should have cost $40,000 to make. But the Beach Boys could afford the expense and Brian was trying to produce a sound that approximated the simplicity and innocent wisdom of Hindu philosophy. The mood was one of childlike wonder, and much of the music possessed a gentle but eerie quality like a breath held too long. Lyrics for "Heroes and Villains," as for a few of the later tracks, were written or initiated by Van Dyke Parks, who worked with Brian Wilson during the months of experimentation. The music for this track was composed of short, undeveloped fragments, typed "scenes or sections, a mood moment" by Wilson. Although a *Cheetah* reviewer characterized *Smiley Smile* as "the most beautiful rock album ever recorded in this country," it fared better in England where the Beach Boys were voted "best group" of 1967.

Before the west coast became a scene of experimentation with electronics and composition, it went psychedelic. Suddenly, instead of floating precipitously on the peaks of ocean breakers, or travelling at suicidal speeds in souped-up cars, youngsters began taking trips of another sort, and rock music developed qual-

ities of a related character. Although the Haight-Ashbury district
of San Francisco soon became the west coast center of psychedelia, as Manhattan's Tompkins Square Park area became the
eastern center of hippiedom, the original source of the new
style was Los Angeles. Quite appropriately, the development
occurred on a recording—a Capitol documentary disk on LSD
on which the narrator alleged that the musicians played while
under the influence of the drug. A weird blend of vocal moan-
ing and vibratory flutes, the music had a strange trancelike
quality.

It was The Byrds, however, that made the ears of Hollywood
hippies perk up and stirred widespread talk, far beyond the Sunset Strip, about the new sound. The medium was the Bob Dylan
song "Mr. Tambourine Man," later widely described as the tale
of a drug pusher. Soon, The Byrds had other songs like "Eight
Miles High" and "5 'D' (Fifth Dimension)," which metaphori-
cally and musically captured the acid aura of the era. By the
time that the Mothers of Invention appeared on the scene in
1966, the locus of hippiedom had shifted from the Sunset Strip
to the Haight-Ashbury district, and the major west coast rock
groups all seemed to come from San Francisco. However, the
movie capital was responsible for The Doors and United States
of America as well as The Byrds and the Mothers.

Freak Out, the title of the first Mothers' LP, was a term that
became prominent. As explained by Frank Zappa, the Dada of
the Mothers: "You get the same effect from a Freak Out as
from taking acid, but without any of the bad stuff. And it's not
like a happening where they try to do something to you. It's
like the audience is all a part of the whole thing. You're integrated into the whole fabric of sight and sound." And that
fabric consisted, as it has since been experienced at the Fillmore
Auditorium in the San Francisco Bay area, or at the Electric
Circus and The Cheetah in New York, of blinding flashes of
strobe light, giant movie images projected at crazy angles on
walls, colored lights blinking on and off, and music played at so

deafening a level that sensory overload is achieved. Freaking-out was a social as well as an esthetic experience. It had something to do with casting off restrictive standards of thinking, dress and social etiquette.

The music on *Freak Out*, a two-record sonic stew of pop, rock, electronic and classical elements, abounded in satire. It included a take-off on early rock 'n' roll with the piano treble-triplets ("Help, I'm a Rock"), a Motown waltz, and an angry song on the Watts riots ("Who Are the Brain Police?"). In the schooled orchestration of "The Return of the Son of Monster Magnet," performed by an enclave that included French horns as well as electric guitars, one heard the Frank Zappa who was writing serious music in his teens, who has scored two films (*World's Greatest Sinner* and *Run Home Slow*) and whose recordings include rock treatments of Stravinsky, Mozart, Holst, and other serious composers. Zappa has named Edgar Varese's futuristic composition "Ameriques" as his "favorite Top Forty record," and in the commentary accompanying the two-record set, enumerates Leopold and Loeb, Sacco and Vanzetti, Sabu and Lenny Bruce as his influences.

Of listener reaction to his far-out musical melanges, he has said: "The kids are ready for anything. . . . Feedback, anything. It's because they've been fed all this garbage for so long. The Beach Boys' *Be True to Your School* and all that. They don't wanna be true to their school, they want *truth!*"

"Kill Ugly Radio!" is a large-as-life caption that greets record-buyers when they open *Absolutely Free*, the Mothers' second LP. "Brown Shoes Don't Make It," the funniest track, and "Ritual Dance of the Young Pumpkins" are each over six minutes long and suggest Zappa's concern with larger structures, a form that might be described as a rock-pop comic operetta, or The Theater of the Absurd played to an accompaniment of surrealistic music. Lyrically, Zappa is a Lenny Bruce of recorded rock, both in his obscenity and the thrust of his satire. Even though radical outlook and rough language have limited the group's exposure largely to underground radio and personal appearances, Zappa was voted Pop Musician of the Year in *Jazz & Pop* magazine's annual poll (June, 1968). *Newsweek* memorialized the award in an article in which it saluted the Mothers as "the most radical and entertaining group in the United States." Shortly thereafter, *Life* ran an outrageously funny and blunt essay by Zappa on "The New Rock." By then, *We're Only in It for the Money,* his third album assault on conformity, passivity and the police state, was selling briskly. The viceroy of verbal violence was in danger of being accepted by the Establishment.

Although the United States of America did not make it with their debut LP, many of the under-thirty critics looked to it as the group that would shape rock into an art or art into rock. Some called Columbia's CS 9614 a milestone in the electronic synthesis of the New Music. Others typed it a magnificent failure. The more guarded concluded that it was both a milestone and a failure. An outgrowth of an environmental workshop run in Los Angeles by Joseph Byrd, an electronic genius, and Dorothy Moskovitz, a Barnard prodigy from the Bronx, the United States of America attempted a sophisticated synthesis of rock and electronic composition. Employing a Byrd-Durrell Synthesizer, analogous to the Moog, to originate melody—not merely to alter or distort it—Byrd worked with densities, textures and sounds as compositional elements. In person, the USA resembled nothing less than a Hollywood movie version of the Electronic Revolution—six small people surrounded and overshadowed by numerous electrical keyboards, amplifiers, transformers, synthesizers, and what-nots. (According to reports, it took seven hours for the group to set up its equipment.) Gene Youngblood, who edits and seems to write most of *Zero,* the informative rock supplement of the *Los Angeles Free Press,* stated flatly: "There is more talent in the United States of America than perhaps in all major American rock groups together." It remains to be seen whether there is more music

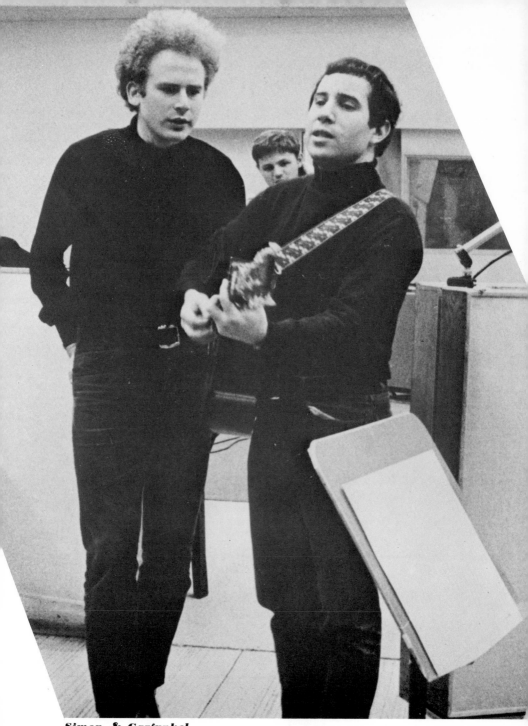

Simon & Garfunkel

James Brown

Martha and the Vandellas

Dionne Warwick

Nina Simone

The Lovin' Spoonful

The Mamas and the Papas

Ray Charles

Diana Ross and the Supremes

**Sam
and
Dave**

Booker T. and the M. G.'s

The Four Tops

Otis Redding

Wilson Pickett

Stevie Wonder

The Temptations

The Miracles

Janis Ian

Aretha Franklin

The Blues Magoos

The Beach Boys

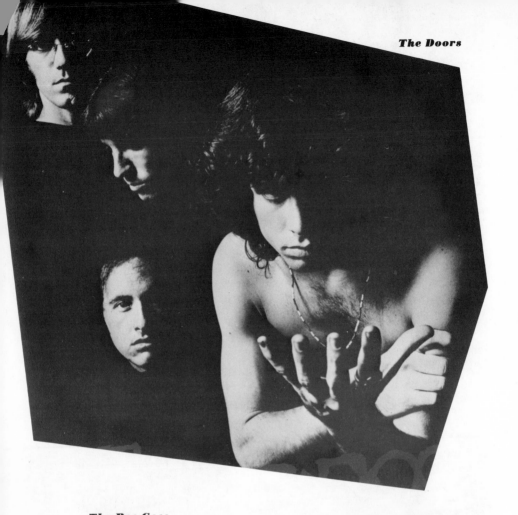

The Doors

The Bee Gees

Donovan

The Mothers of Invention

The Cowsills

Country Joe and the Fish

Spanky and Our Gang

The Rascals

The Monkees

The Cream

Jimi Hendrix

Janis Joplin

and competitive appeal. (Dismal footnote: In July, 1968, despite the ballyhoo and panegyrics, the group folded.)

Like The Mothers of Invention, another Los Angeles group that is much concerned with personal freedom, particularly in the realm of sensation, is The Doors. Although the older generation tends to be offended by vocalist Jim Morrison's overt sexuality and libidinous frenzy, his songs and his performances are the product of a carefully thought-out philosophy. Even the title of the group was selected, not as a put-on or a put-down, but as an expression of outlook. "There are things that are known," the English mystical poet William Blake had written, "and things that are unknown; in between are doors." Novelist Aldous Huxley had adapted the phrase for a book on experiments with mescaline. Morrison shortened Huxley's title *The Doors of Perception* to The Doors. But the concept was there.

"There's a whole region of images and feelings inside us," Morrison has said, "that rarely are given outlet in daily life. And when they do come out, they can take perverse forms. . . . Everyone, when he sees it, recognizes the same thing in himself. It's a recognition of forces that rarely see the light of day."

Appearing on-stage in a black leather jacket and skin-tight black vinyl pants, Morrison gives rather vivid visceral as well as violent aural expression to the repressed feelings. "The more civilized we get on the surface," he says, in almost Freudian terms, "the more the other forces make their plea. We appeal to the same human needs as classical tragedy and early Southern blues. Think of it as a seance in an environment which has become hostile to life—cold, restrictive. People feel they're dying in a bad landscape. People gather together in a seance in order to invoke, palliate and drive away the bad. Through chanting, singing, dancing and music, they try to cure an illness, to bring harmony back into the world."

Morrison's extreme personal drives coalesce with the group's sublimating role. "I think the highest and the lowest points are the important ones," he says. "I want freedom to try everything—I want to experience everything at least once." And he explains: "I am interested in anything about revolt, disorder, chaos, especially activity that seems to have no meaning. It seems to me to be the road toward freedom—external revolt is the way to bring about internal freedom. Rather than starting inside, I start outside and reach the mental through the physical."

The Whiskey-A-Go Go in Hollywood provided the opening for The Doors, who came together during the summer of 1965. Organist Ray Manzarek, a Chicagoan who hung around South Side clubs to hear Muddy Waters, had known Morrison at UCLA, where the latter was an advanced student in the Theater Arts Department. ("The good thing about film is that there aren't any experts," Morrison has said. "There's no authority on film. Anyone can assimilate and contain the whole history of film in himself, which you can't do in other arts.") A secondary hinge for The Doors was the Meditation Center established by the now famous Maharishi at Third Street in Los Angeles. Here Ray Manzarek met the two other members of the group: drummer John Densmore and guitarist-songwriter Robert Alan Krieger, both of whom are still strong advocates of meditation. The group went through several transformations and hard times. They were fired by the London Fog where Morrison's style was rather reserved, and also by the Whisky-A-Go Go, where they were signed by Elektra Records and where Morrison's frenzied and erotic presentation took shape.

Their debut album, released in January, 1967, contained "Light My Fire," their first big single. This invitation to unknown ecstasies was written not by Morrison, as is frequently assumed, but by Bobby Krieger, who also is responsible for another of their hits, "Love Me Two Times." But Morrison has himself explored the orgiastic theme in "Moonlight Drive" and "Break On Through." The group's most powerful and provocative number is "The End." According to reports, it was Morrison's presentation of this eleven-and-one-half-minute Walpurgisnacht dramatic dialogue, with its pointed Oedipal imagery, that resulted in the group's dismissal from the Whisky-A-Go Go.

Early in 1968 The Doors attained national notoriety as the result of an appearance in New Haven. Backstage, words between Morrison and a policeman led to his being squirted in the face with Mace and arrested. Discovering their error, the constabulary apologized and permitted Morrison to continue with the show. But then during "Back Door Man," Morrison began to tell the audience about the backstage incident. Contending that his narrative was abusive and inflammatory, the police turned up the lights in the hall, dragged Morrison off the stage, and charged him with committing a breach of the peace, resisting a police officer, and "giving an indecent or immoral exhibition." Arrested with Morrison were three journalists who protested the action of the police: Michael Zwerin, music critic of *The Village Voice*; Tim Page, a free-lance photographer who aroused police ire when he photographed a cop roughing up a kid in the audience; and Yvonne V. Chabrier, a researcher for *Life*. The incident did not hurt the sales of "Unknown Soldier" backed with (b/w) "We Could Be So Good Together," their spring 1968 release.

Morrison, who was a student of Roman and Greek classics on his own while a cinema student at UCLA, thinks of rock in terms of Greek drama. "In its origin," he says, "the Greek theatre was a band of worshippers, dancing and singing on a threshing floor at the crucial agricultural seasons. Then, one day, a possessed person leaped out of the crowd and started imitating a god. At first it was pure song and movement. As cities developed, more people became dedicated to making money, but they had to keep contact with Nature somehow. So they had actors do it for them. I think Rock serves the same function and may become a kind of theatre."

Morrison's knowledge of Greek drama doubtless accounts for certain changes he has made in his personal appearances. Aware that Greek actors used the buskin (an oversized, built-in shoe) and stately movements so that they could be seen and their gestures understood in the huge amphitheaters, he has said: "I was less theatrical, less artificial when I first began performing. But now the audiences we play are much larger and the rooms are bigger. It's necessary to project more—to exaggerate—almost to the point of grotesqueness." Well, the New Haven police and over-thirty viewers have other explanations of Morrison's outsized manifestations of sexual behavior. Some characterize his on-stage conduct as evil. He argues the appropriateness of the term "primeval."

Regardless of which interpretation one accepts, the power of the group to provoke audiences led to riotous developments in several cities. But it was also reflected in the sales of the group's albums. By August, 1968, all three LPs of The Doors on release were certified as Gold Records, with *Waiting for the Sun,* their then most recent album, occupying a slot among the country's three top bestselling LPs.

The Doors are, perhaps, the only west coast group who are outspoken partisans of the Los Angeles scene as against San Francisco. "Here we have no scene," says Jim Morrison, who lived in a shack in Laurel Canyon and who doubtless forgot about the 1966 Sunset Strip confrontations between Hollywood hippies and the fuzz. "We're on our own." And the group's pianist-organist Ray Manzarek adds: "There's a placidity about San Francisco. It's really the dropout city. It's where you retire whether you're sixty-five or fifteen. Here in Los Angeles the young people especially are very excited, very alive." In *Song Cycle* Van Dyke Parks characterizes Laurel Canyon as "the seat of the beat." And Frank Zappa said, after an eighteen-months stay on the east coast: "New York is a good city to make money in. But I can't write there. I have to be in L.A. There's something very creative here."

A different opinion was voiced by Ralph Gleason, once a columnist of *Rolling Stone* and long a commentator on entertainment in the Bay City, originally and still as jazz critic and columnist of the *San Francisco Chronicle*. "In Los Angeles," he contended in a talk with me, "a group heads for the recording studio almost before it's formed. Not so with the San Francisco groups, virtually all of whom start out as live performing combos. Long before they saw the inside of a studio, the Jefferson Airplane, the Grateful Dead, Country Joe and the Fish, Big Brother and the Holding Company all paid their dues gigging around the clubs and ballrooms of the Bay area. That's what makes the difference. San Francisco has the Fillmore Auditorium, the Avalon Ballroom, the Carousel and a string of clubs in Sausalito and Berkeley where groups can keep playing. They play for dancers and for listeners. All this gives them a sense of control and an ease in improvisation, which you can't hothouse in a recording studio. There is no California Sound. But if there were, it would have a Bay City freshness rather than a Hollywood slickness."

The first Bay group to gain national recognition was the Jefferson Airplane, whose music has been described as love rock and as "trans-love airplanes" by Donovan in his song "Fat Angel." A folk-rock group of the post-protest era, they were performing at The Matrix, a local San Francisco nightclub, when Gleason brought them into the national limelight in the fall of 1965 through his syndicated column in the *Chronicle*. Founder and leader Marty Balin is Ohio-born, California-bred and a former singer-dancer in musical comedy. The voice most frequently heard above the others and largely responsible for the group's impact is that of Grace Slick, ladylike daughter of a Palo Alto banker, former "regular suburban preppy" (in her words), dropout of Finch College (an elegant, private New York girl's school), University of Miami dropout—where, she says, she could have earned a degree in foul language, and a singer whose robust sound recalls Ronnie Gilbert of The Weavers.

Sometime in 1965 Grace went with her husband, moviemaker Jerry Slick, to The Matrix, to listen to a fledgling group known as the Jefferson Airplane. As a result of this encounter, Grace,

Jerry, his brother and three friends formed a unit called the Great Society. They recorded an album, *Conspicuous Only in Its Absence,* which included "Somebody to Love" and "White Rabbit," two songs that Grace wrote in this period, but which occasioned only modified rapture. (Columbia re-released the album after the songs and Grace struck pay dirt on RCA Victor.) The Great Society began to fall apart just about the time when the Airplane lost the female singer who had been part of its original personnel. Grace's acceptance of a berth on the then low-flying combo proved of significance to her, the Airplane and rock.

Jefferson Airplane Takes Off, released in August, 1966, did not make a record-breaking flight, despite the group's mastery of The Beatles' art of putting-on and -off inquisitive interviewers. But two hit singles "Somebody To Love" and "White Rabbit" laid the groundwork for the success of their second LP, *Surrealistic Pillow.* "White Rabbit," written and soloed by Grace Slick, displayed a musicality and a feeling for dynamics and buildup rare among rock groups, who are prone to deliver on one level—loud. "White Rabbit" also contained references—one pill makes you larger, one makes you small—which could be read on an *Alice in Wonderland* level or in terms of the pills prevalent on the psychedelic scene. Similar two-level imagery was to be found in "She has Funny Cars," "3/5 of a Mile in 10 Seconds" and "Embryonic Journey." In "Plastic Fantastic Lover," wailing, weird-sounding guitars against a steady thumping beat project a crazy world of strange surrealistic images. Whether it was the imagery or sheer musicality of the album, *Surrealistic Pillow* earned a Gold Record.

To produce a more recent album, *After Bathing at Baxter's,* the Airplane remained grounded in recording studios for three months. The LPs most interesting and impressive track, "re-joyce," composed and arranged by Grace Slick, encountered radio censorship. It was the text, based on Molly Bloom's soliloquy in James Joyce's *Ulysses,* that troubled many station managements. Slick's music was unstructured, electronic rock, a direction that the more musical California groups have taken since the collapse of the hippie movement. "We start with a single element—a bottom," Miss Slick has said. "Then we try to build on it. We don't really know how any of the pieces are going to sound until we've finished them. . . . But all sounds are within the scope of music." And many of the selections in *Baxter's* are extended pop songs from which traditional circumscriptions as to structure and musical and lyrical context have been eliminated. It was greeted with hosannas by young and old, particularly for the beauty and originality of Paul Kantner's songs and the artistry of Jorma Kaukomen's guitar work.

During the two-year period in which the San Francisco Bay area flourished as the heart of Hippieland and the Liverpool of the West, new electric groups proliferated like jet-age amoebas. *Newsweek* stated that at its peak, there were 1,500 groups using the city's electricity. Ralph Gleason claims that this was a typo and that the figure should have read 150. Regardless of which figure one accepts, the number of groups that had something to offer is small by comparison with the current consumed. Nevertheless, a surprising number came up with hit records, if not fresh ideas.

Formed early in 1965, The Association worked together for a long while before it scored on wax. But its first single "Along Came Mary," its second single "Cherish" and its first LP *Insight Out* all became Gold Records. On the appearance of the last mentioned in the fall of 1967, *Look* hailed the group as "an American combo, for a change, that is witty, literate and freshly bathed." Hardly an exciting advertisement for a musical group! But The Association as a musical quartet relies little on electricity for its impact and sells an appealing folk-type rock, one of whose attractions is Terry Kirkman's performance on a tiny wooden recorder. Their second album, *Birthday*, released in the summer of 1968, shows signs of duplicating the appeal of the first.

The Grateful Dead, out of the Palo Alto area that nurtured Grace Slick as well as Joan Baez, has been unable to translate its reputation and prestige into sales. "Extremely driving, amplified and hirsute, even by San Francisco standards," wrote a commentator in *The New York Times*, who reported on an open-air concert in Central Park. The Grateful Dead are among the groups who display a large sense of theater in their appearances, a fact that duly impressed the *Times* reporter. "In their finale," he observed, "one of the drummers—there are two in the combo—appears to run amok and savagely attacks the cymbals, while another member of the band sets off an explosion." Released in May, 1967, the group's debut album sold so little, despite their visual impact, that no new LP appeared until *Autumn of the Sun* in the summer of 1968.

The concert at which the Grateful Dead performed, along with the Paul Butterfield Blues Band and the Jefferson Airplane, drew over six thousand listeners to the Mall in Central Park. It was a free concert, in keeping with a tradition that has developed particularly among the San Francisco groups. "We almost always do free gigs," the road manager of the Dead explained. "Sometimes after the paying concert, we go outside and do another show for the kids who couldn't get in."

Another San Francisco group whose debut LP was something of a bust was the oddly named Moby Grape. Unlike most Bay area groups who came to be known in the underground rock audience long before they signed a recording contract, the Grape received an expensive, hard sell by Columbia Records. Apart from pulling out all the stops on promotional gimmicks, Columbia released five singles simultaneously from their first LP. While the unheard-of ploy drew large attention to the group, it did not succeed in putting it over. A number of critics contend that the Grape's natural audience was alienated by the blitz. Curiously, while the critical acclaim visited on the debut album did not carry over to *WOW: Grape Jam*, the second album was on its way to becoming a bestseller in June, 1968.

In both the contents and the promotion of *WOW*, the group

again seemed to be "reaching." Advance ads explained that WOW was MOM upside down and cited two lines from a song called "Motorcycle Irene": "Super-powered, deflowered/ Over eighteen Irene." Mention was also made of "Just Like Gene Autry: A Foxtrot," a song that featured Lou Waxman and his orchestra and stirred Arthur Godfrey on banjo and ukelele. They were not kidding, and to emphasize the nostalgic put-on, this track of the LP had to be played at 78 r.p.m., an item that irritated some listeners and critics. WOW included a bonus record titled "Grape Jam" on which guitarists Al Kooper and Mike Bloomfield temporarily deserted their own groups and instruments to improvise on piano. Many commentators rejected the album as a too-studied attempt at originality and the preservation of a sense of self-importance.

Despite its position as the psychedelic pivot of rock, the purveyor of Total Sound and the locus of fuzztone and feedback, California has contributed to the growth of soft rock. Scott McKenzie's "San Francisco (Be Sure to Wear Some Flowers in Your Hair)" comes quickly to mind. In 1966 a group called The Mamas and The Papas swept the country with "California Dreamin'," a song written by John Philips, one of the Papas and the author of the Scott McKenzie hit. Other bestselling disks followed—"Twelve Thirty," "Monday Monday," "Words of Love," "Creeque Alley." The arrangements were so original and the blend of voices so rich that the foursome quickly gained recognition as one of the great vocal quartets of rock. Thanks to the raunch-and-rock quality of big Mama Cass Elliot, however, it never sacrificed the big beat. Many hear her influence in the vocalizing of Spanky and Mama Cowsill, and to a lesser degree in Janis Joplin and Grace Slick. The group also boasted the songwriting talent of John Philips, who eventually displayed skill as a record producer. Many of his songs, including "San Francisco," which went to # 1 in England, may be heard in *The Voice of Scott McKenzie*, an album he co-produced with Lou Adler, mentor of The Mamas and The Papas.

John Philips' heady songs and textured arrangements also

161

enrich *The Papas and The Mamas* (note the inversion), an album issued in the summer of 1968 after many rumors of the group's dissolution, retirement, and splintering. Mama Cass did appeared high on single record charts with a solo of the oldie "Dream a Little Dream of Me"—and there were reports that Philips was planning to turn to film production. Marked by a melancholy moodiness, the album presented at least one explanation of their troubled outlook and uncertain future. From the start, they had been anti-middle class and anti-star, displaying amusement, in the manner of The Beatles, at their rising fame and fortune. Their new album suggested that they felt themselves being suffocated by success.

Some of the San Francisco groups have a kooky quality that seems indigenous to the California climate or scene. To be free in their thinking and to find the largest possible audience, Country Joe and the Fish perform wherever there are people willing to listen. This includes parks, municipal squares and even parking lots—and they do not concern themselves about the profit. They have also participated in yippie protests and freak-outs.

"We were all misfits when we started," says Joe McDonald, the Country Joe of the group. "We're going to do our thing and refuse to sell out. We've refused to do certain commercials for this reason. . . . We may look and sound strange, but that's because we don't consider ourselves slaves to any audience. . . . We want to be trusted, to be heard. We'd like to stimulate people to wake up, to think and to create."

The ambitions are lofty and their readiness to enunciate them bespeaks a rare degree of naïveté. But McDonald is equally direct in songs like "Don't Drop That Bomb on Me," "I-Feel-Like-I'm-Fixin'-To-Die Rag" and other topical, satirical numbers. ("Be the first on your block," he sings in the "Rag," "to have your boy come home in a box.") The other Fish in the group share McDonald's penchant for plain speaking. Guitarist Barry Melton, whose nickname is Blind Ebbets Field, believes in naming

names and muckraking. The catalyst in bringing the group together, he knew organist David Cohen from a band in which
they worked together and Bruce Barthol from high school.
Barthol, who is proficient on folk instruments like the harmonica, autoharp and banjo, was a participant in the Berkeley
Free Speech Movement, CORE and Young Democrats for Action and McDonald were doing a folk act at Jabberwock in
San Francisco when they decided to form a group and found
their drummer in a young man known as Chicken Hirsch.

In October, 1966, they began playing in a Berkeley coffee
house. Their sound was jug band to rock. After a time, they
went electric, Eastern influences crept into the down-home
sounds, and the topical tune was added to the tender love
ballad. "Not So Sweet Lorraine" was their debut single, and
it was a chart-climber. Their follow-up single "Janis" was a
tribute to Janis Joplin of Big Brother and the Holding Company.

The Buffalo Springfield is symptomatic of the obsessive concern with image among today's rock groups. Names have always
been an important consideration in the development of a successful singing act. But the current craze involves total concept.
The Springfield found its name by accident. As they rehearsed
one day on a deserted road, a steam roller came by. The name
of the manufacturer was on the side: Buffalo Springfield. The
attire they adopted was, by contrast, an expression of personal
preferences. "Odd" describes it better than western, though
there are touches of things associated with buffaloes and Springfield rifles.

Steve Stills—leader, second lead vocalist, second lead guitarist and responsible for their first national hit "For What It's
Worth"—wears moccasins, his blond hair long, and custom
Brioni suits. Rhythm guitarist Richie Furay dons cowboy boots
and East Indian shirts. Lead guitarist Neil Young, a Canadian
who made the trip to Los Angeles in a hearse he bought, prefers
fringed jackets, custom-made, of course. Bassist Bruce Palmer's
garb includes Indian shirts, sandals, sunglasses and a French

beret. Drummer Dewey Martin, who came to Los Angeles from Ontario by way of Nashville—he played record dates with Roy Orbison and Carl Perkins and was a regular on the Grand Ole Opry—leans to Edwardian jackets, silk scarves and leather clothing.

Neil Young has characterized their sound as "summer, now, soft, hard." It is apt in suggesting that their music is a salmagundi, with ingredients that range from hard-core rock ("Mr. Soul") to back-country banjo stuff. Having passed beyond its psychedelic adolescence, rock is becoming a musical amalgam of sounds from around the globe.

By August, another Los Angeles-based group composed largely of Canadians, Steppenwolf—so named after the novel by Hermann Hesse—was at the top of the charts with a hit single "Born To Be Wild" and in the Top Ten with its debut LP. A medley, *Berry Rides Again* reflected the quintet's debt to one of the early purveyors of r&b. But in *Steppenwolf the Second,* a new album then just on release, the group expressed its feeling for funky country blues. And yet the verbal content of its songs, as exemplified by its hit single, was socially oriented.

Commenting on the source of the group's name, lead-singer John Kay, one of its founders, acknowledged a philosophical kinship between its outlook and that of novelist Hesse's hero. "He rejects middle class standards," Kay stated, "and yet he wants to find happiness within or alongside of them. So do we. He is constantly pursuing something—an ideal—he is not sure of. So are we, in a way." In short, as "Born To Be Wild" suggests, the group is rebellious without a cause and its idealism lacks focus—a state of mind which appeared increasingly to characterize many members of the rock generation in the year that saw Nixon running against Humphrey.

Like the Jefferson Airplane, Big Brother and the Holding Company is composed of four boys and a girl. Like the Airplane's Grace Slick, Janis Joplin can cut through any wall-of-sound with her pipes. "Life is primarily to live it," the Holding

Company explains, "and to get into it, to be able to do something so that if you're going to die, like everybody is, it'll be OK. You won't feel like you're being burned. Like for example, if I had to go to Vietnam and die, I'd feel I was being burned." But despite its outlook and satiric name, the group has been unconcerned with Now themes like alienation, flower power, Hindu philosophy or psychedelic sensation.

With Grace Slick, Janis Joplin, who has been called a female Leadbelly, is the most admired white, female rock singer of the day. Reviews are splattered with epithets like "very tough, very raunchy and very beautiful" (Paul Williams in *Crawdaddy*) and "best rock singer since Ray Charles" (Robert Christgau in *Esquire*). Her performances are such a profligate expenditure of explosive energy and unrestrained feeling that many have wondered how long she can last. To which she responds: "If I hold back, I'm no good *now*, and I'd rather be good sometimes than holding back all the time. I'm 25 [April, 1968] and, like others of my generation and younger, we look back at our parents and see how they gave up and compromised and wound up with very little. So the kids want a lot of something now rather than a little of hardly anything spread over seventy years."

Of her first appearance at the Avalon Ballroom where Big Brother was the unofficial houseband, Janis has said: "It was the most thrilling time in my life. It was the first 'hippie' dance I had ever seen. I couldn't believe it—all this pulsating rhythm. I exploded. It made me stoned, like the best dope in the world. It was so sensual, so violent." But what happened that first time apparently is a continuing reaction: "When I'm singing," she says, "I'm inside of it. . . . I feel, oh, like I feel like when you're first in love, when you're first touching someone. . . . Chills, things slipping all over me. . . . A lot of times when I get off, I want to make love. . . ."

Janis' sure-fire showstopper is the soulful "Love Is Like a Ball and Chain," a song created by and the trademark of Big Mama Willie Mae Thornton. Miss Joplin contends that soul, two of whose components are feeling and sensuality, is not exclusively a black patent: "White people don't allow themselves to feel things," she has said. "Housewives in Nebraska have pain and joy; they've got soul if they'd give into it. . . . It isn't all a ball when you do. . . . Now, though, I've made feeling work for me through music, instead of destroying me."

But soul is not the only quality in her voice. "I've got country in my music, too. But what changed things was singing with an electric band. All that power behind you—that pulsating power. . . . You can't sing a Bessie Smith vocal with a rock beat." Making a clear distinction between rock and jazz singing, Miss Joplin asserts that she is not a jazz singer. "I don't feel quite free enough in my phrasing," she says. "I sing with a more demanding beat, a steady rather than a lilting beat. I don't riff over the band. I try to puctuate the rhythm with my voice. That's why Otis Redding was so great. You can't get away from him. He pounds on you; you can't help but *feel* him."

Having exploded nationally in the summer of 1967 at the Monterey Pop Festival, Big Brother and the Holding Company appeared on wax in the spring of 1968. Its debut album on Mainstream Records pleased neither the group nor the public. By the time their new LP was released by Columbia Records, the group had scored at the Newport Folk Festival and *Cheap Thrills*, as the album was titled, had the omens of a bestseller. Nevertheless, it left much to be desired as a revelation of the group's musicality and the depth of its feeling for the black idiom it affected. Although many observers felt that Janis Joplin was basically a visual performer, she was able to project in the album the furious energy and the feverish excitement, if not the coarse and, at times, vulgar sexuality of her on-stage appearances. (Rumors of Miss Joplin's break with Big Brother and the Holding Company were confirmed in September, 1968.)

On October 6, 1967, the Psychedelic Shop of San Francisco whose doors had opened for business on January 3, 1966, closed them with a debt of $6,000. On the same day, the remnants of the hippie movement held a widely publicized funeral in which they buried the remains of hippiedom and simultaneously celebrated the birth of a new Be Free movement. The concept of the Free Man, which was to supersede moribund hippie ideas of flower power, sexual ecstasy and heightened living through drugs, was rather unformed. But the freedom and unrestricted experimentation with which they were concerned had become well-established tenets in pop recording and creativity. And the freedom could be costly: the removal of restrictions on time and charges led to records that were dull, tiring and filled with arid patches of formless and meaningless sounds.

Partisans of the San Francisco scene maintain that, despite the demise of hippiedom, the Bay area remains a haven for creativity and creative spirits. To bolster their thesis, they point to the Youngbloods, a group that hit with "Grizzly Bear" early in 1967. Proponents of a style they describe as "rag 'n' roll," fusion of a 1920s ragtime beat with the electric drive of the 1960s, the Youngbloods have had two album releases. Neither their debut LP nor *Earth Music* has proved earthshaking. Drummer Joe Bauer comes from the jazz world of Memphis. Guitarist-harmonica player Jerry Corbitt hails from the blues-and-ragtime scene of Georgia. Bassist Jesse Colin Young is partial to country blues though he was born and raised in New York City. Only the young man who plays electric piano, looks like Harpo Marx and goes by the strange name of Banana, is a native Californian. The group was formed before claims were made for a Bosstown Sound in the locale of the nation's most celebrated Tea Party where Young and Corbitt worked as a coffee house duo. But for the past year or more, the Youngbloods have been Bay City dwellers. Only time will tell whether the scene will be as favorable to creativity as San Franciscans contend.

Neither Los Angeles nor San Francisco was the birthplace of The Union Gap, a group that performs in blue-and-gold Civil War uniforms and that took its name from the historic town of Union Gap, Washington. Led by "General" Gary Puckett, lead guitarist and vocalist, the quintet was formed in San Diego where the next in command, "Sergeant" Dwight Bement, was a music major at San Diego State and a part-time tenor saxist. The other members of the quintet are "Corporal" Kerry Chater (bass guitar) and "Privates" Paul Wheatbread (drums) and Gary "Mutha" Withem (piano and woodwinds). In 1967 the group would have been dismissed as shlock rockers. But in the post-*John Wesley Harding* critical climate, they stand forth as exuberant representatives of the return to "Music is fun-joy-motion." Although Puckett and Chater have contributed songs to the Gap's repertoire, they have mostly recorded songs by their hot songwriting contemporaries—Dylan, Lennon & McCartney, Jim Webb, Tim Hardin, Sonny Bono and the Gibbs Brothers. Three song hits give them a place in the story of rock: "Woman, Woman" by J. Glaser and J. Payne, "Young Girl" by Jerry Fuller, their record producer, and "Lady Willpower," also by Fuller. All three have accounted for Gold Records.

The year 1967 was one of songwriting *wunderkinder,* all of whom seemed to emerge from the west coast: Los Angeles and not San Francisco. None was really a native Californian. Jim Webb was born and raised in Elk City, Oklahoma. John Hartford, born in New York City, grew up in St. Louis, Missouri, developed as a singer-writer in Nashville, but became nationally known only after he settled in Hollywood. And Van Dyke Parks, whose artistry flowered in the California sunshine, was a migrant born in Mississippi and educated in New Jersey and Pennsylvania.

The youngest and most successful of the three was Jim Webb, who was just twenty-one when he made the leap from a $50 a week music copyist, sleeping on bare floors in a Hollywood apartment, to the highly remunerative multiple role of hit song-writer-producer-conductor-arranger-singer-publisher. At the 1968 annual ceremonies of NARAS, Webb collected eight Grammy awards for "Up, Up and Away," a 1967 smash for The Fifth

Dimension, and "By the Time I Get to Phoenix," a hit for Glen Campbell. While both of these were still being played on the country's radios, Webb wrote, arranged and produced an album for actor Richard Harris, his first attempt at singing on records. Out of *A Tramp Shining* came "MacArthur Park"—Harris sang "MacArthur's Park"—a seven-minute twenty-second surrealist song named after a park in downtown Los Angeles, which, despite its length and the known aversion of stations to play long singles, became a top five best-selling single record.

One of the more interesting facets of Webb's success story was that he had written the "Phoenix" song while working as a copyist in the lobby of a Hollywood recording studio. "It was kind of like shining shoes," he has said. The son of an Oklahoma Baptist minister and a songwriter from age thirteen —"As a matter of body chemistry," he has said, "I wrote three songs a week"—he had come to the film capital in a decrepit Volkswagen after dropping out of San Bernardino Valley College. "Phoenix" interested the manager of an unknown group (later The Fifth Dimension), who brought the song to the attention of writer-singer-producer Johnny Rivers. The latter included it in an album where, despite his success with "Memphis" and "The Poor Side of Town," and a track record of six successive Gold Records, "Phoenix" remained unheralded. It took the Glen Campbell version to make the song. But Rivers—himself a migrant from New York City, Baton Rouge and Nashville who struck paydirt in 1963 as a result of appearances at Los Angeles' Whisky-A-Go Go—was sufficiently impressed by young Webb so that he bought his songwriting contract from a small publisher. It was a brilliant move, particularly after he put Webb in charge of The Fifth Dimension's first album, which became the first release on his newly formed Soul City record label.

In addition to Johnny Rivers, Webb credits Dunhill record executive and producer Lou Adler for his "course" in recording techniques and studio musicianship. Despite his youth, Webb's songs display a remarkable mastery of melody, harmony and lyrics, fresh, appealing melody, literate, frequently surrealistic lyrics and sophisticated, show-type harmony. As this is written, Epic Records is about to release an album *Jim Webb Sings Jim Webb*, reportedly consisting of demos he had made in his indigent days and now embellished with many instruments. Another record company is about to release an instrumental single in which an orchestra of sixty-five musicians will perform the "Allegro" from the Richard Harris hit "MacArthur Park." He has been flown to New York by Frank Sinatra who wanted to do an album of Webb songs tailored for him. Already the composer of the title theme for the movie *How Sweet It Is*, he has been signed by Universal Pictures to score a new Mel Ferrer production. Webb asserts that he never received formal training either in theory or orchestration. "I just jumped into arranging," he says, "but you should have seen when I first heard a chart of mine being played."

Housing Project is the title of John Hartford's newest LP, his fourth on RCA Victor and the first since he won a Grammy for "Gentle on My Mind." The title has a double significance. "I have been moving," he told me, "toward the concept of an album as more than a collection of separate tracks. And then, a song is like a room or an environment in which a listener lives with you for a spell. This housing project has a number of rooms, spanning different places and periods of time."

Hartford does not regard himself as a country writer even though, prior to his settling in Hollywood, he lived for nearly four years in Nashville, made appearances on the Grand Ole Opry and recorded three of his albums in Music City's Victor studios. In this respect he is characteristic of the new breed of writer, singer and instrumentalist, all spawned by the Rock Revolution, for whom categories do not matter, musical creation is a fusion of many sounds and the only important thing is "doing your own thing" but doing it meaningfully and well. Born in New York City in December, 1937, while his father worked as a hospital intern, he was raised in Missouri where his father settled as a professor of medicine at St. Louis' Washington University. His mother, an accomplished painter, doubtless inspired his study of art at the University—the collage on the cover of *Housing Project* is his own creation. But after working briefly as a sign painter, he functioned as a disk jockey, a deckhand and a sideman before he turned to writing songs in 1963. He acknowledges many, varied influences in his work— Hank Williams, Truman Capote, Allen Ginsberg, Carl Sandburg and others—but he names Bob Dylan as the writer who turned him on. What ignited him was that Dylan wrote poetry and not merely song lyrics.

"Gentle on My Mind," the song that exploded his career, was the product of twenty minutes at the typewriter. "It took final shape that fast," he says. "But of course I had been working on it mentally for a long, long time. I was moved to put it down after seeing *Dr. Zhivago* at a Nashville moviehouse. There's no connection really, except that that the picture left me in a frame of mind and feeling that was just right for the song." His own version created no sales stir but it did attract a number of recordings. As with Webb's "Phoenix," it was Glen Campbell who came up with the hit version. Shortly after the rhythm ballad became a hit, a disk jockey on Los Angeles station KGBS paid a visit to Nashville. Before long, Hartford received a long distance call from Tommy Smothers. A trip to Hollywood led to his becoming a regular writer-and-performer on the *Summer Brothers Smothers Show*, produced by the Smothers Brothers and starring Glen Campbell.

Hartford approaches lyrics in terms of pictures and feels that he is successful when a song becomes, as he puts it, "a motion picture." He likes to structure a lyric so that instead of developing in a straight line, it takes the shape of a circle and becomes an environment into which one may move and exist for a time.

Although the unbridled rave is an earmark of rock criticism, particularly as practiced by the under-thirty contingent, the

171

accolades showered on a new arranger-producer turned composer-artist seem well earned. The young man was not unknown inside California pop music circles for he had played on the Byrds' "Five 'D' (Fifth Dimension)" disk and the first Tim Buckley album. He had produced the Mojo Men's hit cover disk on "Sit Down, I Think I Love You" and written "Come to the Sunshine," a moderate hit for Harpers Bizarre. Just before he himself stepped into the limelight, as arranger-producers seldom do (unless they're Phil Spector), he had spent the better part of a year working with Brian Wilson on a Beach Boys album that never appeared. But he had contributed to *Smiley Smile*, which did appear, the chorus of "Vegetables" and lyrics used in "Heroes and Villains" and "She's Goin' Bald."

Nevertheless, few rock critics expected what they finally heard in Van Dyke Parks' *Song Cycle*. "I feel like making wild, extreme statements," one under-thirty reviewer wrote, "to the effect that the *Cycle* is a milestone in the development of American popular music, that it explores possibilities that were never even dreamt of before, that it attains a level of complexity and subtlety genuinely comparable to that of 'serious' contemporary music, and that Van Dyke Parks is a genius."

What may have accounted for this panegyric, and others like it, is that Parks displayed a high level of achievement not in one area but in many. He was not only a subtle lyricist but a sophisticated composer, not only a skilful arranger but a man who could play the recording studio as well as the best of the new breed of rock artists. Although he was born in Hattiesburg, Mississippi, once lived in Bayside, New York, went to Columbus Boys Choir School in New Jersey, and studied piano and composition at Carnegie Tech in Pittsburgh, *Song Cycle* dealt with Hollywood, where he lived in a garage apartment house close by the Freeway, and where he had come in 1955 as a child actor, and returned in 1962 as a recording musician-arranger.

His lyrics abound in puns: "Dreams are still born in Hollywood"; "San Fernando/On Hillside Manors, on the banks of toxi*city*" (the shift of the accent to *cit* does it). His music is rich in allusions to Beethoven, Debussy, Mahler and, most of all, the American Charles Ives, and yet sounds like Broadway show tunes written in a country-style idiom. His feeling for orchestral textures and fresh harmonic changes, as revealed in "Donovan's Colors," the sole instrumental track, drew hyperboles for his artistry as an orchestrator.

"What drags me most about pure rock," he has said, "is that it has all these things going about being nitty-gritty and yet it's encrusted with chic." And he adds: "I'm interested in understatement. I don't think it's proper to dominate your audience. I'm trying to stand gracefully, and even to control my presence, without dominating. Through the use of creative energy, I want to give people an excuse to trust me, and pay me."

Although he denies that he has been influenced by The Beatles—he was the first one-man unit to embrace all the talents they embody—he recognizes that their influence helped create the recording climate in which he can mature. He is aware, as he has demonstrated in *Song Cycle*, that it is no longer enough to use electronic sounds, devices and instruments, or just to show a rebellious preference for new forms and structures. In the post-hippie, post-psychedelic music scene, content, creativity, expressiveness and appeal count.

Before we leave the California scene, two disparate phenomena, neither native to the west coast, require attention. One is a group called The Monkees, four actor-musicians brought together for a TV comedy series through an advertisement-audition process and then transformed into one of the most successful of rock groups. "Prepubescent rock" is the term that has been applied to them, for the belief is that The Monkees' audience is largely pre-teen age. It is difficult to give credence to the widespread rumor that the members of the group became instrumentally proficient *after* they began making records. But no critic under or over thirty, has ever discerned any musical distinction in their work, other than an artless commercialism.

Nevertheless, every one of their LPs has grossed over a million manufacturer's dollars, giving them five successive Gold Albums. This is an achievement equalled by no other rock group except The Beatles and surpassed only by Herb Alpert and the Tiajuana Brass.

Now, as we go to press, word comes of a development that is really "blowing the minds" of rock critics. A new album released by Dot Records and titled *The Wichita Train Whistle Sings* is the work of one of The Monkees. Mike Nesmith, who had collaborated on some of the group's hits, is the sole writer of nine of the *Wichita* tunes and collaborator on one. Producer of the album, which he personally financed, he also collaborated with jazz trumpeter-conductor Shorty Rogers on the arrangements. Incidentally, there are no vocals on the LP. Despite the title, the *Wichita Train Whistle* does not sing but comprises a 51-piece band that plays the ten Nesmith compositions.

An unrelated development but one also originating in the Hollywood scene, involves a Lebanese-American of uncertain age, who has long, stringy hair, a nose like a flamingo and teeth like a snarling horse. Singing in a high falsetto voice, which has made him the butt of the usual assortment of sissy jokes, and accompanying himself on an ancient ukelele, Tiny Tim has made a hit of "Tip Toe Through the Tulips" and placed an album, *God Bless Tiny Tim*, on bestseller charts. Composed of oldies of the World War I era, the album is dedicated to his mother and father, New Yorkers in their seventies, with whom Tiny Tim, an only child presumed to be in his forties, still lives.

Although Tiny Tim spent much of his unsuccessful singing career in the East and worked for a period in a Times Square freak show as Larry Love, the Human Canary, he must be regarded as a Los Angeles phenomenon. Given national exposure on the Rowan and Martin *Laugh-In*, managed by a Beverly Hills agent and recorded by a Burbank-based record label, he has had the all-out promotional support of two major Los Angeles rock stations. When KRLA sponsored a monster concert at Santa Monica Auditorium in June, 1968, KHJ gave away $5,000 worth of tickets free. Both stations were on the air, crying "We love Tiny Tim" and "God bless Tiny Tim," hour by hour for weeks. "Tip Toe Through the Tulips" was not only a record "pick." It appeared for weeks in a "Boss Thirty" list, published and distributed by KHJ, which calls itself "Boss Radio in Los Angeles."

Apart from the strange fascination he exercises as an eccentric personality, Tiny Tim has attracted attention through the curious character of his repertoire and singing style. With old sheet music and 78 r.p.m. records as his stock in trade, he claims to know more than a thousand songs, all of them written before, during, or shortly after World War I. Lacking any style of his own, he is quite effective in imitating singers like Billy Williams (1910), Henry Burr (1915), Arthur Fields (1917)—"He makes me swoon," he has said—young Al Jolson (1919), Rudy Vallee and others. "I'd love to sing songs like 'I Don't Want to Get Well, I'm in Love with a Beautiful Nurse' through a megaphone," he has said, "instead of with all that modern electronic equipment."

He adds, "I don't think I'm turning the clock back by doing these old tunes." Whether one regards him as camp, a primitive, an innocent, a specter of Victorianism, a weird-o or a put-on—and he has been described as all of these by different interviewers—it seems clear that if anyone can set the over-thirty counter-revolution in motion, Tiny Tim might.

10 EAST COAST ROCK

The California Sound had no real homogeneity other than its hippie locale. But since the impetus for the use of electronic instruments and psychedelic devices originated in the West, it became a convenient label. There is no east coast sound any more than there was east coast jazz when the west coast was the launching pad of the Cool School. New York is a bouillabaisse of beats, a stew of sounds, some of which we have already covered: Simon & Garfunkel and The Lovin' Spoonful under folk or art rock; the Blues Project and Blood, Sweat and Tears as instances of blue-eyed soul on the instrumental level: and so on. There are, however, a number of New York-based or -originated groups whose contribution to the rock scene warrants investigation.

San Francisco's Mothers of Invention have their shock rock counterpart in a New York group whose recordings have seldom been played on the radio. Many disk jockeys are reluctant even to pronounce on the air the name of The Fugs, a group that developed at the Bridge Theatre on St. Mark's Place, Manhattan's hippie haven. Night after night, Tuli Kupferberg, a

176

beat-generation poet, and Ed Sanders, who came from Kansas to study Greek citizenship at New York University, developed and presented anti-Establishment material that combined stinging satire with shocking obscenity. Eventually their songs became available on ESP Records, an independent label. Despite the lack of air-play, the LP sold well enough as an underground item to attract the interest of Reprise Records. (Incidentally, before Ed Sanders hit upon the idea of using rock to undermine the Establishment, he edited a literary magazine whose two-word, seven-letter title no newspaper would print. Regularly confiscated by the police, the magazine was sold by Greenwich Village shops, including a book store The Peace Eye, operated by Sanders. Peace Eye was a title taken from Egyptian mythology and had to do with discovery of the self.)

When Reprise Records released the second Fugs' LP, *Tenderness Junction*, it ran tradepaper advertisements that read: "The Fugs say today's things with more courage, less compromise than any group ever to tilt at the hypocrisy of a hidebound status quo. Improbably named, impassionately premised—The Fugs are ready for the world! Is the world ready for The Fugs?" In interviews, the company's general manager stated: "This is not pornography, it's not obscene; the four-letter word is today's culture." Asserting that there should be no censorship or repression in the arts, Mo Ostin described the album as a legitimate, artistic expression, in line with the "new morality" expressed in the theater and in motion pictures.

The material of The Fugs runs the satirical gamut from take-off's on pop music like "My Supergirl" to bitter invective, as in "Kill for Peace." On stage, Sanders appeared in red-white-and-blue shorts and an Army helmet. As he screamed the "kill" line, the helmet fell off to reveal Nazi headgear underneath. There's nothing psychedelic about The Fugs, but like The Mothers, they are a Brechtian Theater of the Absurd set to rock.

In the psychedelic realm, the East has The Blues Magoos, a group that outdoes the west coasters both in decibels and lighting. They appear in electric suits costing about $1,000 apiece. Into each outfit, made of black polyester, forty-eight light bulbs have been stitched. Each bulb is surrounded by spaghetti-like strips of fluorescent colors. A flick of a concealed switch ignites the bulbs. These in turn activate the fluorescent strips, transforming each Magoo into a glowing swirl of vibrating colors. In the sound department, they employ every known device—feedback, electronic echo, organ fuzz tone, reverberator—to increase the volume and density of the sounds they produce. Two albums, which have been bestsellers, are not inappropriately titled *Electric Comic Book* and *Psychedelic Lollipop*.

The East has a counterpart even for the west coast's Monkees. In the spring of 1968, a group called The 1910 Fruit Gum Co. scored a bestseller with a rock version of the nursery rhyme "Simon Says." About the same time, the family group known as The Cowsills had "Indian Lake" while the Ohio Express, another eastern group, had "Yummy, Yummy, Yummy." Whether or not bubble gum rock, as it has been called, develops into a trend—in England, Manfred Mann offered a version of the nursery jingle "My Name Is Jack"—it is apparent that rock has dramatically lowered the age level at which consumers enter the record market, and that market, in turn, continues to reflect the tastes of younger age groups. Early rock 'n' roll was recognized as a teenage product. The audience for Monkees records is regarded as subteen. And now with these new groups, we may be dipping down to the nursery level.

The largest number of eastern groups fall into *Esquire's* category of shlock rock. They are effective rather than creative performers and writers. The Four Seasons, oldest of this genre, have sold millions of albums since they had their first hit in "Sherry" in 1962. "Sherry" was written by Bob Gaudio, pianist-organist, who had contributed "Short Shorts" in the early days of rock 'n' roll, and whose songwriting talent has played a large role in giving The Four Seasons their longevity. Gaudio has collaborated on many Seasons' hits with Bob Crewe, who has been their producer since 1962. While the group has a distinctive sound, its style is based on Negro r&b groups that play contrasting high falsetto and low bass voices against the ensemble. Although The Four Seasons have, for many years, been on the Phillips label, they had their start on Vee Jay, one of Chicago's hot r&b labels before it went bankrupt.

At the start, The Young Rascals, a group that broke in 1966, recalled the Seasons with their blue-eyed black sound. Smart promotion by manager Sid Bernstein, who brought The Beatles to Shea Stadium, resulted in an Atlantic recording contract for the quartet after a debut at an obscure roadhouse in New Jersey and a summer sojourn at a floating nightspot in Westhampton, Long Island. "I Ain't Gonna Eat Out My Heart Anymore" was their first hit single while "Groovin' " became their first Gold Record. Their most successful numbers are the work of drummer-lead singer Eddie Brigati and organist Felix Cavaliere, whose vocal on "Groovin" has been compared with some of Ray Charles' balladry. By the summer of 1968 the group had garnered seven Gold Records, four for albums and three for single hits. Included among the latter was the stirring protest song "People Got to Be Free," an unexpected change of pace for the group and, surprisingly, a disk that attained and remained # 1 for weeks.

The # 1 Top Male Artists in *Billboard*'s year-end tabulation of 1967 bestsellers were a group known as Tommy James and The Shondells. Tommy comes from Niles, Michigan, where at the age of fifteen he recorded a song called "Hanky Panky" in the studios of a local radio station. Three years later, a Pittsburgh jockey found the disk, began playing it, and started it on the way to becoming a hit. Their first LP, *I Think We're Alone Now*, cut early in 1967, was a smash seller. It was cut under the aegis of the two men, Bo Gentry and Ritchie Cordell, who serve as their songsmiths and record producers. In styling, they are in the pseudo-r&b bag of The Rascals and The Four Seasons. But the key to their success may lie in the special appeal that

Tommy James makes to female teenagers. He is the male counterpart of Diana Ross of The Supremes, emoting in a soft, deep, buzzing sexy voice.

Two young rock groups that combine showmanship with interesting material are The Happenings and Spanky and Our Gang. The latter are not really east coasters since they made their debut in Chicago where Mercury Records found them at an obscure club, Mother Blues, and signed them to a recording contract (no advance). They were actually without funds when they arrived in New York early in 1967. At the Scene, an underground basement on West 46th Street, they persuaded the owner to let them do a set. Steve Paul, former public relations man who, at sixteen, touted the Peppermint Lounge into the Twist capital of the world, signed them on the spot. By Easter, when they were appearing at the Bitter End in the Village, Mercury released their first single. "Sunday Will Never Be the Same" did the impossible: it took off in New York City, a town known as a place to reap but not to sow. With the Good Guys on WMCA spinning it hard, the disk climbed to # 5 in New York City and eventually to # 9 nationally.

The public appearances of Spanky *et al.* were greeted with huzzahs by a variety of reviewers, including *The New York Times*' Robert Shelton, who characterized their style as "a blend of carnival, camp and corn." In effect, it was no style at all, but an inventive ability to parody a wide range of styles from jugband to vaudeville, from c&w to protest rock. The central figure was Elaine (Spanky) McFarlane, an ex-jazz singer, whom Shelton colorfully described as one who had borrowed charm from Judy Garland, phrasing from Judy Henske and many chins from Lynn Redgrave. Her main assistant was Nigel Pickering, who looked more like an English big-game hunter than a former c&w singer and disk jockey. On third was a man with big, white, horse teeth and a handlebar moustache who went by the strange name of Oz Bach and played a strange-looking instrument called "the electrical banana." It was a dressed-up kazoo.

In their first LP, released in December, 1967, they demonstrated that their wit, musicality and showmanship can be captured on wax. Much of their material had the sophisticated adult-appeal of Beatle spoofing. "Commercial" was a take-off on smoking pot, done in the style of a TV aspirin commercial. "Happy Landing, Amelia Earhart" took a laughable, lachrymose hillbilly shape. They could score with a witty "Five Definitions of Love," based on a verbatim excerpt from Webster's New Collegiate Dictionary, as well as a pop anthem of the depression 30s, "Brother, Can You Spare a Dime?" In the words of drummer John (The Chief) Seiter, they regard themselves as a "bridge thing": "There's a definite gap between the kids today and their parents. . . . We do rock for the teenyboppers and stuff the parents will call music too."

The Happenings are another bridge group. Although their first hit was the youthful "See You In September"—it earned a Gold Record—their succeeding bestsellers were "My Mammy" and "I Got Rhythm," songs that come from the memory books of the older generation. While they are extremely popular on college campuses, their video appearances on *Smothers Brothers, Merv Griffin, Mike Douglas* and *Tonight* shows, demonstrate their adult appeal. Effective on stage as on disk, they do a mixed-generation set of imitations that includes the Rolling Stones, Bob Dylan and the Beach Boys—and Johnny Mathis and Dean Martin.

The eastern rock scene also includes two family groups. The members of the 5 Stairsteps and Cubie from Chicago range from 2½-year-old Cubie through sons aged 14, 15, 16, 17, a daughter aged 18, and Mom and Dad. The Cowsills of Providence and Newport, Rhode Island, are nine if you include father Bud who acts as manager and son Dick who is the lighting expert and road manager. On stage or on mike, there are seven, running the gamut from Susan 8, John 11 (drums), Barry 14 (bass), Paul 16, Bob 18 (organist), Bill 20 (lead guitarist) to Mother Cowsill (harmony singer), a young 40. The story of the Cowsills had its beginning in 1963 when father Bud retired from the Navy as a chief petty officer. Working as a painter-carpenter, he put his earnings into instruments, amplifiers and costumes. The rest of the family was required to rehearse a minimum of two hours a day. Going was so rough that, to heat the 23-room, ramshackle mansion they called home in Newport, they at times used furniture for firewood.

The change in their fortunes came with "The Rain, the Park and Other Things," a record that touched # 1 late in 1967. Three albums later, they occupied three apartments in a new, high-rise, midtown Manhattan building and looked to a future with millions in it. Their repertoire consists of golden oldies from the Top Forty hits. Their audience consists mainly of children who are contemporaries of drummer John, aged 11. Their style is raucous and corny. Theirs is an American success story of the 60s, a tale of the gold in pop and rock.

A survey of the eastern scene would be incomplete without some reference to rock musicals. Two of them were visible during the 1967–68 season, regarded by many as one of the worst in the history of Broadway's musical theater. *Hair*, subtitled an American Tribal Love-Rock Musical, inaugurated the Shakespeare Festival Anspacher Playhouse, a theater that opened on Lafayette Street in what had formerly been the old Astor Library. Written by two actors, Gerome Ragni and James Rado, *Hair* was set to music by Galt MacDermot, a classically trained Toronto pianist who had become a rock-jazz composer. It started as an audience show and eventually drew the plaudits of the reviewing fraternity. Howard Taubman, *The New York Times'* critic emeritus, praised its freshness, exuberance and impertinence, and quite properly compared it to the off-Broadway revues of the 20s that shook up the established musical theater of its day. Clive Barnes, the *Times'* active critic, characterized it as an honest attempt to jolt American musicals into the 60s and applauded two sovereign qualities: the likeability and honesty of the cast, and the rough, tough, lusty music because it was not a pastiche of Rodgers & Hammerstein.

Hair had a framework, rather than a book. Its thin story line dealt with a young man who sought a moment of ecstasy with a desirable lass before he was drafted, and who ended by having his locks shorn. The two were part of a tribe of loving drop-outs who shared a pad called The Intergalactic Bathtub. Employing a mixed-media approach, *Hair* used slide projections, colorful posters and a mishmash of hippie paraphernalia. Its insouciant, under-thirty point of view included angry comments on the Vietnam war, hypocritical public figures, and outworn contemporary institutions. The original cast album on RCA Victor has a monotonous quality, particularly on the rhythmic side, which suggests that the musical approach was too narrowly rock 'n' roll, rather than wide-spectrum rock. In May, 1968, the musical moved to Broadway, where a revised book, additional songs and new staging led to rave notices and a new cast album.

RCA Victor also released the original cast album of *Your Own Thing*, the other rock musical, paying a royalty that startled established composer-producers like Richard Rodgers and Leland Hayward. *Thing* was the work of Danny Apolinar, a Jewish-Catholic Filipino from Brooklyn, and Hal Hester, a renegade southern Baptist from Paducah, Kentucky. They had met in the Village in a spot where Hal, a graduate of the Cincinnati Conservatory of Music, was playing piano, and Apolinar, a commercial artist, came in as vocalist. After writing music, lyrics and the initial book, they were joined in their endeavors by Donald Driver, who made it on Broadway with the American version of *Marat-Sade*, and who shaped and staged the work as a Now musical.

The message of the work, as Driver describes it: "Our brutally masculine world has got to go. The Establishment, the military-economic complex, the Big Brother government must go off to the dinosaur burial ground. Why should we be forced to be any way but the way we want to be, our 'own thing.' Why must the American male be a fighter, play football, be dressed in shades from bleak to drab, knuckle under to all kinds of rigid ideas of what's right. I haven't time to march on Washington, but this play is my protest." But Driver also cites the comment of a little old lady who said after a performance of *Thing*: "I don't know what the message is, but it comes through."

Hester and Apolinar trace the origin of the work to a McLuhan article in which the author of *The Medium Is the Message*, contended that the sexes were moving closer together. In Shakespeare's *Twelfth Night*, with its comedy of sexual confusion, they found a framework for developing their ideas: that the image of the American male as a tough he-man is nothing but myth; that the new male is by virtue of his dress and coiffure indistinguishable from the female; and that so long as love is real, it does not matter which sex loves which. "I've worn my hair like this for years," says Apolinar whose hair-do is typically under-thirty. "The only difference now is that people don't stare any more." And Driver, who has gold-red hair, delights in flaunting at Connecticut commuters a gift given to him by the producer of *Your Own Thing*—a fur jacket made of red fox. The show was named the Best Musical of the 1967–68 season by the New York Drama Critics Circle. It was the first time that an Off-Broadway show received such a citation from the group.

The sound of rock was heard on the screen, of course, long before 1967–68. A long list of Presley films, starting with *Jailhouse Rock* in 1957, have racked up substantial grosses among teenage followers. It was not until 1964 when The Beatles produced and starred in *A Hard Day's Night* that a prestige, adult film made use of an all-rock score. Since then rock has been heard in *Georgy Girl*, *You're a Big Boy Now* (music by John Sebastian of The Lovin' Spoonful), *Privilege*, *To Sir, With Love* (which featured Lulu), Sonny & Cher's *Good Times*, Antonioni's *Blow-Up* (which used The Yardbirds), *The Trip*, *The Graduate* (score by Paul Simon of Simon & Garfunkel) and others.

There are indications that the rock revolution is now finding expression in theaters in other parts of the country. One hears of a Los Angeles musical, *Catch My Soul*, whose book is based on *Othello*, with Iago being played by Jerry Lee Lewis, the early rockabilly screamer remembered for "Great Balls of Fire." At San Francisco State College, Euripedes' tragedy *The Bacchae* has been done with a score written by a local rock group known as Liberty Street. And in New York, students and faculty of Hunter College heard a forty-minute rock 'n' roll opera, based on the Scrooge theme of Dickens and composed by a jazz pianist, Charles Bell, who teaches at Manhattan's P.S. 169 and at Hunter. "Is This Where It's At?" asked *The New York Times* in a Sunday piece on *Your Own Thing*. *Life*, having surveyed the new rock musicals, concluded: "Rock is the only popular sound drawn from today's urban, socially explosive, mixed-media world . . . and the only music that today can lure young people back to the musical theater they long ago deserted."

As rock demonstrates its pervasive impact, invading the Broadway theater as well as the Hollywood screen, new efforts are being made to exploit its sound in promoting new groups and given areas. For a time there was publicity about a nonidentifiable and ultimately nonexistent Chicago Sound. During 1968 the type of manufactured rumor known as "hype" fixed on the Boston Sound. Within a short period of time, every New York record company was taking the air shuttle to the home of Harvard and signing new combos heard at The Boston Tea Party, The Catacombs, or the Psychedelic Supermarket, three of the main discotheques. Before long, ABC Records had Eden's Children, Elektra had Earth Opera, Decca had The Improper Bostonians, Atlantic had Bo Grumpus and The Apple Pie Motherhood Band, and MGM gobbled up four groups: The Ultimate Spinach, The Beacon Street Union, Orpehus and Phluph. There was even a new rock word to identify the new sound—Bosstown.

But what was the Boston Sound? Like many publications, *Newsweek* tried hard to define it. "Anti-hippie and anti-drugs," it wrote. Then, after references to sophistication, wittiness and electricity, it concluded: "However diverse, the Boston groups are held together by their general folk orientation, their subdued, artful electronic sound, an insistence on clear, understandable lyrics, the spice of dissonance and the infusion of classical textures." *Vogue,* which seldom deigns to concern itself with so unchic a matter as pop music, could not resist the vibrations of a Boston Sound. After all, there was Radcliffe to be considered, and not too far away, Wellesley. And so they turned to the crown prince of rock critics for a scholarly disquisition. Richard Goldstein is too knowledgable not to have known that he was being asked to describe something that had no identity. But instead of saying right out that there was no Boston Sound, he referred to "the hyper-orchestrated Broadway slick" which permeates the first albums of Orpheus and The Ultimate Spinach, and added: "The Spinach and Orpheus are as indicative of Boston's culture as baked beans, and as canned."

It finally devolved upon *The New York Times* to put the record straight. "The Boston Sound Is Mostly Puff," read the headline over a Robert Shelton story. Observing that there was a lot of pop activity brewing in the area, Mr. Shelton stated: "The Boston Sound is no more an audible entity than the Long Island Sound." This is not to say that there may not be a Boston Sound at some time in the future. Like jazz, before the 60s, rock has displayed a tremendous receptivity to change, and has undergone unbelievable changes in its short span of life. Nothing less than a revolution within a revolution is audible when one compares Presley rockabilly with the artful music of Van Dyke Parks, the meaningful lyrics of The Fugs, the extended forms developed by The Beatles, and the imaginative use of electronic sounds and devices made by many rock groups.

CODA

In 1962, seven years after the rise of Elvis Presley, Station WINS in New York City switched from a Top Forty programming format to so-called Good Music. By way of signalizing the shift, it played nothing but Frank Sinatra records for a total of sixty-six consecutive hours. Whether the novel programming was spontaneous, as the station claimed, or planned, as some cynical commentators suggested, the Sinatrathon elicited praise around the globe. From Broadway where Jule Styne heralded the return of good music (meaning the type of ballad popular during the 30s and 40s) to Moscow, where *Pravda* congratulated WINS for dropping "that contaminator of American youth" (meaning rock 'n' roll), older generation listeners happily intoned obsequies at the apparent burial of teenage music.

Only, of course, rock did not die. In fact, it was just five years before the older generation did a complete turnabout. By 1967 rock was being hailed as the style that had made an art of pop music. Magazines like *Down Beat* and *Jazz*, which had shunned any reference to popular music, suddenly began covering rock, and the latter pointedly changed its name to *Jazz and Pop*.

Esquire and *Vogue* added under-thirty commentators to their coverage of the lively arts while literary and intellectual publications like *Commentary* and *Partisan Review* printed scholarly articles on The Beatles, Bob Dylan, *et al.* Following the lead of the defunct *Herald Tribune, The New York Times* began reviewing rock concerts and club acts, and devoting copious space in its Sunday pages to record reviews and interviews. In the past two years, Hollywood films and the Broadway musical theater have both begun to use the creative talents of rock composers.

In fairness to the old folks, let it be said that what has happened is the result, not only of the persistence of this new art form, but of the vast changes that it has undergone. The mewling infant that was born with Presley and soon found exponents in Pat Boone, Bobby Darin, Buddy Holly and the Everly Brothers was a primitive, crude and tiresome thing compared with what it has become. Rockabilly and teenage rock were four-chord songs, diapered in dull triplets and pinned with cliché lyrics. With Bob Dylan, poetry and protest were introduced. Humor and adventure were contributed by The Beatles, who disarmed the older generation since they were *for* adolescents without being *against* adults. Rhythm-and-blues, a kind of lumpenproletariat expression in its beginnings, evolved into the musical and expressive soul of Ray Charles, James Brown, Sam Cooke, Nina Simone, Otis Redding and Dionne Warwick. Amplification and electronics added new dimensions to rock, and made new demands on singers, instrumentalists, arrangers and producers.

It is a curious coincidence that the historic Supreme Court decision outlawing school segregation came just about the time that Haley and Presley were siring mulatto styles. The coincidence becomes even stranger when one realizes that in 1954, too, Ray Charles made the first fusion of gospel and blues, of sacred and profane Negro song, that brought him into the mainstream of pop. Sociological and esthetic coincidences of this type seem inevitably to reflect deep-seated psychological disturbances. Although the teenage generation first turned to rock 'n' roll because it offered a happy, exuberant, irresistible dance beat, the heartbeat of rock soon became protest—protest against the static forms, verbal cliches, tired harmonies, instrumental limitations and the vapid romanticism of Tin Pan Alley song; protest against the sexual taboos, racism, violence, hypocrisy and materialism of adult life. The protest took many forms, from the diatribes of early Dylan to the alienation of Simon & Garfunkel, from the escapism of psychedelic rock to the sharp-edged satire of The Fugs and Mothers of Invention. The dissatisfaction of the younger generation and of its song spokesmen created an atmosphere which made for adventure, experimentalism and an unleashing of the creative spirit. Artificial boundaries of structure, content and sound, which had prevailed for decades, were torn down. What counted was sincerity, involvement, saying where it was at, doing one's own thing, blowing the mind. Symptomatic of the generation's receptivity was the emergence of a forty-seven-year-old Indian sitarist, Ravi Shankar, as a rock idol.

In this boil of unrestrained creativity, new forms and styles seemed to develop almost day by day. Rockabilly evolved into folk and protest rock, into psychedelic, shock and acid rock, into baroque and raga rock, into studio and aleatory rock. One day it was the Detroit Sound, the next the Memphis Sound, then the Chicago Sound, later the Bosstown Sound. Some had identity and substance. Others were fictions of record company promotion. Today, few groups are pure examples of any one style of form. Eclecticism and integration are the order of the day. Examine the tastes and performances of any of fifty contemporary groups, and you find such a mishmash of folk, blues, jazz, c&w, r&b, bluegrass, show tunes, and soul that one must recognize rock as an amalgam. It is music from the ghettoes of Chicago and Detroit, from the recording studios of Nashville, from the psychedelic auditoriums of San Francisco, from the docks of Liverpool, and from the foothills of the Himalayas.

At Carnegie Hall in December, 1967, two groups presented a program called "An Electric Christmas." On stage were the members of the New York Pro Musica and the Circus Maximus, the former, twelve musicians who specialize in playing Medieval and Renaissance music, the latter, a five-man rock group usually resident at Greenwich Village's Electric Circus. Also there was an electronic composer, Morton Sobotnick, who contributed original improvisations, and an "electrical designer," Anthony Martin, who presented a light show. Each of the musical groups played material from their regular repertoire. But several times in the course of an eighty-minute program, they joined forces. Then one heard a psychedelic rock number follow a mighty Gregorian chant, which in turn gave way to electronic ruminations by Sobotnick as skeins of colored light danced on the walls of the concert hall. In March, 1968, the Pro Musica group moved into the Electric Circus itself and there gave four concerts, collaborating with the Chambers Brothers, an integrated, soulful rock group.

More than one concert critic felt that the compartmentalization of art, upheld in the nineteenth century, was becoming a nonexistent issue. Harold C. Schoenberg, the *New York Times'* chief music critic, wrote: "All techniques are being synthesized. The Beatles had something to do with it, and John Cage and the Columbia-Princeton Electronic Music Studio, and the jazz boys, and some of the movie composers, and some television commercials, and Viet Nam, and the psychedelics. Young composers today enthusiastically use everything within reach." And a colleague, Donal Henahan, concluded in *The New York Times*: "The wedding of Bach and rock, of Purcell and Pop becomes not only permissible, but inevitable for the predictable future. . . . No one, even in the most respected academic circles, hesitates now to adapt pop music and pop art, along with Schoenberg and Stockhausen. And, although the actual evidence is not yet strong, rock in its many guises seems to be moving into the picture as an energizing influence on serious composition."

But evidence is accumulating. Suddenly, recording companies have begun releasing the work of electronic, aleatory and other avant-garde composers, many of whom have been clamoring for recognition for decades. Last year, Columbia Records devoted one entire release of seventeen LPs to their material. What has rock to do with this? Nothing directly. But it is a fact that the Now Generation first heard the sounds of Stockhausen, Varese, Ives, Cage and other experimentalists in rock records. Through these, young America also discovered the music of nonmusical materials, a field explored by Harry Partch, a self-taught American composer who devised an octave of forty-three tones. Not our concert musicians, conductors, or recording executives, but groups like The Beatles, The Fugs, Mothers of Invention, United States of America and many lesser known combos sowed the seeds that created a taste and market for the "music of sound." Nowadays, the use of electronic synthesizers like the Moog and Byrd-Durrett to *originate*, and not merely to reproduce or alter musical sounds, is becoming a rock commonplace. The appetite of rock producers, musicians and composers for sophisticated sounds and equipment, has compelled recording studios to install twenty-four-track tape machines where a year or two ago, eight-track was considered advanced. These developments, not without the danger posed by the legendary mad scientist, require the corrective influence of a Bob Dylan recording meaningful material with a small combo and acoustic guitar, as he did in *John Wesley Harding.*

Rock has also given a shot in the arm to jazz, stirring many who were saying that Jazz Is Dead—it surely has had a declining audience in the last five years—to hope that a transplant of the heart of rock might bring new life to the ailing form. Whether this will happen or not, jazz and rock are beginning to go together in an exploratory courtship. There has already been some interchange of personnel, with rock artists like guitarist Larry Coryell joining Gary Burton's jazz combo, and jazz flutist Jeremy Steig reconstituting his group as The Satyrs, a rock combo. An increasing number of jazzmen, like Don Ellis, have begun using electric instruments and exploring rock textures, while rock groups like The Yardbirds and many blues bands have shown an interest in improvisation and the brass-and-reed instruments of jazz. The two have a common denominator, of course, in their attachment to the beat. (*Had* would be a more exact word in view of jazz's postbop *listening* or *concert* emphasis and the opposition of today's jazz drummers to acting as time-keepers.) The basis for a courtship was also established when psychedelic rock moved teenage music away from its folk orientation (with the stress on *meaning*) toward soul and jazz (with the overriding drive for emotive and evocative *sound*).

Like hair, horns are increasingly "in." Recently, the sign at the pool of a Hollywood hotel, which long read, "Ladies must wear caps in pool," was altered to read: "All guests with long hair must wear caps." During the past year, the Paul Butterfield Blues Band, The Electric Flag and Blood, Sweat and Tears— to name a few—have all added trumpets, trombones and/or saxes to their personnel, suggesting that the sound of strings is beginning to wear. The natural extension of this development is hinted by the recent amalgamation of seven rock combos into the Kasenetz-Katz Singing Orchestra Circus of 36 pieces (cum horns). Intimations of the possible re-emergence of big bands (though not Big Bands a la the Dorsey-Miller-Goodman era) are also to be found in Van Dyke Parks' *Song Cycle* recorded by an orchestra of 55 pieces, *The Wichita Train Whistle Sings*, an album employing 51 men, and Dave Axelrod's *Song of Innocence*, recorded by a 37-piece band.

Like jazz, country-and-western music has a point of contact with rock in its rhythmic framework. From time immemorial, country singers have hung onto the beat even when they were yodelling the most lachrymose of ballads. But c&w recording techniques, particularly in the use of head-arrangements devised at record sessions, actually antedate studio rock, the Now art of playing the recording studio as if it were an instrument. Of course, the city slickers have not been the same since c&w and r&b were wed in the 50s, and the union produced r 'n' r. But as time has gone on, the country cousins have also changed. The development of a rock-country trend is reflected in the rise of Bobbie Gentry, Billy Edd Wheeler, Glen Campbell and John Hartford. The last two, one as a singer and the other as a writer, accounted for the 1967 award-winning hit "Gentle on My Mind." This song, as well as those by Wheeler and Gentry, are indicative of a new sophistication, a new depth of meaning and feeling in c&w.

Strange though it may appear, rock has invaded even the sanctuary of traditional religion. In Elizabeth, New Jersey, a Roman Catholic priest serves as the lead singer of The Heartbeats, a rock group composed of students of the Sacred Heart High School. Appearing with the group at a benefit concert sponsored by young churchgoers, Father Charles W. Findlay was able to help raise $1,000 for a summer program for underprivileged teenagers. In the spring of 1968, too, The Electric Prunes, a west coast group, recorded in rock style a new *Mass in F Minor*. Convinced that rock could be a "forum for serious messages," the United Presbyterian Church retained the Australian Sleeve to produce a "message" single, "You Can't Hide" b/w "Love Is Everywhere." Perhaps the most unexpected development in this area was the appearance of a lengthy discourse, "Rock Is Salvation," in the Sunday *New York Times*. Contending that "rock can possess quasireligious force," Prof. Benjamin DeMott of Amherst wrote: "It leads me past myself, beyond myself, beyond my separateness and difference into a world of continuous blinding sameness—and, for a bit, it stoneth me out of my mind." Despite the locution, the professor was not indulging in a put-on.

As rock has moved into new areas, leaving the imprint of its rhythmic thrust, it in turn has undergone significant changes. Its melodies have become more evocative, its harmonies more complex, its rhythms more involved. Its resources have been expanded through exotic importations of Middle Eastern and Far Eastern instruments, and orchestral colors have been enriched through the application of electronics. Having explored the esthetics of sensory overload, distortion through amplification, wall-of-sound dynamics and mixed media, rock has become a music for *listening* as well as dancing.)

From simple folklike songs, it has moved into the area of extended forms. From albums consisting of disparate three-minute tracks, it has developed in the direction of the integrated suite and the theater of the sung and spoken word with musical background. To the sounds of spontaneity and surprise, indigenous to jazz, it has added the more complex, improvisatory elements of recording studio creation. From a literature consisting largely of love and sex ballads, it has become an instrument of commentary, introspection, analysis, satire, humor, irony and protest. As its language has become richer and more allusive, it has brought a revival of the bardic tradition, with songwriters performing their own songs, poets chanting their verses to rock musical accompaniment. The blues, now sung to electric instruments and embodying the drive of the Negro struggle for equality and freedom, has become soul—a more sensual, more violent and more propulsive sound.

In 1939, in his history of *Our American Music,* John Tasker Howard observed: "The line between popular music and art music remains sharply drawn, even after many fusions of styles that have been made in the last twenty years." Ten years later, when Sigmund Spaeth revised his lively little book *Read 'Em and Weep,* he wrote: "America's popular music has made such definite advances that it no longer deserves a patronizing or pitying approach." But the fact is that it received both and that songwriters, with few exceptions, continued to be so treated through the 1950s and 1960s until the combination of Dylan and The Beatles brought a revolutionary overturn.

And now that the walls of musical segregation have come tumbling down, there is some indication that we may be moving toward what Harold C. Schonberg of *The New York Times* characterized as "a kind of Total Theater in which the human voice will be mingled with lights, electronic sounds, improvisation and a completely new outlook on what constitutes music." And he added: "Music is becoming a joint effort these days, and the composer is allied with the physicist, the expert in film techniques, the electronic engineer."

We are today still living in a race-conscious world. "The draft is white people," someone says in *Hair*, "sending black people to fight yellow people to protect the country they stole from red people." Musical integration has come more quickly, and with less bloodshed, than racial integration. At this moment, it appears that we are on the edge of a synthesis in which composers will create, not pop, not rock, not folk, not art, but music that will embody the best qualities of each—the involvement of folk, the exuberance of dance and the dimensions of art music. The receptivity to that development, if it ever comes, must be credited to rock and its more inspired creators.

GLOSSARY
OF ROCK

A & R: "A" stands for Artist, "R" for Repertoire. The term A & R department developed in the prerock era when a recording executive's function was to find material and choose the right artist to record it. A & R men still perform this function for artists who do not write their own material. Otherwise, they tend to operate as co-engineers, collaborating with the recording engineer at the control board and later working with him to edit the tapes.

acid rock: See *psychedelic rock* and *freak-out.*

aleatory rock: Chance composition with a beat. Also rock music in which nonmusical sounds and nonharmonic material, as we traditionally understand them, are the basis of a composition. These sounds may be created electronically, through the use of tape, or the employment of noninstruments. Derived from the experimental works of John Cage, Karlheinz Stockhausen, and Harry Partch. The Beatles approach this style in *Sgt. Pepper.* So do Chad and Jeremy in "The Progressive Suite" in *Of Cabbages and Kings.*

attitude rock: Related to protest rock but suggesting an inner-directed approach. Involves a statement of one's feelings about a situation rather than a criticism of it. Dylan in *Highway 61 Revisited* rather than *The Times They Are A-Changin'*.

baroque rock: The sound and also the instrumentation of music of the Bach era. Ensembles were then composed of bowed instruments like violin, viola and cello, wind choir or recorders, valveless horns, coiled trumpets, keyless oboes and pre-Bohm (wooden) flutes, and harpsichord. The style is contrapuntal and fuguelike. Procol Harum's *A Whiter Shade of Pale* is a rock instance.

blue-eyed soul: Whites singing black, for example, the Righteous Brothers.

blues bands: The white equivalent of the *r&b* bands of the 1950s. This is *blue-eyed soul* on the instrumental level.

bozouk: Also spelled bouzouk. The "Never on Sunday" instrument, it sounds like a mandolin with a deeper texture. The mandolin is Italian while the bozouk is Greek, and the latter generally has eight strings instead of four paired. Listen to The Devil's Anvil on Columbia.

bugaloo: One of the many teenage types of dancing together *apart*. Other *no touch* dances include the Monkey, Boston Monkey, Frug, Hitch Hiker, Hulabaloo, Mashed Potato, Shake, Skate and Watusi.

b/w: Abbreviation of "backed with." Generally, a single record has an "A" side, considered the more important or more commercial. This side is b/w the so-called B side.

c&w: Abbreviation of country-and-western. An urban and twentieth-century type of white folk music, it developed in the southeastern part of the United States. Important centers were Memphis, Shreveport, Louisville and Nashville. At one time, the music was known as "hillbilly," a term that was dropped at about the same time that "race" gave way to *r&b*, and for similar reasons.

camp: Something that's so corny it's avant-garde; so out that it's in; so cute and cloying that it's outrageous; so sad that it's funny.

çaz: Anglicized to saz since English typefonts seldom include a "c" with a little tail. A string instrument of the eastern Aegean area, with sixteen movable frets on a long neck, it usually has three strings tuned E D A or G D A. Its exotic sound derives from the melody, played on the A string, sounding simultaneously with its fifth on the low, middle string, or with a single or double drone. The *bozouk,* heard on an LP by The Devil's Anvil, is currently the most-used saz in teenage music.

Detroit Sound: see *Motown* or, if you are near Detroit, look up Berry Gordy, who developed it and, in so doing, became a music millionaire. You can hear the sound on such labels as Soul, Tamla, VIP, Gordy and Motown.

dobro: An unamplified guitar. The typical glissando sound is associated particularly with Hawaiian music. But it has been much used in country-and-western music. You can hear a rock treatment on *The Buffalo Springfield Again.*

dub: An acetate trial copy made on a circular metal disk from master tape.

echo: Years ago, Columbia used to channel sound through a sealed staircase to give it the big, hollow, vibratory quality of music heard in a large concert hall. Now it's all done electronically by turning dials on a control board. In the jaundiced view of older generation singers, many youngsters would be driving trucks or working as bellhops, instead of making records, if echo had not been developed. See *feedback, fuzz tone, tape reverb.*

feedback: The squealing sound heard when a microphone is placed too close to a speaker and the signal loops back and forth, rising to an ear-shattering crescendo. On the disks and in the personal appearances of The Mothers of Invention, The Blues Magoos and other rock groups of the *psychedelic* school, feedback is used as an esthetic device.

fender bass: It looks like an electric guitar but it's tuned as a bass, and played with a plectrum instead of being plucked. It's called a fender after the company that popularized it. The company is now owned by CBS. No self-respecting rock group is without one.

flip side: The other side of a record. See *b/w.*

folk rock: A wedding of folk-oriented song to the Big Beat—instead of "I Want to Hold Your Hand," "I Wanna Change the World" or "I Wanna Change My Life." Also the use of electric instruments, guitar, bass and organ, instead of folk instruments like the harmonica and acoustic guitar. Prophet of the

198

genre was Bob Dylan. More recent proponents are Simon & Garfunkel and The Lovin' Spoonful, both of whom have developed a more musical style in which they seek lyrically and musically to capture the freshness of imagery, the immediacy of feeling and the probing commentary of ethnic song.

freak-out: Of western origin, a term referring to the disorientation of the senses achieved through the use not of LSD, but of sound, light and color. The LPs of The Mothers of Invention· are minus the flashing strobe lights and images that send the freaks—this is not a putdown in their lingo—but you can hear the ear-splitting decibels.

funky: The quality that Negro jazzmen sought to bring back into the music when the cool (white) school was dominant. A return to the blues sound, emotional involvement and playing hard on the beat. The counterrevolution was led by pianist Horace Silver.

fuzz tone: An electronic distortion of sound produced by a contraption known as a fuzz box. By adding overtones and increasing vibrations, it literally smears the original impulse. Beards and longhair may be symbolic of a generation that prefers fuzz to clarity.

go-go: Since discotheques originated in France, it is not surprising that au-go-go derives from a Gallic colloquialism. "Agogo" in French means "full of" or "loaded with." Whiskey agogo signifies a lot of whiskey—which leads to the rock concept of a lot of excitement or a lot of "go."

happening: An event, particularly unplanned, in which one participates. Once it was an event that occurred when artists congregated and interacted—and created. Today, it can just be a spectacle, artistic or not. The phrase "That's where it's happening" means "That's where the excitement is."

latin rock: An intermarriage of Afro-Cuban sounds and the beat of r&b. Examples are to be heard in the recordings of Joe Cuba, Jimmy Castor and Hector Rivera. Herb Alpert and the Tijuana Brass occasionally fall into the groove.

lip sync: Not a new phenomenon, but one that is in evidence on teen TV discotheque shows. Since it is generally impossible to reproduce live what is heard on a recording, singers mouth the words to a playing of the record. To be effective, the movement of the lips has to be synchronized with the words heard on the disk.

Memphis Sound: A product of Stax and Volt recordings out of Memphis, it is more earthy and raucous blues-and-gospel-sounding than that coming out of Detroit. The late Otis Redding was one of its celebrated exponents and producers.

mod sounds: An omnibus expression for all types of music created by today's teenagers, but particularly those aping the British contingent.

modal rock: Modes are the Greek ancestors of our major-minor scales. They are pentatonic, instead of having eight notes, and they have a minor, oriental sound. Just as jazz went modal at one point, so rock is exploring this area.

Moog: Rhymes with "vogue" and is the name of an electronic synthesizer invented by Robert A. Moog of New York. It can duplicate a vast number of sounds, including animal, natural, speech, sound effects and most orchestral instruments (as many as twelve simultaneously). It can be programmed by computer or controlled by keyboard. It is being used by Motown Records and is rapidly becoming a standard fixture in most recording studios. It has been used on disk by Simon & Garfunkel and other rock groups. Those who play the instrument on recording dates must be members of the Musicians Union. It costs $2,000 to $10,000 and ranges in size from a small suitcase to an oversized wardrobe trunk.

Motown Sound: The word Motown is a contraction of Motor Town in whose environs Berry Gordy worked and created the sound. A wedding of rhythm-and-blues (*r&b*) and pop, of gospel rhythms and modern ballad harmony, Motown or Detroit Sound is exemplified by The Supremes, The Temptations, The Four Tops and Martha and the Vandellas.

Nashville Sound: Despite the publicity, there is no Nashville Sound as there is a Motown Sound. This is hardly surprising since Music City has hundreds of working musicians and a large number of recording studios. The arranger, who is such a vital figure in New York and Hollywood studios, also in Detroit, is largely nonexistent in the Tennessee capital. Recordings have, from the beginning of time, been head-arrangements, that is, they have been worked out in the studio. As a result, Nashville disks tend to have a feeling of immediacy and an improvisational quality, which are more common in blues and in jazz than in pop music, and which also gave country or hillbilly music, a rhythmic earthiness. These characteristics, so basic in rock, contributed to the early development of *rock 'n' roll.*

nitty-gritty: Title of an *r&b* hit of a few years ago, it became the "in" word for essence, bottom line, or heart of the matter.

obscene: In the 20s, the expression was "you're the top," thanks to the song of that name by Cole Porter. Later, it became "out of this world." Later still, it was "the end" or "out of sight." Today, the word is "obscene," which some adults take literally.

oud: A lute originating in the Near or Middle East and currently used by some rock groups, also by Herbie Mann in a recent LP. The oud has a bulging belly, four to six pairs of strings, three sound holes, and—outside of rock music—is native to the Arab countries.

overdub: Adding an instrument, part, voice or figure to a previously recorded track.

playback: At a recording session, the playing of something just recorded.

psychedelic rock: West coast in origin, it aims to achieve the mind-smashing effects associated with LSD. Sensory overload is the technique. On records, it's largely a matter of volume and density of sound. In person, visual devices, such as flashing strobe lights, distorted images and kaleidoscopic designs, are added to the aural impact. Apart from The Beatles in *Sgt. Pepper,* examples of the style are to be heard on recordings by The Jefferson Airplane, The Fugs and The Blues Magoos (*Psychedelic Lollipop*). The Byrds also occasionally fly in acid circles (*Mind Gardens*). Some critics describe the development as "music to drive you out of your mind." Others more favorably disposed characterize it as Theater of the Absurd projected in Surrealistic Sound.

r&b: Abbreviation of *rhythm-and-blues.*

raga rock: Although jazz musicians have in the past manifested interest in the music of India, it was not until George Harrison of The Beatles studied with famed sitarist Ravi Shankar and used the sitar on a recording that the raga concept invaded rock. The raga is not a scale, of which there are seventy-two in Indian music, but a modal group of notes serving as the basis for improvisation. Each raga has a different emotional tone. Raga rock uses instruments like the *sarod, sitar, tabla* and *vina*, and pursues complex rhythmic patterns comprehended under such tala or time signatures as 10/8, 7/4, seldom encountered in Western or pop music.

rag 'n' roll: A wedding of ragtime and rock. The union is to be heard in LPs by The Kaleidoscope and various English groups.

reverberator: A device that employs a minuscule delay technique to make one instrument sound like many. The Byrds used it in early recordings.

rhythm-and-blues: (r&b) An urban, band-backed form of the blues that developed in the 40s and 50s and that was to be heard on records made by small independents for the segregated Negro market. These records were first known as race records, a carry-over from the period of classic blues recording. After World War II, the term rhythm-and-blues was substituted. English rock groups like The Rolling Stones and The Animals were particularly influenced by r&b artists like Chuck Berry, Muddy Waters, etc.

riff: A phrase repeated over and over, either as a melodic device to build tension, or as a rhythmic device to create a figure against which a melody can be bounced. Typical of *r&b* in the 1950s but also of swing during the 1930s.

rock 'n' roll: Originally a Negro expression with sexual connotations, not unlike the word jazz itself, r 'n' r became the generic name of Big Beat music. It was the late Alan Freed, a midwestern and later a New York disk jockey, who gave this designation to the merger of *r&b* and hillbilly music that occurred in the early 50s.

rockabilly: The earliest type of rock. It evolved in Memphis on the Sun Record label when white country singers adopted the blues-gospel style of their Negro brethren. The most important exponents of the style were Carl Perkins, Jerry Lee Lewis, Johnny Cash and, of course, the prophet of rock 'n' roll, Elvis Presley.

sarod: A complex Indian string instrument whose greatest master (*ustad*) is Ali Akbar Khan, an idol (like sitarist Ravi Shankar with whom he has recorded) of many rock groups. The sarod has a teak body, a stainless steel fretboard, no frets, and as many as twenty-five strings. Four of these are for melody, two are for rhythm, four others are retuned each time according to the chosen *raga*. The other fifteen strings are drones whose vibrations create a diffuse, echolike effect. Played with a plectrum, it possesses a balalaika tone which has great carrying power.

shlock rock: Music that is uninspired and noncreative, even if it is well performed.

shock rock: Another term for *psychedelic rock*.

sitar: Played with a wire plectrum worn on the performer's right forefinger, it is a long-necked lute with a wide fretboard and from sixteen to twenty movable frets. These are adjusted to the varying arrangement of notes within a selected mode or *raga*. Although the sitar may have four to seven strings, the melody is played on only one, with the others serving to provide a sympathetic drone accompaniment. The instrument can sound like the metallic hissing of many snakes and it frequently has a trancelike quality. It has become so popular because of its use by rock groups that a Broadway publisher has recently released an instruction book, a New Jersey instrument company has marketed an electric sitar, and Ravi Shankar has given a course in Indian music at New York's City College.

soul: The intensity, immediacy and involvement of Negro singing in the era of integration. Perhaps as a result of the struggle for Freedom Now and the growth of black nationalism and Black Power advocacy, today's blues singers have more bite and thrust. James Brown, Aretha Franklin, Otis Redding and Ray Charles are at the top of a long list of soul singers. White rock singers like Mitch Ryder and Mick Jagger try to approach the raucous sense of frenzy, the rhythmic drive and the violence of their soul brothers.

splice: To join two pieces of tape. It can be done with such precision that a single syllable can be cut out of a recording.

studio rock: Not a style but a procedure: arranging and composing in the studio. The technical resources of the recording studio—

different sonorities, types of echo, tape speeds, volumes, textures and densities—all become components of the record or composition.

Surf Sound: A sound originated by the Beach Boys in the early 60s with a hit called "Surfin'," written by two of the group and little more than a typical 12-bar blues. The sound seemed to embody a modified walking boogie bass and a gentle afterbeat device: rest, *clap-clap*/rest, *clap*/rest, *clap-clap*/rest/*clap*. The swell of excitement among West Coast youngsters over the surfing fad carried over into cities where Harley-Davidsons served as substitutes for surfboards.

tabla: Tuned drums used by Indian musicians to accompany the *sitar* and *sarod*.

tape loop: The ends of a piece of magnetic tape are tied together or looped, making it possible to play the same piece of music repeatedly. Rock and jazz groups (Don Ellis, for instance) have used it so that a musician can superimpose line upon line on previously recorded material. In short, a man can duet or "trio" with himself. Without a loop, the tape machine would have to be stopped each time and the tape rolled back to the beginning.

tape reverb: All echo thrives on the time interval between the original sound and its reflection back from a natural or electronic barrier. Tape reverb is a type of echo that exploits the space between the recording and playback heads of a tape machine. The resulting sound: *bowowowowowow*.

Theremin: An electronic instrument devised by the Russian whose name it bears. The public first became aware of it through its use in the score of the Hitchcock film *Spellbound* (1945). Its wailing sound, reminiscent of a musical saw, is produced by interrupting a magnetic field. Vertical motions of one hand over a box, the size of a TV set, regulate pitch while horizontal motions of the other determine durations or rhythm.

touch dancing: Since partners do not touch in virtually all teenage dances, this is how the younger generation designates waltzes, fox-trots or any dances in which the man holds the woman in his arms.

vina: Another Indian instrument that is attracting attention among rock performers. Three of the seven strings are drones. A gourd resonator attached to its upper end rests against the player's left shoulder. As with the *sitar* and *sarod,* the trancelike sound of drone strings apparently accounts for its appeal.

wall-of-sound: A type of recording in which the sound is continuous. Originated by one of the young rock producers, Phil Spector, it envelopes the listener and creates great tension. The electric organ is most frequently employed to achieve this effect. Listen to the Righteous Brothers.

DISCOGRAPHY

Albums are listed for each chapter in alphabetical order according to the names of artists. The choice of albums, particularly with regard to the pioneers of rock, is dictated by the best available LPs.

Titles of albums appear in italics. When an *artist's* name appears in italics, it signifies a debut album. Many carry no title except the artist's name.

1. Where It's At

Bobbie Gentry. *Ode to Billie Joe*. Capitol ST 2830

2. When It Started

Bill Haley. *Rock Around the Clock*. Decca 29214
Elvis Presley. RCA Victor LPM/LSP 1254
———. *Golden Records*. RCA Victor LPM/LSP 1707, 2075, 2765, 3921

3. Where It Started

Chuck Berry. *After School.* Chess 1426
————. *Golden Decade, 1955–1965.* Chess LPS 1514D
Fats Domino. *Rock and Rollin'.* Imperial 9004, 9009
————. *Fats Is Back.* Reprise RS6304
The Drifters. *Rockin' and Driftin'.* Atlantic 8022
B. B. King. *Live at the Regal.* ABC S 509
History of Rhythm and Blues. Atlantic SD 8161–4
Lightnin' Hopkins. *Country Blues.* Traditional 1035
Blind Lemon Jefferson. Milestone 2004
18 King Size Country Hits. Columbia CL 2668, CS 9468
Leadbelly. *Library of Congress.* Elektra 301/2
Little Richard. *Here's Little Richard.* Specialty 2100
Bessie Smith. *Story.* Columbia CL855–8
Muddy Waters. *Best.* Chess 1427
Muddy Waters, Howlin' Wolf, and Bo Diddley. *Super, Super Blues Band.* Checker LP 33010

4. Teenage Rock

Paul Anka. ABC S 371
Frankie Avalon. *Hits.* U.A. 3382, S 6382
Pat Boone. *Pat's Greatest Hits.* Dot 3071, S 25071
The Coasters. Atlantic 33–101
Bobby Darin. *This Is Darin.* Atco S 115
Everly Brothers. *Golden Hits.* WB/7 Arts S 1471
Connie Francis. *Rock 'n' Roll Million Sellers.* MGM S 3794
Buddy Holly. *Story.* Coral (7) 57279, 57263
Jerry Lee Lewis. Smash 27056, S 67056
Ricky Nelson. *Million Sellers.* Imperial 9232, S 12232
The Platters. *Encore of Golden Hits.* Mercury 20472, S 60243
Neil Sedaka. *Sings His Greatest Hits.* RCA Victor LPM/LSP 2627

5. Bob Dylan

Bob Dylan. Columbia CL 1779, CS 8579

————. *Freewheelin'*. Columbia CL 1986, CS 8786
————. *Times Are A-Changin'*. Columbia CL 2105, CS 8905
————. *Another Side*. Columbia CL 2193, CS 8993
————. *Bringing It All Back Home*. Columbia CL 2328, CS 9128
————. *Highway 61 Revisited*. Columbia CL 2389, CS 9189
————. *Blonde on Blonde*. Columbia C21, 41, C2S 841
————. *John Wesley Harding*. Columbia CL 2804, CS 9604
Byrds. *Greatest Hits*. Columbia CL 2716, CS 9516
Leonard Cohen. Columbia CL 2733, CS 9533
Donovan. *Mellow Yellow*. Epic IN 24239, BN 26239
————. *In Concert*. Epic BN 26386
Arlo Guthrie. *Alice's Restaurant*. Reprise R/RS 6267
Tim Hardin. *Tim Hardin 2*. Verve Forecast FTS 3022
Janis Ian. Verve FT/FTS 3017
Lovin' Spoonful. *The Best of*. Kama Sutra KLP/KLPS 8056
Phil Ochs. *I Ain't Marching Any More*. Elektra EKL 287, EKS 7287
Tom Paxton. *Outward Bound*. Elektra EKL 317, EKS 7317
Simon & Garfunkel. *Sounds of Silence*. Columbia CL 2469, CS 9269
————. *Parsley, Sage, Rosemary and Thyme*. Columbia CL 2563, CS 9363
————. *Bookends*. Columbia KCS 9529

6. The Beatles

Beatles. *Meet the Beatles*. Capitol ST 2047
————. *Rubber Soul*. Capitol ST 2442
————. *Revolver*. Capitol ST 2576
————. *Sgt. Pepper's Lonely Hearts Club Band*. Capitol MAS/ SMAS 2653

7. The British Invasion

Eric Burdon and The Animals. *Best*. MGM S 4324
Bee Gees. *Idea*. Atco SD 33–253
Chad and Jeremy. *Best*. Capitol ST 2470
Dave Clark Five. *Greatest Hits*. Epic IN 24185, BN 26185

Petula Clark. WB/7 Arts S 1590
Cream. *Fresh.* Atco S 33–206
———. *Disraeli Gears.* Atco S 33–232
Georgie Fame. *Yeh Yeh.* Imperial 9282/12282
Gerry and The Pacemakers. Laurie S 2037
Jimi Hendrix Experience. *Are You Experienced.* Reprise RS 6261
Herman's Hermits. *Best.* MGM S 4315
Hollies. *Greatest Hits.* Imperial 9350/12350
Incredible String Band. Elektra 4010
Tom Jones. Parrot 61004/71004
Lulu. *To Sir.* Epic IN 24339, BN 26339
Peter & Gordon. *Best.* Capitol ST 2549
Rolling Stones. *Big Hits.* London NP/NPS 1
———. *Between the Buttons.* London 2499/499
———. *Their Satanic Majesties Request.* London NP/NPS 2
Seekers. *Best.* Capitol DT 2746
Dusty Springfield. *Hits.* Philips 200220/600220
Who. *My Generation.* Decca 7–4664
———. *Sell Out.* Decca 7–4950

8. Soul

Blood, Sweat and Tears. *Child Is Father to the Man.* Columbia
   CS 9619
Blues Project. *Live at Town Hall.* Verve/Forecast S 3025
Booker T. and the M.G.'s. Stax 701
James Brown. *Please Please Please.* King 909
Paul Butterfield. *The Paul Butterfield Blues Band.* Elektra EKL
   294, EKS 7294
Canned Heat. Liberty 3426/7526
Ray Charles. *What'd I Say?* Atlantic 8029
———. Genius Sings the Blues. Atlantic 8052
———. *Modern Sounds,* V. 1 & 2. ABC S410, S435
Sam Cooke. *Hits of the 50s.* RCA Victor LPM/LSP 2236
James Cotton. *The James Cotton Blues Band.* Verve FT/FTS
   3023
Electric Flag. *A Long Time Comin'.* Columbia CS 9597

Four Tops. *Greatest Hits.* Motown S 662
Aretha Franklin. *I Never Loved a Man the Way I Love You.* Atlantic SD 8139
Buddy Guy. *A Man and The Blues.* Vanguard VSD 79272
Martha Reeves and The Vandellas. *Greatest Hits.* Gordy S 917
John Mayall's Blues Breakers. *Blues.* London 3492/492
Wilson Pickett. *Wicked.* Atlantic S 8138
Lou Rawls. *Soulin'.* Capitol ST 2566
Otis Redding. *History of Otis Redding.* Volt S 418
――――. *Dictionary of Soul.* Volt S 415
Righteous Brothers. *You've Lost That Lovin' Feelin'.* Philes S 4007
Smokey Robinson and the Miracles. *Greatest Hits.* Tamla 2S 254
Diana Ross and the Supremes. *Greatest Hits.* Motown 2S 663
Mitch Ryder and the Detroit Wheels. *Sock It to Me, Baby.* New Voice S 2003
Sam and Dave. *Hold On, I'm Comin'.* Stax S 708
Otis Spann. Bluesway S 6013
Temptations. *Greatest Hits.* Gordy S 919
Vanilla Fudge. Atco 33–224/SD 33–224
Little Stevie Wonder. *Jazz Soul.* Tamla 233
Dionne Warwick. *Golden Hits,* Vol. 1. Scepter S 565

9. The California Sound

Association. *Insight Out.* WB/7 Arts S 1696
Beach Boys. *Surfin' U.S.A.* Capitol ST 1890
――――. *Pet Sounds.* Capitol DT 2458
Big Brother and the Holding Company. *Cheap Thrills.* Columbia KCS 9700
Country Joe and the Fish. *I-Feel-Like-I'm-Fixin'-to-Die.* Vanguard VRS 9266, VSD 79266
――――. *Together.* Vanguard VSD 79277
Doors. Elektra EKS 74007
――――. *Strange Days.* Elektra EKS 74014
――――. *Waiting for the Sun.* Elektra EKS 74024
Grateful Dead. WB/7 Arts S 1689
John Hartford. *Earthwords and Music.* RCA Victor LPM/LSP 3796

Jefferson Airplane. *Surrealistic Pillow.* RCA Victor LPM/LSP 3766

Scott McKenzie. *Voice of.* Ode Z 1244001/124402

Mamas & The Papas. *Farewell to the First Golden Era.* Dunhill S 50025

Monkees. *Pisces, Aquarius, Capricorn and Jones, Ltd.* Colgems COM/COS 104

Moby Grape. Columbia 2698/CS 9498

Mothers of Invention. *We're Only in It for the Money.* Verve 6–5045

Steppenwolf. Dunhill DS 50029

Van Dyke Parks. *Song Cycle.* WB/7 Arts S 1727

Gary Puckett and The Union Gap. *Featuring "Young Girl."* Columbia CS 9664

———. *Woman, Woman.* Columbia CL 2812, CS 9612

Johnny Rivers. *Back at Whisky-A-Go Go.* Imperial 9284, 12284

Tiny Tim. *God Bless Tiny Tim.* Reprise RS 6292

Turtles. *Happy.* White Whale 7–114

United States of America. Columbia CS 9164

Youngbloods. *Earth Music.* RCA Victor LPM/LSP 2865

10. East Coast Rock

Blues Magoos. *Electric Comic Book.* Mercury 21104, 61104

Cowsills. MGM 4498

Four Seasons. *Gold Vault of Hits.* Philips 200196, 600196

Fugs. *First Album.* ESP 1018

———. *Tenderness Junction.* Reprise 6280

Happenings. B. T. Puppy S 1001

Hair. (Original Cast.) RCA Victor LOC/LSO S 1150

Tommy James and the Shondells. *Hanky Panky.* Roulette S 25336

Sonny and Cher. *Best.* Atco S 33–219

Spanky and Our Gang. *Like to Get to Know You.* Mercury SR 61161

Young Rascals. *Groovin'.* Atlantic S 8148

———. *Time Peace/Greatest Hits.* Atlantic SD 8190

Your Own Thing. (Original Cast.) RCA Victor LOC/LSO 1148

INDEX